Still Pitching

ALSO BY MICHAEL STEINBERG

Peninsula: Essays and Memoirs from Michigan

The Fourth Genre: Contemporary Writers of/on Creative Nonfiction
(co-edited with Robert L. Root Jr.)

Those Who Do, Can: Teachers Writing, Writers Teaching
(with Robert L. Root Jr.)

The Writer's Way
(with Clinton S. Burhans Jr.)

I'm Almost Famous
(stage play with Bob Baldori)

Still Pitching

A Memoir

Michael Steinberg

Michigan State University Press ◆ *East Lansing*

Author's Note: This memoir is in part a work of imagination and memory.
The persons, places, and situations are real, and the dialogue is recon-
structed as best I can remember it occurring. The names and other identi-
fying characteristics of some of the people have been changed.

∞ The paper used in this publication meets the minimum requirements
of ANSI/NISO Z39.48-1992 (R 1997) (Permanence of Paper).

Michigan State University Press
East Lansing, Michigan 48823-5245

Printed and bound in the United States of America.

09 08 07 06 05 04 03   1 2 3 4 5 6 7 8 9 10

LIBRARY OF CONGRESS CATALOGING-IN-PUBLICATION DATA
Steinberg, Michael, 1940–
Still pitching : a memoir / Michael Steinberg.
p. cm.
ISBN 0-87013-697-6 (cloth : alk. paper)
1. Steinberg, Michael, 1940– —Childhood and youth. 2. Brooklyn (New York, N.Y.)—
Biography. 3. New York (N.Y.)—Biography. 4. Baseball—New York (State)—New
York—History—20th century. 5. Baseball—Social aspects—New York (State)—New
York—History—20th century. 6. Brooklyn (New York, N.Y.)—Social life and customs—
20th century. 7. New York (N.Y.)—Social life and customs—20th century. I. Title.
F129.B7S776 2003
974.7'23043'092—dc21
2003009751

Parts of this memoir have been published as stand-alone pieces. The author would
like to thank the editors of the following literary magazines and anthologies:

The Missouri Review; New Letters; The Florida Review; Sport Literate; The
MacGuffin; The American Examiner; Baseball, I Gave You the Best Years of My Life;
Baseball Diamonds: Tales, Traces, Visions, and Voodoo from a Native American Rite;
The Fourth Genre: Contemporary Writers of/on Creative Nonfiction

Two stand-alone memoirs, Trading Off and Chin Music, were cited as Notable Essays
in Best American Essays, 1995 and 1999 respectively. Trading Off was cited as
Notable Sports Writing in Best American Sports Writing, 1995.

Cover design by Erin Kirk New
Book design by Sharp Des!gns, Inc., Lansing, MI

Cover photo, Ebbets Field Exterior, used by permission of
the National Baseball Hall of Fame Library, Cooperstown, N.Y.

Visit Michigan State University Press on the World Wide Web at:
www.msupress.msu.edu

for Carole
with love and admiration

Acknowledgments

My special gratitude to Martha Bates, my editor, who knows a lot more about baseball than I do. Her ongoing support and honest, unflinching critiques made this a much better book. A special thanks as well to Maureen Stanton, who read every word of every draft and offered pointed suggestions and guidance each step of the way.

Thanks also to Jack Driscoll whose friendship, encouragement, and critiques were invaluable.

To Edward Chalfant, Don Murray, Steve Tchudi, Jaimy Gordon, David Bradley, and Robert Shekter—my mentors and teachers.

To Robert Root, Skip Renker, Tim Jeffrey, John Boe, Marc Sheehan, Tom Ray, and Anne Marie Oomen—all of whom read early drafts and offered much needed direction.

To Lev Raphael, Gersh Kaufman, Pauline Adams, Jim Heavenrich, Dr. Mary Berman, Mimi Schwartz, Lee Hope, Jaimee Wriston Colbert, Marcus Cafagna, Sue Silverman, Lynda Reichert, Phyllis Barber, Philip Cioffari, David Cooper, Michelle Cacho-Negrete, Shirley Eicher, Susanne Rose, Tanya Whiton, Gloria Nixon John, Patti Aiken, Trisha Heller, and Nick Z. Monet—for their ongoing support and counsel.

To the staff at the MSU Press: Fred Bohm, Julie Loehr, Sylvia Robine, Julie Reaume, and Annette Tanner—for their enthusiasm, hard work, and dedication to books and literature. My gratitude as well to Kristine Blakeslee for her precise copy edits and knowing advice.

To Philip Spitzer who suggested I write this memoir in the first place.

Finally, to Carole, my partner and kindred spirit who believed in this project and in this writer from the very beginning.

◆

Still Pitching

Nothing flatters me more than to have it assumed that I could write prose, unless it is to have it assumed that I once pitched baseball with distinction.

—Robert Frost, in a letter to a fellow poet

◆

There is nothing greater for a human being than to get his body to react to all the things one does on a ball field. It's as good as sex; it's as good as music. It fills you up.

—John "Buck" O'Neil, Kansas City Monarchs

◆

[Baseball is] America's game; it has the snap, go, fling of the American atmosphere; it belongs as much to our institutions, fits into them as significantly as our Constitution laws; [it's] just as important in the sum total of our historical life.

—Walt Whitman

◆

Prologue

*1950. **An overcast Sunday** morning in early June. I'm ten years old and I'm standing in our driveway on Beach 132nd Street in Belle Harbor. Our two-story, slate grey, wood frame house sits between Jamaica Bay, only a hundred yards to the west, and the Atlantic Ocean, four blocks to the east. Most of the other homes are brick two-stories, like the Ellerstein's next door, or split-level ranch houses, like Frieda Bergman's and the Sloan's across the street. In years to come, these houses would be the backdrop for the marathon stoop ball games my younger brother Alan and I would play all summer long.*

On this particular morning, my grandmother Tessie, a rotund, stern woman, has just finished serving breakfast. My grandfather Hymie has already left to open up the pharmacy. This being Sunday, my mother is typically still asleep.

Out in the driveway, I'm playing catch with my dad. I'm dressed in an oversized New York Giant baseball suit, a uniform I will soon renounce. My father is wearing his own Sunday soft-ball uniform: royal blue tapered cotton pants with white trim down the sides and silver snaps on the bottom. His middle-aged paunch bulges slightly beneath a gold and navy nylon jersey with "Jerry's Esso" scripted across his broad chest. A sky blue cap crowned with a white J covers his bald spot. He looks a lot more imposing than the father I know who dresses in a suit and goes out on the road to sell table linens.

As we toss a grass-stained baseball back and forth, I watch our neighbors pass by. They're heading to early Mass at St. Francis de Sales. The men and boys are wearing dark suits and ties, the women and girls have on tasteful, conservative, long dresses— their Sunday uniforms. I'm feeling smug now that Hebrew School is out for the summer. While Frankie Carney and Billy Creelman are sitting through boring church services, in a few minutes I'll be headed for Riis Park to watch my dad's team play its customary Sunday doubleheader.

A half hour later I'm on the home team's bench at the Riis Park men's softball field. As the guys on the team slowly gather, in the distance I see families in terry cloth robes and bathing suits eating hot dogs and cotton candy as they stroll the raised board-walk that runs parallel to the expansive, sandy public beach.

My father's teammates are warming up for the first game. Most are in their late thirties and early forties, and they're all wearing uniforms like my dad's. Playing catch and pepper, laugh-ing and kidding around, they look to me like the major leaguers I see on TV. They're so easy and intimate with one another—like they all belong to an exclusive club—a club I ache to belong to.

Just before the first game begins, my heart's racing with anticipation. This week it's my turn to be batboy. Last Sunday, Smitty Shumacher's son, Eddie—a pudgy kid with perpetual smudges of dirt on his knees—sullenly performed that chore. To Eddie this is an annoying obligation. But not to me; when I hand a pine tarred Louisville Slugger to my dad, or to Lefty Benton, our stocky, blond first baseman, I feel all tingly inside. And when I watch Smitty glide into the hole between shortstop and third base, smoothly backhand a grounder, straighten up and plant his spikes in the dirt, then rifle the ball to Lefty at first base, I'm overcome by a catch-in-the-throat sensation that rivets my rubber spikes to the ground.

This is the seed *of a dream, the beginning of a passionate obsession with baseball that would dominate my childhood and adolescent years and that—for better or worse—would inform many of the choices and decisions that ultimately shaped my adult self.*

◆

_1.

I came to love baseball in a roundabout way. Until age nine, I had an active distaste for the sport. And for good reason. In grade school pickup games, the neighborhood clique of guys—Louie Mandel, Freddy Klein, Allen Nathanson, and Frank Pearlman—and the top athletes—Rob Brownstein and Ronnie Zeidner—always chose each other first. I was one of the last to be picked. When I did get to play, I batted last and got shuffled out to right field, as far away from the action as possible. I also recall being ridiculed by the clique for "throwing like a girl" and for swinging the bat "like a rusty gate." I was so afraid of making a mistake that I'd stand out in right field praying that the ball wouldn't be hit to me.

I was so ashamed of my incompetence that for years I refused my father's offers to play catch in the backyard and his invitations to watch the Sunday softball games at Riis Park. He didn't let on to me how disappointed he was. But I found out one day when I overheard him talking to my mother.

"It's unnatural, Stell," he said. "I don't want him to grow up to be a sissy."

"Don't push him Jack," my mother said. "He'll come around when he's good and ready."

It was an off-handed remark, but a perceptive one. No one understood me or my idiosyncrasies better than my mother did. She knew exactly how I operated. Perhaps, it's because for the first nine years of my life, I spent more time at home with her than I did with my father.

For as long as I could remember, my mother, an ex–pre-school teacher, was a voracious reader. I recall that a lot of books, newspapers, and magazines—like *Reader's Digest* condensed editions, dictionaries and encyclopedias, *Sunday Times*, *Life*, *Colliers*, *Harper's*, *New Yorker*, and *Saturday Evening Post*—were always strewn around all over our kitchen table and living room floor.

According to her I was an avid reader and a bright, curious kid. Maybe that's how I seemed at home. But in school I was shy, scared, and withdrawn.

My aversion to school began in kindergarten, when Mrs. Buckley, our blue-haired teacher, singled me out because my finger paintings didn't look anything like the models she'd posted on the blackboard. From then on, I felt light-headed and nauseated every time we had to paint or draw. One time, she tacked my drawing up on the wall. I knew she'd be using it as an example of how not to draw. I felt a deep, sinking feeling in the pit of my stomach. So before she could say anything, I threw up all over the floor. After that everything became a blur. All I recall is my cousin Doris escorting me out of class and walking me home. I was so embarrassed by my behavior that at dinner I begged my mother not to send me back to school the next day.

My mother and Mrs. Buckley met a few days later. I don't know what transpired, but when my mother came home she told me I didn't have to go back to kindergarten that year. As soon as my father found out, he as much as ordered her to send me right back to school.

My mother stood her ground, and as it turned out, I didn't attend kindergarten. But all year I felt ambivalent and guilty that I hadn't "toughed it out," like my father said I should have. I don't remember much else about that year except that until summer recess I went out of my way to avoid facing the neighborhood kids who were in my kindergarten class.

It was with much apprehension, then, that I started first grade. Every morning before I left for school I felt so sick to my stomach that I couldn't eat breakfast. It took a week or two to get over my fear of what I imagined the other kids might be saying about me. After that, I began to enjoy first grade. I even recall winning a class spelling bee and receiving a "word wizard" button from *Junior Scholastic* magazine.

Then it happened again. When Mrs. Krisberg was teaching us how to hold a pen, I got nervous and began to panic. After that my penmanship was so bad that at parent-teacher night Mrs. Krisberg told my mother that I had a motor skills deficiency.

Once more, over my father's objections, my mother pulled me out of school. I couldn't face the prospect of being at home again while the other kids were in class. I whined and pleaded, but it didn't matter. My mother was determined to see that the school system wasn't going to get away with miseducating her son.

She did, however, propose a compromise. She would work with me at home until the mid-year break—after which, I could go back to school. I wasn't happy about it, but at age six what were my options? That fall, we did my school lessons every day at the kitchen table—the same reading, writing, arithmetic, arts and crafts, and drawing assignments that everyone else was doing in class. When I tried to play with the other kids my age, they taunted me and called me names like "momma's boy" and "retard." So I withdrew deeper into myself. That's when I discovered my first real passions: reading and writing.

It was my mother who introduced me to books. Every night, before sleep, she would read to me from her collection of children's stories. At first, she read me the usual fairy tales and kid's books:

Uncle Remus, Hans Christian Anderson, Grimm's, Winnie the Pooh. Most of these blur in my memory, though I vividly recall being enthralled by outcasts like Cinderella, Jack from *Jack in the Beanstalk*, and Pinocchio. It wasn't just their misfortunes that attracted me. I admired their resilience, their determination to overcome all obstacles. The seven-year-old "schlepper" that I was, I wanted to prove to all the kids in school that I could be as persistent as those characters and as tenacious as the Little Engine That Could.

What I remember best, though, is what it felt like to read: the exhilaration of discovering kindred spirits—authors and characters alike; the thrill of finding secret joys and hopes that I shared with fictional beings; the colorful pictures I could conjure up in my imagination; and the sense of being fully absorbed in the moment—suspended in time and space. I can remember times when I would start a book in the afternoon, and I would be shocked to find when I picked my head up that it was dark outside and that I'd forgotten to turn on the lights or take my afternoon nap.

At home I read wherever I could find a spot to hide out—in the bathroom, my bedroom, the basement. I was intoxicated by language and stories. When I didn't understand something, I loved looking it up in the dictionary or the encyclopedia. Often I was lonely and sad for days after I finished a book. It felt as if I'd lost one of my closest friends. On the other hand, it was so satisfying to struggle through a story until I reached the end. It soon became a matter of pride to finish everything I read, no matter whether I loved or hated the characters or plot. Over time, the compulsion to finish *anything* I started would become a habit that would carry me into adulthood.

As I got a little older, specific books and characters—like the Hardy Boys and Chip Hilton, Speed Morris, and Soapy Smith—the star athletes in Clair Bee's Chip Hilton series—felt more real to me than the neighborhood kids I knew. In fact, it was those Chip Hilton books that first made me aware of just how much attention and recognition you could get from being an accomplished athlete.

I loved the books themselves—their feel, their smells, their textures. While my mother shopped for groceries and clothing on 116th Street, I haunted the Rockaway Beach Public Library, eagerly pulling books down from the shelves and sitting cross-legged on the wooden floor, inhaling the musty aromas and running my fingers over the grainy textures of those volumes. When I'd crack the binding and bend the book open, my heart started racing and my hands trembled with anticipation.

While I was out of first grade, I also began to write. I'd scribble notes in the margins of books, or I'd write in a hand-sized spiral bound notebook I kept in my pants pocket. Sometimes, I'd pretend I was the author and rewrite the story. Or if I wasn't satisfied with a character's decisions, I'd write what I would have done in the same situation. When I didn't like the way a certain book began or ended, I'd make up my own beginning or ending. If a story seemed too predictable or boring, I'd change it. If I felt an affinity for a certain character, I'd pretend that he or she was my friend and I'd write that character a letter. Once in a while something I wrote would stop me in my tracks. Other times I'd be thinking about one thing and an unbidden thought or idea would appear on the page.

I liked writing for many of the same reasons that I loved to read. Once I got going, I could write for hours without thinking about anything else. I loved the sensation of feeling both transported and in control. I never felt inadequate or self-conscious when I was writing. I could imagine anything I wanted to, make myself into anyone I wanted to be. I also liked the challenge of finding the exact language to express some of the doubts and fears I couldn't reveal to anyone else. And if I couldn't think of the right word, I'd look it up in the dictionary or in my mother's thesaurus.

I was just beginning to enjoy my involuntary furlough from school when my mother announced that it was time for me to go back. For the first few weeks I was self-conscious and tentative—so afraid the kids would start taunting me again. But once I got used to being back in school, I remember feeling disappointed that the reading and writing we did in class did not provoke nearly as many supercharged moments as those I'd experienced alone at home.

In those early years of school, I didn't get to spend much time with my father. For much of his adult life, Abraham Jacob "Jack" Steinberg was a traveling salesman. He worked for a Manhattan table linen manufacturer when I was a kid. His territory was Ohio, Michigan, Illinois, and Indiana.

My father disliked being away for such long stretches, but he was a lot happier on the road, where he could be his own man, than he was in the home office. Whenever he took me with him to Manhattan, he'd balk at doing the routine paperwork they gave him. And it irritated him when he'd have to take orders from his bosses, some of whom were younger and less experienced than he was. But he put up with it because, like so many Jews of his generation, he believed it was his responsibility to work hard and provide for his family. This was the ethic he lived by until the day he died in 1989.

I admired my father's persistence, but I felt sorry for him because he never got the chance to follow his dreams. As a kid I had no idea what I wanted to be when I grew up, but I knew I craved a more romantic existence than the unremarkable life my father and mother led.

My father knew this about me, and he was always urging me to get my head out of the clouds. At the same time, he never stopped encouraging me to better myself. His standard lecture was about missed opportunities. He made it clear that he wanted me, his first-born son, to go to college and get an education—as well as to seek out and do whatever it was that would make me happy.

"If you settle for anything less, you'll always regret it," he said.

While my father offered me this permission, he was never able to give it to himself. I learned how to follow my own dreams, not from his advice, but from my grandfather Hymie's escapades.

In his prime, Hymie Frankel was a robust, gentle man. Almost six feet tall, he liked to wear grey cardigan sweaters and smoke pungent White Owl stogies. By his late forties his hair was already thinning, and his shoulders were rounded from bending over the prescription counter at the pharmacy. Yet my grandfather had an aura about him, a tangible presence that attracted women and men alike.

As a young boy I was enamored of him. My mother claimed that Hymie fawned all over me, the family's firstborn son. Allegedly, he took me for rides on Sundays in his beat-up old DeSoto, just so he could parade me in front of all the uncles, aunts, and cousins. And, as the story goes, he flashed my baby pictures to the regulars at the pharmacy every chance he could.

But my most vivid memories of him don't involve Sunday car rides. By the time I was nine Hymie and his buddies were smuggling me into the harness racing tracks at Roosevelt and Yonkers. The first time he took me to the races he said, "Don't tell your mother or Grandma Tessie. If you do, Mikey, we'll never hear the end of it."

That was the start of our conspiracy.

Whenever he planned to take me to the harness races, he'd tell my mother we were going to the movies. She knew Hymie wasn't playing it straight with her, but what could she do? He'd been taking *her* to the track since she was a young girl. Besides she also knew that the serious betting action was at "the flats," Belmont Park and Aqueduct ("The Big A").

"Swear to me Hymie that you'll never take him there," I once heard her urge him. And, despite my pleading, he honored that request. He didn't take me to Belmont until I graduated from high school.

The family mythology only added to Hymie's aura. According to my mother, in the Roaring Twenties my grandfather owned two Manhattan pharmacies near the Ziegfield Theater. And she liked to boast that Al Jolson, Jimmy Durante, Georgie Jessel, and Burns and Allen hung out at Hymie's stores before and after their shows. She also claimed that he loaned Jessel some big money when the future star was just getting started.

"He might as well be giving it all away," she frequently said. And in some ways she was right. Whenever Hymie was flush he gave his money to show biz and racing buddies, and to the down-and-outers and hangers-on who regularly tapped him for cash. But once when I pressed her on the issue, she admitted that most of the luxuries she enjoyed came from money he'd won at the track.

Hymie was so fond of my mother, his eldest daughter, that for her eighteenth birthday he bought her a canary yellow Ford roadster and then enrolled her in an exclusive women's teaching college. And her younger sister, my aunt Ruthie, claims that she would have enjoyed the same privileges had it not been for the stock market crash of '29. My mother's version, though, was that Hymie lost the pharmacies not on account of the crash, but because he ran up so many debts with the bookies.

Whatever the case, Hymie characteristically took the loss in stride. He moved the family to Rockaway Beach, a resort community on the south shore of Queens, where he bought a small pharmacy in partnership with his three nephews, Mickey, Sam, and Abe Neiman. Together they began to rebuild what he had lost.

By the time I was born, in the early 1940s, Hymie was earning what my mother called "a decent living;" and he and my grandmother Tessie were living in my mother's and father's house on Beach 132nd.

My father was on the road so frequently that for a time Hymie became a permissive surrogate father to me. On racing nights Hymie would have me meet him at five o'clock at Neiman's Pharmacy. The ritual went like this: first he'd slip me a twenty and we'd go up the street to Sam Cahmi's deli, where he'd sit me down at the counter and order me a lemon coke and a hot pastrami sandwich, then he and Sam would duck into the back room to wait for Willie and Ralph—from the butcher shop—to arrive with the racing programs.

Those two guys were right out of a Damon Runyon novel. During the day, Willie and Ralph cut meat and wore bloodstained aprons and baggy brown wool pants. But at night, when we went to the track, they were decked out in three-cornered hats, shiny black suits with diamond stickpins and vests, and pointy shoes with white spats.

I used to love to hang around and listen to them handicap.

"Doc Robbins says to put the long green on Adios Harry in the third," Willie would boast. And Ralph would counter with something like, "I have also got an inside tip. From Shermie. He says number three's got the post. And mark this down, Will, the horse is runnin' on greenies."

When the four of them disappeared into the back room, I wasn't supposed to know what they were up to. But it didn't take a lot of smarts to figure it out. Guys with wallets bulging like egg rolls paraded in and out of that room as if it had a revolving door.

Once at the track, Ralph, Willie, Sam, and my grandfather would go back to the stables to get inside tips from the trainers and stable boys. They always had the lowdown on which horses were running on Bute, who was lame, and who was the heavy favorite. They also studied the drivers' records, each horses' winning times, the track conditions, the horses' blood lines, even the wind velocity and direction. They bickered over which horses were the "mudders" and which ones were "rabbits." They always knew who you could count on to "crap out in the stretch."

Hymie was their leader—always the taciturn, dignified patriarch. When he walked through the admissions gate at Roosevelt, Hymie headed straight for Doc Robbins's office under the grandstand. Doc was an old racing crony, a fellow pharmacist who'd

retired in his mid fifties to pursue his real passion. He owned the
track's program concessions, and when Hymie and the guys showed
up, Doc gave them box seats right at the finish line. More than once
I heard my grandfather telling Willie, Ralph, and Sam that he wished
he could do exactly what Doc Robbins had done. It was something
I never forgot.

Hymie also kept company with the top drivers, and he traded
tips with the Mafia types—the big-time shooters in sharkskin suits,
black silk shirts, and white ties. Everyone looked up to my grandfather—the bookies, the touts, the trainers. They took his marker,
came to him for advice, asked him for handouts. And he acknowledged them all. He'd give money to Jimmy Sparrow, the retarded
kid, and to old Shep, the shell-shocked local "village idiot." He even
bankrolled Hilda Bells, who was a bag lady long before bag ladies
became part of the landscape.

But he didn't just hand them the money. In his way, he made
them earn it. I remember once when old Hilda hit him up for a loan.
Hymie pulled out his wallet, but before he handed over the cash he
flipped open the plastic sleeves that contained his family photos.

"Look at my grandson," he said. "Isn't he a beautiful kid?" The
gesture embarrassed me, but I enjoyed watching old Hilda grimace
and nod her head in mock agreement.

Grandparents and grandchildren are natural allies. Both
have a common adversary: the parents. Hymie wasn't responsible
for bringing me up, so he could afford to indulge us both. And what
young kid wouldn't enjoy that kind of permission?

The first time I went with him to Roosevelt Raceway, we sat in
the grandstand high above the oval dirt track that circled the green
infield. I took in the scene through Hymie's old Zeiss binoculars. To
my right, just beyond the lip of the grandstand roof, were the finish
line and the tote board that flashed the odds every few minutes.
Below, between the railing and box seats, were swarms of people:

parents and kids sitting on blankets, eating out of wicker picnic baskets; dapper men and flouncy women who looked like they just
stepped out of "Guys and Dolls"; faux aristocrats with porkpie hats
and chauffeur's caps who sat on folding chairs studying the racing
form; and the touts and hangers-on who scurried around like worker
ants. It was the most enchanting spectacle I'd ever seen. I felt as if
I'd been transported to another dimension

Even though my grandfather was a gambler, the money that
traded hands seemed less important than being part of the spectacle and milieu. Ten minutes before the first race, my grandfather sat
me down and said, "Mikey, I want you to understand that there's
more to this than the money." Then he walked me through the racing form, explaining the Byzantine symbols: the post position numbers, the horses' best and worst times, their previous finishes, their
breed, the trainers' record, the jockeys' track record, the racing conditions, and the stakes. Then there were the times when Hymie took
me back to the stables and introduced me to the trainers and jockeys. He had them explain to me how the horses were bred, trained,
and developed into trotters and pacers. It was the first time I had
truly felt like an insider.

During the racing season Hymie couldn't stay away from
the track. Whenever he could get cousin Sam or Mickey to cover at
the pharmacy Hymie would fill prescriptions from six A.M. till noon,
and then he'd head for Belmont or The Big A. After a dinner break,
he'd drive twenty-five miles to Roosevelt Raceway in Westbury in
time for the nightly double. When the ninth race ended, he and his
cronies went over to the Sunrise Highway Diner for a cup of coffee
and the ritual post mortem. He'd get home after midnight and slip
into bed, always remembering—win or lose—to leave a rose and a
fifty dollar bill on the dining room table for Tessie and his two daugh-
ters. It was Hymie's way of buying them off.

By eight the next morning he was back at the deli making book on the day's races, before heading up the street to the pharmacy where he'd fill prescriptions and indulge his other passion: shmoozing the regular customers.

Though cousin Sam and Mickey were never easy with Hymie's gambling, they had to keep quiet about it. Whatever reservations they harbored, they knew he was never negligent or irresponsible. He'd get up at three in the morning to deliver medicine to a sick friend or customer; he'd fill the paregoric scripts that no one else wanted to make; he'd work the counter, sell cosmetics to the women, order the supplies, keep the books, pay the bills, listen to salesmen's stories, and place the weekly ads in the *Rockaway Beach Wave.*

But at home Hymie was restless and impatient. Sometimes he'd get up from dinner to call Sam or Ralph to check the latest racing information. Or he'd listen to the sports news on the radio to find out the results from the afternoon card at The Big A. Still, when my mother scolded him for not being around often enough, he neither argued nor defended himself. He'd acknowledge that she was right, and he'd apologize. Then a day or two later, he'd bring her flowers and take her out to dinner and the track—just as if she was his date.

When Hymie took me to the track, I loved watching how excited he and his cronies would become when a horse they'd spent days researching, studying, and inquiring about, won a race. It was as if they'd accomplished something significant. And given their otherwise mundane lives and jobs, who could begrudge them those brief moments of fulfillment? Isn't that what we all yearn for?

Then there were the aesthetics. I'd listen with rapt attention when my grandfather would describe to me how he loved watching a thoroughbred racing at full speed—muscles taut, tail whipping in the wind, outstretched legs seeming to float above the brown clay. Who but an aficionado would describe that scene in such passionate, reverent detail? It was as if he was talking about a work of art.

Another reason that Hymie was so driven to pursue his racing pleasures was, I believe, because of a mid-life bout with tuberculosis.

When he was in his early forties, the doctors removed a diseased lung and told him that if he wanted to live more than another five years, he would have to quit smoking and chasing the horses. To my grandfather, it was a worse punishment than the diagnosis. So he made the only compromises his temperament would allow: in place of the stogies he started smoking Tipperillos, and for six months he skipped the trotters and went only to the flats in the afternoon. But as soon as he could convince my grandmother he was healthy, Hymie was back at the pharmacy in the mornings and doing his usual double shift at the tracks.

Anyone looking for a cautionary tale here will be disappointed; my grandfather lived this way for the next thirty years. He died, appropriately enough, at Roosevelt Raceway. It was a sudden heart attack, and he went quickly. When the medics found him, he had four winning tickets in his shirt pocket.

◆

_ 2.

If you grew up in New York City between 1947 and 1957, you were witness to a period that sportswriters and baseball historians still refer to as the golden age of New York baseball. That reign began with the Dodgers signing of Jackie Robinson, the first Negro ball player in the major leagues, and it ended with another first—the Dodgers' and Giants' migrations to Los Angeles and San Francisco in 1957.

What's most remarkable about those years is that at least one, and most often two, of the three New York teams—the Yankees, Dodgers, and Giants—appeared in the World Series. This streak was interrupted only by the Cleveland Indians–Boston Braves Series in 1948. Even more extraordinary is that from 1947 until 1957 the three New York teams won a total of nine world championships. The Yankees won seven of the eight World Series they appeared in, the Giants won one of their two appearances, and the Dodgers won a single championship along with six National League pennants. All of the city's newspapers—and there were more than a half dozen dailies back then—routinely referred to the World Series as the Subway Series.

My parents, and it seemed most of the men and women of their generation, rooted for the Giants. On hot summer nights they'd sit with our neighbors out on the front stoop, swatting mosquitoes, sipping coffee or beer, and listening to Russ Hodges and Ernie Harwell broadcast the games. Every so often, something one of the announcers said would trip off a memory. Then my dad and Mr. Creelman, the police detective from down the street, would start reminiscing about the great Giant teams of the twenties and thirties. Mostly, they'd boast about their Hall of Famers: Frankie Frisch, Bill Terry, John McGraw, Carl Hubbell, Mel Ott. I was envious that they'd actually seen these players in person.

If my father's friends were Giant rooters, most of the guys in the neighborhood clique and the rich kids from Neponsit were Yankee fans. When they weren't playing ball at recess, they'd smugly invoke their team's immortals—Babe Ruth, Lefty Gomez, Lou Gehrig, and Joe DiMaggio—as if they'd actually grown up with those players. They'd lord it over everyone in the schoolyard that their Bronx Bombers, their Yankees were "becoming a dynasty."

That kind of gamesmanship was de rigueur. Bragging rights were important currency in the schoolyard. One time, I heard Frank Pearlman ragging on poor Sherman Carlson for being a Brooklyn Dodger fan. Sherman was one of those guys who was always getting picked on. He was a math brain, a slight skinny kid with bad skin and horn-rimmed glasses. Every day, he wore rumpled brown corduroys with a slide rule attached to his belt. He was a walking target for mean-spirited jerks like Pearlman.

"Why do you root for such a loser team?" Frank taunted. "It makes you a loser too."

"The Yankees are lucky," Sherman shot back. "And, they have more money than the other teams."

I was surprised by his comeback. And I was glad to see him fight back. Just when I thought the dispute was over, Sherman launched into a passionate monologue about Jackie Robinson breaking the color line, and Duke Snider being the best center fielder in the city—maybe even the whole universe. By the time he was done, Sherman was red in the face.

I'd always thought of this kid as somewhat of a loser. But I found myself admiring his passion and fierce defense of this much maligned baseball team. That's when I asked my father if he'd take me along with him to one of his Sunday softball games.

In real life, most of my father's teammates lived pretty ordinary lives. They had families and respectable jobs. Some were salesmen like my father, while others worked for banks, insurance agencies, and firms in the city. But when they put their uniforms on, they were transformed into ball players, guys who razzed each other and shouted obscenities at the opposing team, who yelled stuff like "attaway to go" and patted each other on the back and said "great play" or "good hit."

I was captivated by how intense and animated those grown-ups were—my father included. It was only pickup ball, but they played with such determination. They argued with the umps when calls went against them, and they bickered with each other about strategy decisions and "what ifs." But as soon as the games were over, they'd head for Johnny's Bar and Grill on 129th where they'd replay the highlights and mistakes over a few beers.

I especially loved watching my father play. He seemed so alive, so vibrant when he was out on the field. It was the only time I'd ever seen that side of him. Sometimes he'd get so caught up in the game that he'd barely remember he'd brought me with him. I'd have to reach up and tug on his jersey just to remind him I was still there.

At first I felt privileged just to be on the fringe of this inner sanctum. It was like being at the track with my grandfather. Was there anything, I wondered, that could ever absorb me the way horse racing engaged my grandfather—and the way baseball excited my father?

Once I began to take an interest in the game, baseball became the common ground between the two of us. Whenever I rode with him to his Manhattan office, my father would tell me stories about his old ball playing days. I remember how exuberant he'd get when he reminisced about playing shortstop for George Washington High. One of his teammates, he said, was Lou Gehrig, the Yankee Hall of Famer. My father's voice rose whenever he invoked Gehrig's name. He'd talk about how badly he too wanted to go to Columbia and play ball, just like Gehrig did.

But college wasn't an option. His family, first generation Polish immigrants, couldn't afford it. Nor was it part of the family ethic. Instead, he worked in his father's tailor shop and played semi-pro ball on weekends. That was before he became a traveling salesman, married my mother, and started a family.

My father's biggest regrets, he once told me, were that he never got to fight in World War Two, never went to college, and didn't get to pursue his dream of playing baseball.

To compensate for the loss of his baseball dreams, he began to educate me about the game. Sometimes on weekends, he'd take me up to the Polo Grounds to watch the Giants play. He taught me how to keep score, and he kept pointing out nuances and strategies: how infielders and outfielders positioned themselves differently for left- and right-handed hitters, when a bunt or steal or a hit-and-run were imminent, what kinds of pitches would exploit a given hitter's tendencies, and so on.

I caught on fast. The "inner game" appealed to me. And I was also impressed by my father's insider's knowledge of baseball. He was as much of an aficionado about this game as my grandfather was about the horses.

Once, he took me to see the Giants play their hated rivals, the Brooklyn Dodgers—the same Dodgers that Sherman was so eloquently defending that day in the school yard. I was immediately drawn to them—especially to Jackie Robinson, their Negro second baseman. He was like a lightening rod. He played with such reckless

So much "I"

abandon that it seemed to energize the entire ball club. The whole team, in fact, played with a kind of furious intensity—as if they had something urgent to prove.

I was beginning to understand why these scrappy, spirited Dodgers made the more businesslike Yankee fans and lordly Giant fans feel so uneasy. This was a team I wanted to learn more about.

My love affair with the Dodgers began in earnest in the spring of 1950, just before I turned ten. As soon as school let out, I started spending my days in the public library reading books about the Dodgers, biographies of Dodger greats, popular coffee table books like *Big Time Baseball*, and standard reference books like *The Official Encyclopedia of Baseball.*

As far back as the '20s, the Dodgers—whose nickname was "Dem Bums," and whose slogan was "Wait till next year"—were characterized, even by their own fans, as perpetual also-rans. The most famous chapter in the team's mythology would of course become the pennant race of 1951, when they blew a thirteen-and-a-half-game mid-August lead and lost the final playoff game to the Giants on Bobby Thomson's "shot heard 'round the world."

But even before that collapse, the Dodger legacy featured anti-heroes like Mickey Owen, whose ninth inning, two-out passed ball against the Yankees was the turning point in the team's loss of the 1941 World Series. Then there was George "Babe" Herman, who had the ignominious distinction of winding up on third base with two other teammates. The same Babe Herman got hit in the head trying to catch a routine fly ball. These were guys I could identify with.

The team's fortunes changed drastically in the late 1940s, when they signed Jackie Robinson, the first Negro to break the major league's color barrier. Had it not been for the great Yankee teams of the '50s, the Dodgers would have been the best team in baseball. The truth is that the Dodgers were a team of highly skilled players that happened to flourish at the same time as the great Yankee teams and fine Giant teams of that era. They were so resilient. No matter how many times they lost the pennant or World Series, they'd be right back in the race the next season.

The Dodgers' luckless history and its star player Jackie Robinson's determination and tenacity were irresistible attractions for a kid who already saw himself as a congenital underdog and outsider—always persevering, always having to prove himself to others.

It wasn't long before I became an aficionado. By mid July, I was reading the sports pages religiously each day—a first for me. And for the entire 1950 season, I followed Robinson's and the Dodgers' exploits via radio broadcasts of their games.

Part of the mystery and allure of baseball was learning the language of the game. Understanding the lingo—that hip vernacular— made me feel like I was an insider. At night, I'd listen late through the red plastic Philco's crackling static to Red Barber and Connie Desmond broadcasting Dodger road games from Cincinnati, Chicago, and St. Louis—the exotic western cities that lie beyond the Hudson. From "the catbird seat" high above the diamond, the Alabama redhead would sigh "ohhh doctor" and inform us in his smooth drawl that when Duke Snider camps under a lazy fly ball "it's an easy can of corn." When we were beating Cincinnati by five runs in the ninth, Red would say that we've got the Redlegs "sewed up in a crocus sack." After the eighth place Cubbies beat us, Red's recap informed us that we lost it in a "squeaker." And when Cardinal lefty Howie Pollett threw a bean ball at Jackie Robinson's head, Red described the bench clearing brawl as "an old-fashioned rhubarb." My favorite Barbarism was his description of those games when the Dodgers were beating up on their opponents. That's when he'd announce that "the Brooklyns are tearin' up the old pea patch."

That same summer, I invented board and street games that revolved around the Dodgers. I also began to learn more about the other major league teams. I read the sports pages in the New York papers as well as old yearbooks and programs. I collected Topps and Bowman bubble gum cards and stashed them in cigar boxes under my bed. I subscribed to *The Sporting News*, the Bible of the sports world. By mid season, I knew the uniform numbers, bios, and batting averages of everyone on all three New York teams. And, of course, I'd memorized every piece of trivia I could uncover about the Dodgers.

By the end of the summer, I'd become an expert, a walking encyclopedia of information about the Dodgers and their legacy, and about baseball lore in general. A whole new world, it seemed, was beginning to open up. In less than two months, I'd gone from being a curious observer to a baseball fanatic.

As soon as fifth grade was out, I begged my father to take me to Ebbets Field. But he was already scheduled to be on the road for the entire month of June. So in early July, just after I turned ten, he gave me permission to accompany Heshy, Kenny, Billy, and Ira— neighborhood boys, all of whom were a year older than I was.

The two brothers, Kenny and Heshy, wore yarmulkes (scull caps) and went to shul regularly. Ira was a science nerd with acne and a bad haircut. Billy was skinny and gawky looking. He had a drooping jaw and his shirts always looked too baggy. Some of the kids on the block referred to him as "slow."

This group of outcasts was even lower on the neighborhood food chain than I was. I felt superior to all of them. Even at my age I was so much more informed about baseball than they were.

It is a crisp, unclouded mid July Saturday morning, and the Dodgers have just returned from a nine game Western swing. After a sleepless night, I spring out of bed at eight o'clock, my stomach churning so hard that I cannot eat breakfast. I'm headed for Ebbets Field to watch my first unchaperoned Dodger game.

After I grab my blue Dodger cap and baseball mitt from the hook on the cellar stairs, grandma Tessie hands me an oil-stained

I always like the showers

brown paper bag, the mayonnaise from the tuna salad already leaking through the wax paper. I then sprint up the block to pick up Heshy, Kenny, and Billy, and we trek through the dew-stained vacant lots and past the shuttered houses until we get to Beach 138th Street. When we get there, Ira is still asleep. Mildly irritated, I wake him up. Then we have to watch him eat his soggy Kix and Cheerios.

I strum my fingers on the kitchen table wondering how in the hell he can be so damn blasé about something so sacred as an excursion to Ebbets Field. A half hour later, we finally head for the bus stop at Newport Avenue and 142nd Street.

This would be the beginning of a series of summer pilgrimages that would soon become a ritual, one that I'd perpetuate until the Dodgers moved west seven years later. Every Saturday home game until late September we'll ride the Green Bus Line to Flatbush Avenue, then transfer to the IRT where we'll stand perspiring in the stifling heat and humidity of a packed subway car, just so we can buy seats in the third base upper grandstand at Ebbets Field and watch the Dodgers play.

Each of the New York ballparks, Yankee Stadium, the Polo Grounds, and Ebbets Field were shoe-horned into their surrounding Bronx, Manhattan, and Brooklyn neighborhoods. But each had its own unique character. The left and right field foul lines at Yankee Stadium were less than 300 feet from home plate, while the left and right center power alleys were over 400 feet away. The Polo Grounds was shaped like a horseshoe with even shorter foul lines—279 down the left field line, and 257 in right field. The clubhouse in dead center field was almost 500 feet from the plate. Both parks had seating capacities of over 50,000.

Of the three though, Ebbets was the quirkiest one. I took special pride in knowing its history and its idiosyncrasies. A 32,000-seat bandbox of a park set in the heart of Flatbush, it radiated a cozy intimacy and an inviting familiarity that the others lacked. From the center field bleachers you could hear left fielder "Shotgun" Shuba yell "I got it, Duke." And from the upper deck behind first, you could see the grimace on Jackie Robinson's face as he went head-to-head with umpire Jocko Conlin.

At Ebbets the double-decker grandstand in center field jutted away to a forty-foot-high black concrete scoreboard, crowned by a ten-foot screen. Our right fielder, Carl Furillo, "the Reading Rifle," knew how to play every carom off that wall. Another thing I'd brag about was Duke Snider's uncanny ability to crank "Bedford Avenue rain makers" over the huge scoreboard.

From the minute we reach the bus stop until an hour later when we get off the subway at Eastern Parkway, we chatter non-stop about the upcoming game. As we're walking up the subway station stairs, Ira asks, "Who do you think'll pitch for the Brooks? The Preach, Ersk, or Newk?"

Jesus, I can't believe he doesn't know this, but I am smart enough to keep my mouth shut. They'd already begun to berate me for being a smart-ass know-it-all.

"Dunno, but for sure it'll be Sal the Barber for the Giants," says Heshy. "He murders us." I think it odd that Heshy can know who is pitching for the Giants but, like Ira, he doesn't know who's pitching for us.

I want to blurt out "It's Newcombe, you knucklehead."

But I decided to bank this information and wait my turn.

"He's a slow starter," Kenny counters. "We can beat him if we get on him early. Pee Wee and Jackie have to get on base in the first inning, so Duke, Campy, and Gil can bring 'em around."

Kenny's right about that much. At least someone in this crowd is paying attention.

We walk down Franklin Avenue and pass right by Lou Eisenstein's sporting goods store, where we gaze in the window and gawk at the expensive, genuine cowhide Rawlings and Wilson baseball mitts—the top-of-the-line merchandise that we all covet but no one can afford.

I wait for an opening and casually mention that during basketball season Lou Eisenstein, the store's owner, referees the New York Knick games at Madison Square Garden.

Ira takes the bait. "How'd you know that?" he asks.

"My dad and I go to the Garden every winter," I counter—hoping to make them jealous.

My heart's pounding with anticipation when we approach the rotunda entrance to the old grey concrete and steel ballpark on the corner of Empire Boulevard and Bedford Avenue. I feel a catch-in-the-throat sensation—a sense of wonder and awe that still overwhelms me every time I visit a baseball stadium. It's a signal that I'm about to cross a sanctified threshold and enter a world of gods and heroes, a universe where ordinary life falls away, where the stakes are high and the outcome is always in doubt.

It's only ten o'clock, and we have three more hours until the game starts.

"I'll get the tickets," I say to my pals.

This assertiveness is part of my plan. Because, when I step up to the general admission window, I feel grown-up and important—so different from the self-conscious, insecure kid I am in school and at parties.

Squinting through the narrow opening in the wire mesh screen, I'm face-to-face with the chubby, bald-headed ticket seller. He's wearing a green see-through visor and puffing on a soggy cigar. Knowing that the guys are watching, I bark out, "Gimme your four best general admissions, upper deck between third and home. And not behind a post, ok?"

The ticket guy blows stinky smoke in my face. Without looking up, he fans the vertical orange tickets like a deck of cards, before pulling four from the middle.

"That'll be five bucks, Jack," he barks. I casually toss a five spot under the wire mesh window.

"Step up, pal. Who's next?" he says, as he slaps a small white envelope on the counter, the tickets spilling out of the flap. For a buck and a quarter apiece, we get our chosen seats—upper deck, right between third and home, just like the ones my dad would always get us when he took us up to the Polo Grounds.

Now I've got the guys just where I want them.

"These are fantastic. How'd you get 'em?" Billy asks. As usual, he's right on cue.

"Man, I told you, I know how to talk to these ticket guys," I say.

My cool pose dissolves when we sprint up the third base ramp. As soon as we pass through the open portal, I stand frozen, rapt, while the other four heathens keep right on going. For a long moment I survey the field: the black scoreboard in right field; the emerald green, manicured grass that surrounds the smooth, tannish-brown infield; the powdered sugar foul lines and the chalky, white-washed bases; the multicolored outfield billboards that advertise "Abe Stark: Hit This Sign and Win a Suit," and "Fill 'er up with Tidol, 'Flying A.'"

The organ strains emanating from beneath the press box inter-rupt my reverie. For a moment I've forgotten where I am. The scene reminds me of the feeling that overcomes me when my parents take me to St. Patrick's Cathedral for Midnight Mass on Christmas Eve.

As Ebbets fills up, we hear the lazy hum and buzz of the pregame crowd, smell the pungent odor of stale Schaeffer's beer, munch on a brown bag of Planter's salted peanuts, and gape at the guys in white aprons and chef hats as they pluck Harry M. Stevens' hot dogs from the huge bubbling vat.

At eleven o'clock we scramble down to the first base field boxes to watch the Dodgers play "pepper" and prepare for pregame batting and infield practice. From any section of the stands you can hear that solid, reverberating "thwack" as wood connects with horsehide. The echo resounds throughout the caverns of the slowly

[handwritten margin note: like it better when he uses verbs]

filling ballpark, while outside on Bedford Avenue neighborhood kids with old leather mitts camp under the scoreboard, waiting to pounce on the batting practice "dingers" that will clear the wall.

For the entire three hours, Billy, Heshy, Kenny, Ira and I keep up a steady stream of chatter: quoting stats, playing baseball initials, kibitzing with neighboring fans about the new pennant race, and reliving "classic" Dodger home games from the past. Heshy tells us about the time Jackie Robinson stole home in the ninth inning to beat the St. Louis Cards. Kenny and Ira brag about the Duke hitting three homers onto Bedford Avenue against the Boston Braves. Billy replays the moment when Furillo threw the Pirates' Mel Queen out at first base on a line drive to right field. Most of those stories are apocryphal. I know that none of them have actually attended any of those games. Yet, they're replaying these moments as if they are their own memories.

A part of me feels it is a sacrilege for them to pretend they've witnessed those events. To make my point, I've deliberately saved my story for last. Once I have their attention, I draw out all the details, embellishing them wherever I can.

On an early June afternoon, I tell them, my father took my brother Alan and me to a day game against the Cubs. This was Alan's first time at Ebbets, and for the first few innings he was flushed with the kind of euphoria that comes from watching your first big league game. But by the fifth inning, he was bored. While my kid brother nodded off, Carl Erskine retired the last twelve Cubbies to complete the first live no-hitter I ever saw.

I pause here to let everyone take in the importance of this event. Then I punched up the climax.

"I still remember the last play of the game," I say. It was when Eddie Miksis hit an easy ground ball to Pee Wee Reese. I neatly penciled 6-3 in my scorecard and jumped to my feet to watch as players and fans headed for the mound to celebrate.

Later on, whenever I told that story, I made sure to emphasize the fact that I attended the game—that I didn't watch it on TV or read about it in a book or in *The Sporting News*. Part of it of course was to show off. But I also wanted my cronies to be more respectful of the game.

After we finish reminiscing, we watch batting practice. Baseball gloves in hand, the five of us stand behind the box seats between third and home. When a foul fly twists toward us, bouncing crazily off the concrete promenade, we wrestle with two Flatbush Avenue hoods—kids our own age who sport greasy DA haircuts and wear pegged pants, motorcycle jackets, and black shit kickers.

If I saw them in the street or on the subway, I'd cut out as quickly as possible. But here on my turf, I wasn't afraid to tangle with them. It's an Ebbets Field baseball at stake here—one of the most coveted souvenirs you can bring home. Worth at least a day or two's bragging rights in the schoolyard.

An hour before game time, we drift over to the right field bullpen to watch "The Knothole Gang," WOR-TV's pregame show. Wearing a blue Dodger warm-up jacket and cap, today the rotund host, Happy Felton, introduces Gil Hodges, our team's first baseman, to the TV audience. Gil grabs a bat and hits a bunch of easy grounders and pop flies to three kids. They are all twelve or thirteen years old, and each is wearing his Little League baseball uniform. One of them in a baggy, "Brooklyn Kiwanis Club" shirt wins an autographed baseball. He also gets to go to the dugout with Hodges. We walk away grousing about this injustice.

"How come those kids got picked?" Billy asks.

Heshy yells "Hey, Happy Man, how do we get on the show?"

"Yeah, how come we don't get picked," I mumble to myself under my breath.

Old Hap looks up and smiles at us. Then he turns away, unclasps his microphone and shuffles his cue cards.

Just before game time, Dodger players perch on the top step of the dugout. A wave of cheers cascades up from the lower stands.

This lets us know that up in the "old catbird seat" behind home plate, Red Barber has just announced, "And the Dodgers take the field" to everyone listening in on the radio and watching on TV. Gladys Gooding plays the National Anthem on her Hammond organ, Lucy Monroe sings "Oh say can you see . . ." in her high-pitched soprano, and I watch as fathers in shirt sleeves and fedoras and young boys with Dodger caps and two-toned reversible jackets tied around their waists place their hats in front of their hearts and sing along.

No matter how corny this ritual is, for those few moments, I feel as if I belong to a coterie of kindred spirits.

Out on the field, the players in their starched white uniforms stand silent and still. When they place their hats over their hearts I notice that Pee Wee's sandy blond hair is thinning on top, and that the Duke is prematurely graying. For a brief moment, the spell is broken; they look almost like the guys my dad plays ball with on Sundays.

Then Tex Richart's voice reverberates over the P.A., "*Ladies-dees and-nd Gentlemen-gentlemen. Batting first-first, for the Giants-Giants, number nineteen-teen, Alvin-Alvin, Dark-Dark, shortstop-stop.*" The home crowd boos loudly. But everyone quickly settles in, and the game is underway. I sit quietly, scorecard resting in my lap, recording each put-out neatly in pencil.

It's as if I've crossed over into another firmament. The game is a closed universe where I exist from put-out, to strikeout, to base hit—where innings seamlessly slip by without any sense of time passing.

There are moments when I am so deep in concentration that I don't even hear the crowd cheering. The only other times I'd experienced this sensation were when I was writing or engrossed in a book.

When the reverie breaks, I start looking around, picking out the oddballs in the stands. In the fifth inning of this scoreless tie, old Hilda Chester, a stout, white-haired woman dressed like a rag picker, runs through the stands, her hands waving wildly. She's clanging a

I would eat this - it has no urgency. "I look around."

set of metal cowbells and leading cheers. We stand up and yell with everyone else. She's accompanied by the Dodger "Sym-Phony," a group of rag-tag local musicians decked out in tattered tuxedos and stovepipe hats. I instinctively start tapping my toes as they play tinny, off-key Dixieland jazz. During the seventh inning stretch, Gladys Gooding urges the fans to sing along as she plays the "Follow the Dodgers" theme song. Like a church choir, we all join in.

On this day Don Newcombe and the Dodgers beat their nemesis, Sal Maglie. The game winner is a three run homer by Gil Hodges in the bottom of the seventh. As the ball disappears over the Brass Rail sign in left field, the people behind me begin showering the lower grandstand with confetti. All around us, we see grown men and women jumping up and down on their seats and hugging one another. I'm happy too; it's another win for the underdogs. Maybe this'll be their year.

When the game is over, the euphoric crowd refuses to leave until the team emerges from the dugout to wave their hats at us. Later, we linger at the third base exit outside the park and watch as the younger kids spot the players. A little blond boy in an oversized Dodger hat yells "Hey, there's Pee Wee and Robbie," and they all mill around their heroes—thrusting scuffed baseballs, Topps bubble gum cards, and black vinyl autograph books at them. Some players, dressed neatly in cubaveras and slacks, impatiently sign for a few minutes. Then they duck into touring cars or taxis taking them, I imagine, to exotic Manhattan destinations.

I feel an odd mix of envy and awe. A piece of me knows that I could never even hope to be like one of those players. Yet, I can't help but wonder what it would feel like to receive that kind of attention and adulation.

During the hot, crowded subway and bus rides home, we keep the afterglow alive by replaying the day's highlights to one another—complete with simulated crowd noises and sound effects. Heshy imitates Red Barber saying "Hodges has just parked one in the left field seats, and that's all she wrote for Maglie."

Fellow strap hangers applaud. Others look at us like we're crazy. I don't care: just knowing I have a Dodger/Giant ticket stub in my pocket makes me glow inside. For the rest of the ride home, I daydream that I'm part of an elite, secret society—a fraternity of select fans, all of us chosen in recognition of our vast knowledge and appreciation for this game.

◆

_ 3.

Being a Dodger fan was a fortunate match, but it didn't satisfy my deepest longings. I desperately wanted to play in the schoolyard choose-up games. After two years of being a spectator, I felt left out, excluded. It was becoming too excruciating to sit in the cheering section behind Elaine Hirsch, Alice Rosen, and the other popular girls. Even if I failed, I had to try and make myself into a ball player. If my father and his middle-aged teammates could do it, then why couldn't I?

I started by asking my father to teach me how to bat, field, and throw. He was only too happy to oblige. Whenever he was home, that is. On those nights, we'd go out in the backyard after dinner and he'd throw me ground balls and pop flies until the sun set behind the Union Carbide gas tank and it got too dark to see. Once in a while we'd drive to the batting range to work on my hitting. Other nights, I'd play punch ball with my Ebbets sidekicks, Heshy, Kenny, and Billy—none of whom were very good athletes. Sometimes, I'd go over to the schoolyard and watch the junior high school guys play softball. Just like I did at Ebbets Field, I studied the best players—analyzing their hitting mechanics and watching the ways they positioned themselves in the field.

I also honed my skills by teaching my kid brother how to play. Alan had just turned six when I started showing him how to bat and throw. He took to it so quickly that we were soon playing our own invented version of "stoop baseball."

On Saturday evenings, we'd huddle around the radio and listen to *Today's Baseball*, with Ward Guest, Marty Glickman and Bert Lee Jr. These dinnertime broadcasts were recreations of a selected afternoon Giant, Yankee, or Dodger home game—complete with simulated crowd noises and the crack of the bat meeting the ball. When the program ended, Alan and I would put on our hand lettered Dodger uniforms and our black Converse high tops, and we'd head out in the street to play "Dodger stoop baseball." To begin, we'd each take turns imitating Red Barber's southern drawl. When I'd shout out, "And the Dodgers take the field," Alan would hum the organ strains and mimic the crowd's roar, as we both ran out into the street to take our positions.

While the imagined TV cameras panned the field, we'd impersonate the entire starting team. First, the infielders, Hodges, Robinson, Reese, and Cox, then the outfielders, Pafko (or Shuba), Snider, and Furillo. And when Alan crouched down in imitation of Campy, I'd mimic the bear-like round-house pitching motion of Don Newcombe taking his warm-up tosses.

Right in the middle of the street, we'd remove our caps and place them over our hearts. I remember that Alan's sandy crew cut stood straight up like porcupine quills whenever we'd bow our heads and begin to lip-sync the National Anthem. Then the "game" would begin.

Alan would whip a pink "Spauldeen" high bouncer against the front stoop. Whenever the ball hit the point of the step, it would spring off the wood and skip into the road, where I'd scoop it up and casually toss it back to my brother.

"And that retires the side," I'd report in my announcer's mode. "Whitey Lockman's out of there, Reese to Hodges. Easy out," I'd say. "Six to three if you're scoring at home."

At the end of each half inning, we'd record the put-outs in one of the Ebbets Field score cards that I'd picked up in the aisles.

By design we could produce line drive outs, pop ups, bunts, and long fly balls. We set boundaries for base hits: a single had to reach the other side of the road, a double had to land on Gail Sloane's lawn, a triple would have to hit Sloane's house above the second floor bedroom window, and a home run would have to clear either Sloane's or Frieda Bergman's rooftop on a fly.

The simulated game would continue until the streetlights flickered on and twilight obscured the flight of the ball. By then, the heat and humidity of the day had yielded to evening's cool ripeness. As neighbors kibitzed out on their front steps, and kids flipped baseball cards against the stoops, Alan and I would trot off the "field" into our imagined dugout.

I loved playing that street game. But beyond that, it helped sharpen my fielding skills, and it offered me a chance to think strategically under game conditions. What's more, it gave me some confidence and hope.

My only friends in sixth grade were Peter Desimone and Mike Rubin, an oddly matched pair of outsiders. Peter was the Italian bakery owner's son. Lanky and angular, he was unathletic and wholly indifferent to what the popular crowd thought of him. In fact, Peter deliberately went out of his way to provoke them. Each day he wore what he called his "bohemian threads"—black turtle neck shirts, a chic beret, and snakeskin leather boots. Some of the nastier guys in the clique called him a "fag" behind his back. But he ignored their taunts.

I admired Peter's independence, as well as his unconventional tastes. While I was still reading the Hardy Boys and Chip Hilton books, he could already talk intelligently about *The Great Gatsby* and *Of Human Bondage*. He was also the only boy my age who was interested in jazz. Late at night, Peter listened to Al "Jazzbo" Collins,

Long John Nebel, and Jean Shepard, the WOR hipsters whose shows came on after midnight.

Peter was an authentic jazz buff, an aficionado like Hymie. On rainy days we'd lie up in his room and listen to old Lester Young and Charlie Parker records, while Peter would tell me apocryphal stories about the musicians and point out subtle shadings in the music.

His worldliness fascinated me. Instead of the usual pictures of movie stars and cars, Peter's bedroom walls were decorated with neatly arranged posters from Broadway musicals, opera, and ballet. Monet and Picasso prints hung side by side above his bed, along with framed color photos of exotic European locales like the Riviera and the Greek Islands. Peter acted as if he inhabited a larger, more cosmopolitan realm. Even as a sixth grader, he'd transcended, at least psychologically, the small-time schoolyard hierarchy.

Mike Rubin, my other friend, was short and chubby—like me. The popular crowd shunned Mike because he tried too hard to impress them—always telling lame jokes and boasting about where he could get cut-rate cigarettes for everyone.

Two jock wannabes, we became known as the "twin Mikes." After school we'd play fierce, competitive stickball matches in his sloped driveway. I had to teach myself how to pitch just to keep up with him. When it rained, we played bruising games of indoor football and basketball, using jerry-rigged equipment that we'd set up in his knotty pine basement. It was not a hostile rivalry—just two disenfranchised kids, each trying to assert his superiority over the other.

After school, Peter, Mike, and I would be out on the streets playing punch ball or stickball. On weekends, I'd round up a bunch of younger neighborhood boys and, along with my other two friends, we'd ride our bikes up to Riis Park where we'd play marathon choose-up baseball games on the grass and dirt fields. Even on those rare September beach days, the first thing I'd do was stake out a patch of hard packed sand near the water's edge and get up a diamond ball game.

In the schoolyard before class, at recess, or in the lunch room, Rubin and I would huddle together and talk about—what else?—baseball. We argued and sang the praises of our favorite players. We bet nickels and pennies on the games. We traded Topps and Bowman baseball cards and played "leaner/lapper" against the handball court wall. All of it was contrived, at least in part, to draw attention from the clique and their girlfriends. It didn't work. The only guys who joined us were fanatic baseball nuts like ourselves.

By this time, my longing to be acknowledged by the guys in the clique was becoming so acute that it felt like a persistent ache. I was also persona non grata with Elaine Hirsch, Alice Rosen, Sandy Kaufman, Bonnie Lerner, and Linda Firestein—the girls they hung out with at lunch and recess. If I couldn't draw the popular kids into my world, I'd have to meet them on their own turf—a daunting proposition to the likes of me.

As much as I hated mixers and dances, I decided to attend the first Temple Beth-El dance of the fall. Maybe if I got up the courage to ask one of the popular girls to dance, the rest of that crowd would take notice.

I'd had a crush on Elaine Hirsch since the second grade. So did everyone else. All the guys in the clique fawned all over her. She was slender, about my height, with dimples and sandy blonde hair that curled in ringlets around her ears. Word had it that she was snotty and stuck up.

Normally, I wouldn't dare approach someone who was so far out of my league. But I thought I might have a chance with Elaine because back in fifth grade I'd helped her with a book report on *The Yearling*. In fact, when she asked me for help, I couldn't say yes fast enough. I even wrote the whole book report.

It got an A, so I felt a little let down that all she said was "Thank you." But at least she always waved or said hello to me before class or at recess. That was just enough to build some hope on.

Temple Beth El mixers were typical of most grade school dances. I'd always shied away from these kinds of social events. The guys—even the clique—stood around on one side of the rec room, while the girls clustered on the other side. The boys shuffled their feet, nervously laughing, telling jokes, and making snide comments about the girls, who in turn giggled and pointed across the dance floor at the boys.

That night, I stood off to the side rehearsing what I'd say to Elaine. She was standing with Alice Rosen, another popular girl who'd never acknowledged me. I could feel the lump in my throat tighten as I walked across the room. For a moment, I wondered why I was doing this. I imagined that every eye in the room was on me. I thought again about chickening out. But I was already halfway across the dance floor. Alice spotted me first. She signaled Elaine with a slight tilt of her head.

Just as I blurted out "Would you like to dan—" Elaine cut me off. "Sorry, but thanks anyway," she said.

Then she turned back toward Alice, and both of them started to giggle. I trudged back to the boy's side of the gym. I didn't dare pick up my head for fear of having to confront all those laughing faces. My scalp tingled and my face was flushed with embarrassment. My legs were so wobbly I felt like I was slogging through a mud puddle. The last time I felt so mortified was six years ago when I threw up in Kindergarten class.

Before I'd even crossed the floor, I heard Alice say—loudly enough for all the others to hear—"I'd never dance with him; he's too short. Besides, he hangs around with those two other losers. All they ever talk about is stupid baseball."

I swallowed hard and tried not to cry. My legs were so heavy that I wondered if I had enough energy to make it to the double doors at the entrance. Knees shaking, I skulked out of the rec room and headed straight home. I crawled into bed without saying good night to anyone. I was too numb to even take off my clothes.

The next day, I ducked around stairwells and hid in dark

corners of the hallway. I kept my head down during class, at lunch, and at recess. I even avoided Peter and Mike. Every two minutes, it seemed, I checked my watch. By three o'clock, I couldn't wait to get the hell out of there.

After school, I ran home and grabbed a broomstick out of the closet. I put on my sneakers and old torn pants and raced down to Casey's Lot—a weed choked, rock-strewn open field on the corner of 129th and Beach Channel Drive. As I swatted handfuls of stones into Jamaica Bay, I pretended I was Duke Snider, then Jackie Robinson, then Gil Hodges. I kept it up until the broom handle was covered with nicks and cuts, and my palms had sprouted blood blisters.

It was early October, just before the World Series was about to begin. Three days earlier, the Dodgers had lost the National league pennant to the Giants on "the shot heard 'round the world"—Bobby Thomson's playoff winning homer off Ralph Branca. I could still hear echoes of the Giants' announcer, Russ Hodges, screaming above the Polo Grounds' pandemonium, "The Giants win the pennant! The Giants win the pennant! The Giants win the pennant!"

I'll never forget the moment and how I felt. It was late afternoon recess at Hebrew School. Mike Rubin and I were sitting outside on the back lawn, huddled around the portable radio I'd brought with me. We were tuned in to the rubber game of the Dodger-Giant playoff. The winner would face the Yankees three days later in the opening game of the '51 World Series.

I'd been counting on the Dodgers to win the pennant, if for no other reason than to take my mind off of the humiliation at the Saturday dance. Not to mention the schoolyard bragging rights that it would bring me. Wasn't it my turn to cop a break?

I'd been agonizing over the Dodgers' collapse since mid September when the Giants had cut a thirteen-and-a-half game mid-August lead to under five games. But now, in this crucial season ending game, the Dodgers were ahead 4-1 in the bottom of the ninth. I was certain that they had it locked up.

When the Giants scored a run to make it 4-2, I began to worry. Then with two on and one out, Thomson hit the game winning, season ending homer. I sat stunned under a tree and began to cry. I was so distraught that no one could console me. Not even Arthur Hoffman, my teacher, could coax me back inside.

For the next week the schoolyard taunts and epithets were cruel and merciless, just as I'd expected they would be. The entire chain of events, from the dance to the Dodgers' loss, had me so rattled that I couldn't bring myself to watch the World Series. The underdogs had lost again. Was it another portent? A signal that mine and the Dodgers' misfortunes were hopelessly intertwined?

A week after the baseball season ended, my sixth grade teacher, Mrs. Carlin, chose me to write the sports column for the class newsletter, the *6-2 Shooting Star.* How and why she picked me is still a mystery. Did she overhear the recess skirmishes? Did she feel sorry for me? Did she see something in me that other teachers had missed? Whatever the reasons, it came at just the right time.

My first response was to write something about the Dodgers' recent collapse. But once I got going, I found myself writing instead about their determination not to give up on the last day of the regular season.

The Giants had already won their game, putting them a half game up on the Dodgers. The Dodgers were playing the Philadelphia Phillies, the team that had beaten them out for the pennant on the last day of the 1950 season. They were trailing the Phillies 8-5 in the eighth. I'd just about given up hope, when they somehow rallied to tie the game and send it into extra innings. Even if they lost the game, the comeback made me feel proud to be a Dodger fan.

In the bottom of the 12th, the Phillies loaded the bases with two out. Their first baseman, Eddie Waitkus, hit a sizzling line drive just inside the second base bag. Jackie Robinson made a spectacular diving catch of what looked like the game winning hit. Then in the top of the 14th, with two out Robinson hit the most dramatic (and overlooked) home run in Dodger history. The Dodgers won the game 9-8. Three days later, they lost the playoff to the Giants.

As I scribbled pages and pages of notes, I was almost paralyzed with doubts. How would I find the right words to express what I was feeling? Would anyone like it? Would anyone even care? This was so different from writing alone at home. It would be published. My name would be on it. Everyone in school—including the teachers—would see it.

In the finished version, I mentioned the Bobby Thomson home run in passing. The column's real emphasis was the tenacity and courage the Dodgers, and Jackie Robinson in particular, had displayed in the last six innings of the must-win Philadelphia game.

When the purple-inked newsletter came out, the two teachers who'd told my mother that I was a slow learner were among the first to praise my writing. Boys who'd ignored me for years sent notes saying things like, "I never told my friends, but I was crushed when Thomson hit that home run," and, "I don't care about baseball, but I felt the same way when my cat died." Even though they'd missed the point of the column, it was gratifying to hear the praise.

Bolstered by those responses, my second piece was more ambitious, even self-aggrandizing. It was about Jackie Robinson's quest to break professional baseball's color line. In it, I compared Robinson's struggle with my own determination to become a better ball player. I got fewer reactions to this one. "Jackie Robinson is my hero too," a classmate lamely told me one day at lunch. Then a couple of other kids came over to tell me that they liked the column.

It wasn't exactly immortality, but I was savvy enough to see that this 300-word sports column had gotten me more attention than anything I'd ever done. Hopefully, in my classmates' eyes, I'd no longer be just the short, chubby baseball nut who sat behind Myrna Stein in the fifth row.

Just before Christmas break, word got out that in April the sixth grade softball team would be competing in the newly formed Rockaway Peninsula League. The winner would get to play for the Queens championship. For the next three months, the only thing I could think about was making that team. I'd show Alice and Elaine what "stupid baseball" meant.

Ever since I'd watched Smitty Schumacher, the slick fielding shortstop for my dad's team, I'd wanted to be a shortstop. Most shortstops though, were big and rangy like Smitty was. Except, that is, for Phil Rizzuto. The Yankee shortstop was only five foot six.

In an interview with *The Sporting News*, Rizzuto said that he'd compensate for his lack of size by cheating a few steps to the left or right depending on a hitters' stance or swing. The interview also said that Rizzuto carefully scrutinized his catcher's signs so he could anticipate what the pitcher would be throwing. It all made perfect sense to me.

When school started again in January, I convinced Peter and Mike to work out with me after class in the gym. Peter wasn't the least bit interested in tryouts, but Mike was as driven as I was to land a spot on the team. On those gloomy winter afternoons, we took turns hitting dozens of ground balls to each other. For batting practice, I concocted a new drill. I thought we'd improve our batting eyes if we used stickball bats and tennis balls instead of baseball bats and softballs, both of which had a larger circumference.

In class that winter I was just going through the motions. When I tried to do my homework, I could only concentrate for a few minutes before I started thinking about tryouts. I skimmed the assigned readings and I daydreamed in class. I even began to lose interest in writing the column.

One day in mid February, Mrs. Carlin asked me to stay after school. Never one to hedge, she asked me point blank why I seemed so preoccupied. I wanted to tell her that I loved her class, to say how much I appreciated her picking me to write the column. But I didn't want her to think I was a brown nose. So the only thing I could muster was a meek, "I'll try and work harder from now on."

Soon after that, I began to feel guilty. Mrs. Carlin was the first teacher who showed any confidence in me. Now, I was letting her down. I was also becoming aware that lately my love of books and writing was beginning to wane. My obsessive desire to make this team was starting to monopolize almost all of my sleeping and waking thoughts.

In late February, I found out through the grapevine that the team's co-captains, Rob Brownstein and Ronnie Zeidner, had already selected the four guys in the clique—Mandel, Klein, Nathanson, and Pearlman. Plus, Stan Weingarten, Zeidner's best friend, had volunteered to catch—a position nobody else wanted. That left only two open spots on the starting team.

I didn't expect an invitation, but I was still upset by the news. Brooding about it though, wasn't going to do me any good. So two weeks before tryouts began, I snuck into a dark corner of the gym and watched the team practice. I could see right away that Mandel was a far better shortstop than I'd ever be. Like Smitty, Louie was slender, fluid, and very agile. In contrast, I had only average reflexes and virtually no experience at the position. And despite what Phil Rizzuto had said, at five foot two I was too small to compete.

As I watched Louie glide into the hole to backhand the ball, I was burning with envy. Ever since early grade school he seemed to possess everything I yearned for. He played lead trumpet in the school band, he was a great dancer, and he was voted class president three times. The popular girls, of course, loved him. To make it even worse, he was now going steady with Elaine Hirsch.

The two starting positions still open were third base and right field. I didn't want to be dispatched to right field again, so I'd have to settle for third base, the least glamorous infield slot. The big problem was that third base was also Mike Rubin's position.

All of a sudden, the stakes were much higher. If one of us was chosen over the other, I knew it could be the end of the friendship. Yet, I wanted to make this team so badly.

I agonized for days before I told Mike. He was predictably surprised and disappointed. I'm sure he took it as a betrayal of the friendship. For the next two weeks, he stopped talking to me. Poor Peter was caught in the middle, so he proposed a compromise. He and Mike would work out together every other afternoon. On the days in between, Peter would work out with me.

At tryouts on the school playground, neither Mike or I looked particularly impressive. Both of us were jittery and on edge. But Zeidner and Brownstein picked us both for the squad. I was surprised and elated that I'd gotten past the first hurdle. I was also relieved that Mike had made the team. Things were still strained between us, but the next day we were at least talking to each other again. There was still a month of practice before the first game. Rubin and I were an equal match. One of us was going to be the third baseman.

Right from day one, practices seemed poorly organized. If you weren't up at bat, you stood around in the field waiting for your turn to hit. Even infield and outfield drills felt chaotic. I knew I'd be a better organizer than either Zeidner or Brownstein—neither of whom, I could see, really wanted to spend their time setting up practices. I'd watched enough Dodger games to know how to set up a fast-moving "around the horn" infield drill, while at the same time keeping the outfielders busy shagging fungos. I also had an idea for setting up a batting practice routine that would involve everyone on the team. But who was I to think I could take over? I was still auditioning for a starting position.

In time, I began to sense an opening. When it got warm enough to go outdoors, I took the liberty of arranging practices, reserving the field at Riis Park, and telephoning all the guys. That alone wouldn't be enough to sway things in my favor. But it wasn't going to hurt my chances.

During the first scrimmage, neither Zeidner or Brownstein wanted to take charge. Ronnie wanted to concentrate on pitching, and Rob simply was not an assertive type. I took a chance and volunteered to coach third and relay the signals. Both of them seemed relieved to be off the hook.

It soon became evident that I knew more about game strategies and tactics than anyone else on the team. So the co-captains agreed to let me run the next practice and coach the last game scrimmage.

It paid off. On the day before the first game, they picked me to start at third. Then they surprised us all by appointing me team manager. It would be my job to coach third and give the signs. I was grateful and flattered. But I knew I'd earned it.

Once I became part of the brain trust, I had some leverage. I suggested to Zeidner and Brownstein that Mike Rubin and I should alternate positions. For the first few weeks, I played third for a game and he'd play right field. Then the next game we'd switch positions. Mike quickly became one of our best outfielders and hitters. By the middle of the season he chose to stay in right field.

Now that I belonged, or so I thought, I looked forward to every practice and game. I was even able to concentrate better on my schoolwork. The team went undefeated, and on Memorial Day weekend we beat a team from Jamaica to win the Queens championship.

At parties and dances that spring I got a lot more attention than ever before. The big disappointment was that away from the ball field the guys in the clique continued to ignore me. Plus, they'd get all riled up whenever any of the popular girls so much as even talked to me.

From the time I was appointed team manager, it was clear that the guys in the clique weren't happy to be taking orders from an underling like me. This was their way of retaliating—by letting me know that on their turf, they were still the top dogs.

Even at eleven, I knew that team sports aren't a popularity contest. If you can help the team win, it doesn't matter if you're well liked or the most obnoxious s.o.b. out there. Still, the clique's off-the-field rejection was hard to take.

That season, I played well enough to make a contribution. I hit for a pretty good average, and my limited range and slow reflexes were offset by a strong and accurate arm and by my ability to position myself in the right spot. But my greatest value was as team manager. In the last year or so, I'd become a passionate and informed student of this game. Making tactical decisions on the field seemed to come easily to me.

The day after the championship game, our team picture appeared in the *Rockaway Beach Wave*. That afternoon, we all rode down Rockaway Beach Boulevard in open Lincoln Continentals and Cadillac convertibles, while our parents and friends lined the street cheering and tossing confetti. It was as if we'd won the World Series.

I'd struggled so hard to earn this moment of recognition. But the feeling lasted only for a few days. In less than three months, we'd all be moving on to junior high. As entering seventh graders, we'd be at the bottom of the pecking order. Which meant that even after so much hard work and suffering, I'd have to prove myself all over again.

♦

_ 4.

In the summer between the end of sixth grade and the beginning of junior high, Ira, Billy, and I were still making our Saturday pilgrimages to Ebbets Field. Now that they were eighth graders, they had a terrific time scaring the hell out of me with lurid tales of the horrors I'd soon encounter on the bus ride to and from school.

"The Arverne greasers have switch blades and zip guns," Billy said with a note of awe in his voice.

He was positively wild-eyed when he told me about the hazing that the Belle Harbor kids had to endure. "If they pick you out," he said, "they'll hang you upside down on the hand rails and turn your pockets inside out till your lunch money spills out."

I was chewing on that image when Ira broke in. *null*

"That's not the worst," he said. "Just pray they don't cut off your belt and pull your pants down."

"Yeah, I saw it happen to Sandy Dorfman," Billy chimed in. "Right in front of all the girls."

They had these big smirks on their faces. It was all a prerehearsed act. A little bit of one-upmanship—payback for all the times I'd accused them being such irreverent, uninformed Dodger fans.

If I wasn't already spooked, Ira made certain to warn me about "Big Tom" Sullivan, the Phys Ed and Hygiene teacher.

"Sullivan's got it in for Belle Harbor Jews," he said. "In Hygiene, he called Eliot Reiss and Danny Klein 'candy ass sugar babies.'"

"And you'd better watch your own ass when you do the rope climb in Gym," Billy said.

"Right, if you're too slow" Ira added, "Big Tom'll whack you across the butt with his paddle."

Ira forged on, describing in detail the notched wooden paddle that Sullivan kept in his office just for such occasions. Even if I could get out of Hygiene and Gym, there was no avoiding Sullivan. Not if I wanted to play baseball. He coached the VFW summer team.

The Sullivan stories weren't the first time I'd encountered anti-Semitism. Over Easter break Mike Rubin and I tried to get into a pick-up basketball game at the St. Francis De Sales playground. As soon as we were inside the gate, Larry Keeley and three other Irish Catholic kids descended on us. All four were scruffy looking urchins with holes in their shirts and sneakers. They reminded me of the orphans in *Oliver Twist*.

Larry was a short, scrawny kid with a legendary mean streak. We'd all heard the stories about his gang—how they liked to lay in wait for the school bus on 129th and Newport and then terrorize the Jewish kids who got off there.

"Can't you boys read the sign?" Larry said, loud enough for everyone to hear.

He was the ringleader. When he spoke, everyone stopped playing.

"No Jews allowed," he said. His three toadies laughed on cue.

We were too scared to respond.

"Everyone knows that Jews can't read," one of them said. More laughs. No one went back to playing ball. They were all waiting to see what was going to happen. If we didn't get out of there fast, we were in for it.

Keeley motioned with his left hand, and the four of them began pelting us with small stones that they'd fished out of their jacket pockets. I started running, with Mike trailing right behind. We sprinted through the front gate and up the block while they chased after us, still throwing stones and yelling, "Chicken-shit Jew boys," and "the Jews killed Christ, the Jews killed Christ."

We were lucky to get out of there without a fight. But when I got home, I was angry at myself for not having the nerve to stand up to them. How could I ever tell my father? Every time Billy Creelman from down the block would beat me up, my father told me, "The only way you'll get any respect from a bully is to stand up to him."

It's the same story almost every father tells his son. What he neglected to inform me of, however, was how to stand up to four of them at once. *NICE POINT*

All summer, I continued to follow the Dodgers' fortunes. Few of even their most loyal fans believed that the team could live down the disgrace of the previous season's disaster. But I didn't share that view. I was confident they'd make a comeback.

They did it, as usual, the hard way. Despite an off year by their best hitters, fewer victories from Carl Erskine and Preacher Roe, a key injury to Ralph Branca, and the loss of their ace, Don Newcombe, to military service—the Dodgers managed to fight off another Giant stretch run and win the pennant by four and half games. They lost the World Series to the Yankees again, but it took the Yanks seven games to beat them. When the season ended, the New York press once again wrote the Dodgers off as inveterate underachievers, if not out-and-out losers. But to my mind, they'd made a remarkable recovery by just winning the pennant.

The team's resurgence was in part due to the performance of a rookie pitcher, Joe Black, a previously unknown twenty-eight-year-old pitcher. Pitching mostly in relief, Black won fifteen games and saved fifteen more. Except for the Yankees' Joe Paige, the Giants' Hoyt Wilhelm, and a few select others, relief pitchers in the early '50s were undervalued role players. For most of the game, they'd huddle together in the bullpen, apart from the rest of their team-mates, watching and waiting for a chance to contribute. Often with the game on the line, they'd be called in to pitch. If they succeeded, they'd earn what, in baseball lingo, is called a save.

I could identify with these relief specialists a lot more easily than I could relate to most of the other players. Their borderline status, coupled with the pressure of having to come though in clutch situations, made them perfect role models for a kid who had an aching need for the spotlight.

By midsummer I was starting to obsess over the prospect of having to defend myself in school this fall. So I took out three library books: *The Amboy Dukes, A Stone for Danny Fisher,* and *Knock on Any Door*—all of which were about teenage street gangs. Two of the three main characters, Frank Goldfarb and Danny Fisher, were Jewish. Nick Romano, the third one, was Italian Catholic. They were all roughly my age.

The book that captivated me most was *The Amboy Dukes.* The gang leaders and henchmen had hoodlike names like Black Benny, Moishe, Larry Tunafish, Bull Bronstein, and Crazy Sachs. They sported Vaseline-slicked duck tailed (DA) haircuts and wore pegged pants—and they belonged to exotic sounding clubs like the Sutter Kings, the Killers, the D-Rape Artists, and the Enigmas.

All of them grew up in post-Depression New York—in rough neighborhoods like Brownsville and East New York. They regularly cut school and hung around pool halls and seedy clubhouses—smoking reefers and planning petty crimes. To maintain respect or stature they had to prove they weren't afraid to fight, steal, lie, cheat, and deal drugs. They picked up young girls and bragged about having sex with them. They robbed neighborhood candy stores and shops, often at gunpoint. Some gang members even put their lives at risk.

The character I felt the most sympathy for was Frank Goldfarb.

He was more intelligent and compassionate than the rest of the gang. His dream, in fact, was to marry his girlfriend and go to college. But he was too caught up in that world to ever escape. In the end, his misplaced loyalty to the group cost him his life.

I couldn't be more unlike these characters—even Frank. Yet there was something compelling about them and the world they inhabited. I yearned for the kind of camaraderie they shared. Sometimes, I even wished I had the chutzpah to live as close to the edge as they did.

P.S. 44 was less than a five mile bus ride from my house. The turn-of-the-century red brick building and its fenced-in schoolyard sat squarely in the heart of the Arverne-Hammels-Holland section of Rockaway Beach—one of the roughest, most rundown areas in south Queens. But it might as well have been on another planet. Nothing we'd experienced, either at home or in six years of grade school, could have prepared us for this junior high.

The forty-five minute bus ride to school took us through neighborhoods our parents had warned us about since we were kids. Once you got past McGuire's Bar and Grill on Beach 108th, all you'd see were seedy looking bars, gated liquor stores, rundown markets, weed choked vacant lots, shuttered stores, ramshackle houses, and shops with iron bars on the windows. I'd been idealizing neighborhoods like these all summer. But when I saw them in person, I was unnerved by the ugliness and squalor. I couldn't imagine growing up in these conditions.

The kids who got on the bus after Beach 100th street were predominantly Irish and Italian Catholics. Most lived in dilapidated old wooden homes with two or sometimes three other families. The Blacks and Puerto Ricans lived in the city funded housing projects close to the El.

A lot of the white guys belonged to street gangs like the South Arverne Boy's Club and the Hammels' Raiders. They took special classes like automotive shop and woodworking. Many were just biding their time until they turned sixteen and could legally quit school.

We all knew better than to mess with them. Like the characters in *The Amboy Dukes*, they had slicked back DAs and wore the same uniform each day: black motorcycle jackets with upturned collars, tight black T-shirts with cigarette packs rolled up in the sleeves, Garrison belts and dungarees, or pegged pants with white stitches running down the sides, and black shit kickers (steel-toed boots with straps and buckles).

The girls frequently came to school with curlers in their hair. They wore breast-hugging black sweaters, tight black wool skirts with slits down the side, black nylons with seams running down the back, and open-toed flats. Some had black cloth jackets with club names, like Pink Pussycats embroidered on the back. Most of them smoked and chewed gum.

The greasers and their girlfriends sat in the back of the bus, their feet up on the seat backs, smoking and cursing loudly enough for everyone to hear.

The school bus was a microcosm of the junior high social hierarchy—a pecking order that had even more sharply defined boundaries than those we'd established in grade school.

Up front were the guys in the clique—who I now thought of as Archies and Reggies. They preened and held court with their Betty and Veronica girlfriends. The kids in the clique were clean-cut preppies. The boys—future class presidents and G.O. leaders—had VO-5–styled crew cuts, and they wore blue oxford button downs, khaki pants, and dirty white bucks. Their companions—would-be cheerleaders, baton twirlers, and boosters—were well-scrubbed, pony-tailed girls who dressed in starchy white blouses, plaid pleated skirts, and white bobby sox with saddle shoes.

Sitting behind them was a most unusual group, comprised of

four guys I thought of as "genteel greasers." All four were from my grade school, and none of them were athletes, big brains, social movers, or even hardcore hoods.

Their leader was Manny Angell—a ruggedly handsome Sephardic Jew whose father was rumored to be in the Jewish Mafia. Manny was tall, lean, and broad-shouldered, with a chiseled profile and a thick mane of dark, unruly hair. He had a brooding insolence that was reminiscent of a young Marlon Brando or the James Dean character in *Rebel Without a Cause*.

Manny's comrades—Stuie Issacs, Jerry Shapiro, Paul Goldman, and Larry Ramis—were always in some kind of trouble it seems. The buzz back in sixth grade was that Manny and Larry had already been to reform school. They'd got caught hot wiring other people's cars and taking them for joy rides in the Riis Park parking lot. I also heard that all of them smoked reefers, and that Paul and Larry raced souped-up Harleys. But the most titillating rumors were the ones about Manny and Stuie "going all the way" with the rich high school girls from the Five Towns—an exclusive enclave of gated villages just across the Queens county line.

I was thinking about those guys while I was reading *The Amboy Dukes* in the summer. Back in grade school, Manny and Stuie played punch ball with some of us. Both lived a few blocks away from me, so occasionally I'd walk to school with them.

On the school bus, they had an air of defiance that bought them a kind of unspoken respect. The greasers, I noticed, never taunted them like they did everyone else. And the girls who hung around with the clique would steal furtive glances at them when their boyfriends weren't looking.

The most hapless group was the losers and outcasts. They had no choice but to sit near the back between Manny's boys and the greasers. Poor Eli Rubinstein and Bernard Schoenberg still had Vitalis-trained hair and wore blue or brown gabardine pants and Buster Brown shoes. The girls, Stephanie Sterner and Francine Leibler, were both overweight and had oily skin and acne. They wore grey felt poodle skirts to school. At dances and make-out parties they'd always wind up doing the Lindy Hop with each other.

The greasers and their "gun molls" taunted the two guys unmercifully, sometimes calling them "kikes" and "dirty Jews." I felt sorry for them, and yet, like everyone else, I kept my distance.

Where did I belong in this deviant hierarchy? As ambivalent as I felt about the clique, I still held out hope that those guys would someday warm up to me. I sat right behind them on the bus, listened in on their conversations, and tried to put in my two cents worth every so often. But not one of them went out of his way to include me in the group's activities—either the Friday night make-out parties or the after school pick-up basketball games in Frank Pearlman's driveway. The snubs were painful, of course. Yet the more indifferent they were toward me, the more I courted their approval. Whenever I asked myself why I was so desperate for their attention, all I had to do is look at the circle of popular girls and guys who were also vying for their attention.

I'd been at P.S. 44 for less than two weeks, and already I was an invisible nobody. Writing the sports column and playing on the sixth grade softball team were the only things that had brought me any recognition. But even those possibilities were closed. The junior high newspaper had been disbanded a year ago. Lack of interest, I was told. I thought about trying to enlist some help to revive the school paper. I even posted a notice on the announcements bulletin board. No one responded.

To my chagrin, the school also didn't have the budget to support any competitive sports—football, basketball, or baseball. That left only softball in the spring. And according to those in the know, the school team was a virtual nonentity.

Back in sixth grade I could share my misery with Peter or Mike. But since junior high began we'd all been drifting apart. We had different homerooms, class schedules, and teachers.

Complaining to my parents wasn't even an option. Because of unexpected setbacks, they'd been struggling to make ends meet. Three years before, during the summer when my grandmother died, my father and Hymie had a falling out. My grandfather then sold his share of the pharmacy to his nephews Abe, Sam, and Mickey Neiman, and moved in with my aunt Ruthie and her family. My parents assumed responsibility for the mortgage. Which meant that my mother had to work a half day at the pharmacy, while my father took a second job as a clothing salesman in a department store.

I could feel the tension between them whenever I was home. My mother blamed my father for driving Hymie out. She also resented having to work. My father tried to explain that it was only a temporary setback. I felt embarrassed and sorry for them. But what could I do? I was too preoccupied with my own troubles. I'm sure I made matters worse by moping around the house all the time.

To distract themselves from their hardships, every Wednesday night my mother played mahjong in the living room with her friends, while my father presided over the pinochle game in the smoke filled kitchen with the other husbands. On Saturday night the card games shifted over to the Platts' house. What little spare time my parents had, they spent over at the West End Temple Men's and Women's Club. It seemed like they were moving in separate orbits.

Lately I'd noticed that my mother had lost interest in reading, which left us little to talk about. My father and I had been growing apart ever since the summer, when he broke his leg sliding into second base. I remember the exact moment it happened. I heard the bone snap just as his foot jammed into the bag. When I ran out on the field, I saw the fractured bone protruding from his ankle. It made me sick to my stomach.

After a slow, painful rehab, he quit playing. Then he stopped watching the Giant games on TV. Without baseball to talk about, we didn't have a lot to say to one another.

I couldn't look to my brother for companionship. He was only seven. And as soon as school started, we weren't playing street games anymore. That was about the only thing we had in common.

So I began to brood and withdraw. After dinner, I'd retreat to my room to read or do homework. As a diversion, I listened to music. I wasn't much of a *Your Hit Parade* fan. The Perry Comos, Guy Mitchells, Patti Pages, and Eddie Fishers seemed unexpressive and bland. The songs were too old-fashioned and sappy for my tastes.

But after midnight, I'd listen under my pillow to the Al "Jazzbo" Collins show. The music's soaring leaps and abrupt transitions, the unpredictable chord changes, the complex riffs and improv solos surprised and delighted me. Even the musicians' names—Bird, Monk, Duke, and Diz, were personal and fraternal—like the nicknames of professional baseball players.

The music conjured up images of a downtown Manhattan nether world—an arcane universe of smoky lounges and Bohemian Greenwich Village clubs where artists, musicians, and writers all congregated. It was an exotic, fascinating universe that I dreamed of being a part of someday.

At best, I was a neophyte jazz buff. But knowing even a little bit about this music made me feel a bit like I did when I hobnobbed with the aficionados at Ebbets Field. Jazz lovers were a select aristocracy of sophisticated, informed hipsters who appreciated the music and who, on cue, could cite its history and invoke its dignitaries. The problem was that, aside from Peter, there was no one else I could share my enthusiasm with.

The only class I looked forward to was Language Arts. The reason I was so taken with it was because of my teacher. Whenever Mr. Aaron lectured on an assigned book, he'd close his eyes and wave his hands around like an opera singer belting out an aria. I loved watching him get all cranked up about whatever novel we were reading at the moment. I knew exactly what it felt like to be so enthralled by something I'd read.

Mr. Aaron's freckles and buzz cut made him seem almost boy-ish looking. He was tall and wiry, and his shoulders were too wide in proportion to his slender frame. Danny Ocasio, the class clown, called him "the human coat hanger." Two of the more savvy greasers, Martin Ackereizen and Vinnie Kay, poked fun at Mr. Aaron's first name.

"Oh Marvin, could you help me with my homework?" Ackereizen would say when Mr. Aaron was out of the room.

But everyone—even the one-book boys—respected him. That was because he didn't let you get away with anything. It didn't mat-ter who you were. If you cut class or didn't do your homework, he'd take it off your grade. If you mouthed off or he caught you day-dreaming, he'd write up a pink slip and send you down to assistant principal Sanders's office.

I too respected his tough, fair-minded ethic. It was like my father's belief that you have to earn what you get. But Mr. Aaron wasn't just a disciplinarian. During tests or grammar quizzes he'd walk around the room and put his hand on your shoulder. It was a disarming gesture. I also suspected that it was his way of checking to see that no one was cheating.

Tom Sawyer **and** *The Adventures of Huckleberry Finn* **were** the first two books we read in seventh grade. I'd read both a few years earlier at home. But I was only nine then. This time I saw them in quite a different light—especially *Huckleberry Finn.*

I identified with Huck's struggles to be more like Tom Sawyer and his gang. It was like wanting to be part of Manny's group. And I understood Huck's ambivalence about trying to please his Aunt Polly and the Widow Watson while also wanting to be part of Tom's mis-chievous gang. Though I didn't fully grasp Huck's moral dilemma, I still cheered his decision to help Jim escape from slavery. I was glad he'd subverted his guilty conscience, even if it meant that Huck would probably go to hell.

Like me, Huck was a lonely outsider. And so I tried to emulate him. While we were reading the book, I had a daydream fantasy where Otis Smith, one of the poorest black kids in class, became my best friend, and I became his protector. I'd take him home for dinner, and we'd pal around at school. It was like having an imaginary companion who relied on me to be his advocate and ally.

Mr. Aaron saw me as a model student. He was always praising my book reports and papers, which only made me want to work harder to please him. When he gave my Huck Finn paper back, he handed me a hardcover novel, *The Catcher in the Rye.* He suggested I read it and then write a personal response for extra credit.

"If you liked Huck," he told me, "You'll really get with this Holden Caulfield character."

His gesture caught me off guard, the same way Mrs. Carlin's had the year before, when she chose me to write the sports column. Both teachers had obviously seen something in me that each wanted to encourage. I'd disappointed Mrs. Carlin the year before. This time, I promised myself I'd follow through.

Holden quickly became my new role model. He seemed to embody my own deepest yearnings. I understood his angst and self-imposed isolation, identified with his compassion for all the losers and outcasts, and shared his disdain for the "phonies." For weeks, I went around imitating the hip, witty way he talked. I even wrote an unmailed fan letter to J. D. Salinger.

Back then I idolized certain writers the same way I worshipped professional baseball players. They were Olympian gods whose powers sprang from some magical source that would always remain elusive to me. But it didn't stop me from wanting to write. For my project, I did a series of Holden Caulfield knockoffs—short sketches that plumbed my deepest fears and secret prejudices. I wrote about dark thoughts and harsh, judgmental attitudes I harbored toward classmates, teachers, friends, my family, and myself. These were things I'd never fully acknowledged before.

I felt strangely elated, even liberated by what I'd discovered. Yet

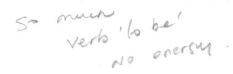

when it came time to turn the paper in, I hesitated. Maybe, I'd revealed too much of myself. But Mr. Aaron, bless his heart, praised my candor. He even urged me to show the sketches to the school yearbook editors. I was flattered, but I wasn't sure I could show anything this personal to strangers. Suppose they hated it? What if they wanted to publish it? Then everyone would know what I was thinking.

I'd always been somewhat intrigued by Rita Caselli and Sarah Broomfield, the yearbook editors. I'd observed them in the halls and in the cafeteria talking to their Bohemian friends. Both were eighth graders who looked older and acted more sophisticated than any of the other girls. Both had dark, braided long hair, and they dressed like identical twins: loose fitting black cable knit sweaters, black wool scarves that hung down to their knees, baggy black skirts, black socks, and either black boots or Indian moccasins. Their faces were pale and washed out looking, and they never wore makeup or lipstick. They always looked like they'd stayed out all night at some jazz club, smoking reefers and drinking hard whiskey. I could imagine them five years from now studying literature at Mount Holyoke, Smith, or Radcliffe.

Both girls seemed deliberately stand-offish. If they deigned to talk at all, they'd speak with affected British accents. Their presence, to say the least, was unnerving. The girls in the clique referred to them as eggheads and bohos. In turn, the two characterized the popular girls as bourgeois conformists.

Their pretentious airs put me off. But their pseudosophistication appealed to me. Whenever I'd see them in the cafeteria, they'd be hanging out with a small entourage of eighth grade girls who looked and dressed just like they did. I'd sometimes eavesdrop while they spoke in hushed, serious tones about the books they were reading and the hip musicians who were "gigging down in the West Village." They'd shake their heads and sigh, as if they were privy to profound ideas and arcane theories that the rest of us were too obtuse to comprehend. They dropped words like *abstruse, esoteric,* and *recondite* like they were part of everyone's normal conversation. For people who claimed to be nonconformists, it sure seemed that they dressed and acted a lot alike.

I wasn't "far-out" enough for this crowd. Yet, except for Peter Desimone, these girls were the only peers I'd encountered in seven years of school who even talked about books and writers. Moreover, their impressions of the clique were right on target—just like Holden's knack for spotting the "phonies." For a moment, I entertained the notion that perhaps they might even like my sketches.

I knew where the yearbook office was. But I couldn't just barge in there and say, "My teacher, Mr. Aaron, told me to give these to you."

The yearbook "office" was at far end of the third floor, right next to the fire escape. The room was a converted supply closet that reeked of stale cigarette smoke, Clorox, and coffee grinds.

For all its grunginess, the place had kind of musty old bookstore charm about it. The chipped peeling walls were covered with black-and-white posters of writers from the '20s and '30s: Hemingway, Fitzgerald, Gertrude Stein, Edna St. Vincent Millay, and Steinbeck.

When I peered through the half opened door, the two girls had their backs to me. They were leaning over a scratched old oak desk that was strewn with sheets of wrinkled, typewritten pages. Both were chain smoking and sipping coffee as they passed pages back and forth. I could hear faint muted strains of music coming from a radio. It sounded like the jazz I listened to late at night.

I felt a sharp pang in my chest. I pictured myself sitting with Rita and Sarah at some imagined jazz club in the West Village, smoking, talking about our favorite books and writers, and intermittently downing shots of Scotch.

After a week of worry and procrastination, I finally put my sketches in a brown manila envelope and wrote my name and home-room class on the front. Then I held onto the envelope for two more days. On a Friday afternoon when I knew everyone would be gone, I slid the envelope under the office door. I immediately wanted to take it right back. I even tried to slide my hand under the door crack before giving up.

I fretted for days over what they'd think of my writing. Then one morning during homeroom, a hall monitor handed me a coffee stained envelope. The stains had blurred all but my last name. I could barely make out the homeroom number. I knew it was bad news. Why else would they be sending back the envelope? My ears burned and my heart was thumping so loudly that I was sure every-one could hear it.

I thought about it all morning until I couldn't stand the tension any longer. In fourth period Social Studies I asked for a bathroom pass and ducked beneath a staircase where no one could see me. All I could hope for was a polite rejection. Or some suggestions on how to improve the writing. I ripped the envelope open and inside was a handwritten note. Two short sentences: "We don't accept work like this. Besides, it isn't even typed." It was signed "The Editors."

My knees began to shake. I read those heartless comments over and over again. What did they mean by "work like this"? I felt a momentary stab of anger. It was all Mr. Aaron's fault. Why did he subject me to this? When the anger passed, I began to blame myself. I should have known better. I hadn't felt so humiliated since the sixth grade dance.

All afternoon, I walked around in a stupor. In the halls, I avoided eye contact with everyone. On the bus ride home I sat alone and buried my head in a book. The rejection stung so much that, finally, I couldn't keep it to myself. I blurted it out to my parents at dinner.

"That's OK," my father said. "You took a chance and it didn't work out. You'll bounce back."

Easy for him to say. I wish I had his resilience.

My mother felt sorry for me—which was, of course, the reaction I was looking for. She suggested I talk to Mr. Aaron. Maybe he could say something to the two editors. It was good of her to take my setback to heart. But the last thing I wanted was to give those two harpies the satisfaction of knowing how I felt.

Every time I saw them at lunch I'd imagine them in that broom closet, laughing and making fun of my writing. When I passed them in the halls, I couldn't bear to look them in the eye. Even if I did have the balls to stare them down, they wouldn't have had the slightest idea who I was.

Which is worse, I wondered: rejection or invisibility? Lately, those seemed to be my only two options.

◆

_ 5.

Just before Thanksgiving break, I was walking into homeroom, head down, feeling sorry for myself. I was a few minutes
early, and Madeline Feeney, a pale, angelic-looking blonde girl, was
a couple of steps ahead of me. I happened to pick my head up just
in time to spot Edward Farley standing in front of the big windows
on the other side of the room. He had a crazed look in his eyes.
Farley was the last guy you'd want to be alone with in a room. We
all knew that he'd been to reform school. His idea of a good time
was to grab some poor schlemiel in the hall or at recess and smack
him around with his open hand. Everyone in homeroom kept a distance from him. Even the street gangs didn't want any part of this
guy. They knew he was a dangerous psycho.

Nobody knew anything about Farley's family or his home life.
He looked like a derelict. Every day he wore the same ratty clothes
to school: ripped, grease-stained dungarees, scuffed leather boots,
and tattered, hand-me-down shirts. His disheveled blonde hair and
perpetual scowl made him seem even more menacing.

Last week in the schoolyard he picked a fight with Martin
Ackereizen, who was not exactly a slouch when it came to defending himself. When Ackereizen got back from the nurse's office he
had a half dozen stitches and a bloody bandage on his forehead. A
bunch of eighth graders had witnessed the fight, but no one had the

guts to rat on Farley. All he got was two days of detention before he was back in class.

And now I was looking right into his steely green eyes. Before I could figure out what to do, he cocked his right arm behind his ear and released what looked liked a yellow pearl handled knife, its open blade glinting in the sun. I yelled "Head's up!" and Madeline jerked her head forward just as the knife whizzed between us and lodged in the bulletin board, its handle vibrating and rattling in the cork.

Madeline was too stunned to even scream. Farley just stood there with a sneer on his face—as if he was challenging me to do something. But I was frozen in my tracks. Then the recess bell sounded and the classroom began to fill up. When homeroom was over, I got out of there as fast as I could.

All night I agonized over whether to tell someone about what I'd seen. I needn't have worried, though. During homeroom the next morning, I got a note to report to the assistant principal's office. Madeline's father, it seems, had already reported the incident.

Madeline, Farley, and I were each called in separately. When it was my turn I described to Mr. Sanders about what I'd seen. He took notes on a clipboard pad, and then he abruptly ordered me to go back to class.

Was he nuts? Who would protect me from Farley? I had a momentary urge to sneak out of the building and go hide in my bedroom. It was one of the few times that I actually *wanted* to be invisible.

All day I worried about encountering Farley. Sure enough, he was waiting for me outside of seventh period biology. While the other kids headed out to catch the bus, he wrapped his right arm around my right shoulder blade and steered me down the empty hall. How could Sanders have been such an asshole? If I got killed, it would be his fault. I wanted to scream for help. But suppose this psycho had another knife on him?

When we were far enough out of sight, Farley grabbed me by the shirt collar and slammed my head against the concrete wall. The pain shot up my neck to the back of my head. Cascades of splintered lights erupted behind my eyes.

"You'll pay for this, Jew boy," he said. I was sure he was going to smack me around some more. Maybe even cut me. He was that crazy. But he just laughed and walked away. I was too numb to remember how I got home.

I couldn't decide what to do. If I told my parents, my mother would surely order me to stay home from school. My father, I was certain, would tell me to go back. And he'd have been right. If I didn't show up, things could go a lot worse with this weirdo.

I stayed up all night rereading *The Amboy Dukes*, asking myself what Frank Goldfarb would have done had he been in my place. Then it came to me. Of course, he'd have packed a weapon and arranged for the other Dukes to watch his back.

That's when I hatched my plan. I'd been looking for an excuse to approach Manny and his guys. Now I had one. They thrived on this kind of stuff.

The next morning, just as the bus made the turn past McGuire's, I leaned over in my seat, casually took out the switch-blade I'd brought with me, and showed it to Manny and Stuie. Then, as if we'd been cohorts for years, I told them what had happened. I was hoping they'd see my dilemma as a big adventure. They did. Both of them volunteered to follow me around in the halls between classes. I was so grateful, I wanted to hug them.

I stuck close to them in the schoolyard until it was time to go to homeroom. They escorted me right up to the door.

"Don't walk in the halls by yourself," Stuie said.

"Pick anybody, even a couple of dorks," Manny added.

Good. They were taking charge.

I walked into homeroom head down, frozen with fear. When I got to my seat, I turned around slowly. Farley's desk was empty. My heart skipped. *He's probably waiting for me right outside the door.*

Who could I walk with to first period Algebra? Before I could decide, the bell rang and Mr. Aaron called me up to his desk.

I was in a panic watching everyone file out for first period classes. The idea of walking the halls alone terrified me. When the room was empty Mr. Aaron sat me down and calmly explained that Farley wouldn't be back.

"He's already on his way to reform school," he said. The knot in my stomach began to dissolve.

I found out later that Mr. Sanders had alerted every teacher in school, in addition to calling my parents. It was the right thing to do. But it seemed odd that no one had bothered to inform me until now. Still, I was elated by the news. At lunch, I told Manny and Stuie what had happened. I could see the disappointment in their eyes.

By the end of the day, the story had already made the rounds. On the bus ride home, everyone—even the clique and the greasers—were anxious to hear about what had happened. Of course, I exaggerated. When would I get this kind of attention again?

While I was holding court I wondered what Manny and Stuie were thinking. If I built myself up too much, maybe they'd blow my cover. But neither one said a word. I could have sworn that Stuie gave me the thumbs-up sign.

When the bus got to Beach 132nd Street, Manny got off with me—at my stop, not his.

"Drop by some night for a game of pool and a few beers." He said it like we were best friends.

Me, play pool? Drink beer? My impulse was to say yes immediately. But I held back. This time, I'd play it cool—like Frank Goldfarb, or even Manny himself would have done.

"Thanks," I said. "I just might take you up on it."

I was wildly ambivalent about Manny's offer. A part of me was curious to see what went on inside his inner sanctum. But compared to those guys, I was a Goody Two Shoes. How would I ever fit in?

It's funny how something like the Farley incident can take on a life of its own. My worst nightmare had turned into a brief moment of celebrity. As word began to spread, I became more and more of a hero in each new version of the story. One particularly outlandish variation even had me putting a switchblade to Farley's throat.

Needless to say, I thrived on being in the spotlight. When questioned, I neither admitted nor denied what had happened. My answer frequently was that "My lawyer advised me not to talk about it." The fib embarrassed me, though obviously not enough to remove it from my repertoire.

The fallout from the incident had even gotten me a moment of attention from the clique. And I wanted to make it last for as long I could. That week, Mandel invited me to fill in for him in one of Pearlman's pickup basketball games. And when Freddy Klein had a Friday night Bar Mitzvah lesson, I got asked to a party at Bonnie Lerner's house. There was no turning that invitation down.

I was beginning to think that maybe I'd finally arrived. Perhaps this would be my big chance to make an impression on the popular crowd. Two nights before the party, I was already rehearsing what I'd say to anyone who asked me about the Farley episode.

As soon as I arrived, the first thing I saw was the coterie of popular girls surrounding Manny and his boys. They were fawning all over them. That evening, no one paid any attention to me. By the end of the night, I felt like an idiot. I was disappointed and angry with myself for being so hopeful and so naive. By the time the lights were lowered and the make out music was on, I was burning with envy. How could stuck-up, prissy girls like Elaine and Alice be attracted to such cocky, crude guys? How come those guys could get away with it and I couldn't? What was their secret?

The next morning, I decided to take Manny up on his offer.

Manny's parent's rec room had faux knotty pine paneling, a well stocked Naugahyde and stainless steel bar with a mirror behind it, a green felt pool table, an oversized sofa, a Dumont TV set, a roulette wheel, a card table, and a Schaeffer Beer wall clock. Where on earth did Manny get all this stuff? Maybe his father really was in the Jewish Mafia.

The basement room was an ultra stylish version of the Amboy Dukes clubhouse. Depending on Manny's whim, the group would shoot pool, or play five card stud, black jack, or roulette. It was also the setting for the monthly circle jerks.

All the guys—Stuie Issacs, Jerry Shapiro, Paul Goldman, and Larry Rabin—looked and dressed just like Manny: slicked back DAs, and sculpted, rooster-like pompadours with a wispy spit curl winding down the forehead. They had expensive black leather jackets, tight Levi's or pegged pants, and black motorcycle boots. Each one carried a switchblade in his jacket pocket, a packet of Trojans or Ramses in his wallet, and a comb in his back pocket. Like every other group in junior high, they thought of themselves as trendsetters.

For the next few weeks, I tagged along wherever they went. On weeknights, they hung out in Manny's basement or at Art's candy store a few blocks away on 129th Street.

The neighborhood stores were all located on 129th, between Cronston and Newport Avenues: Tishman's tailor shop, the Peter Reeves market, the Shell station, Johnny's Bar and Grill, and Willie's butcher shop. Art's was right next to Sam Cahmi's deli, a few stores up the block from Neiman's Pharmacy.

At Art's, the five guys would sit at the soda fountain, sipping egg creams and shooting the breeze. Each month when the new magazines came in, they always pulled the same scam. Three of them would talk to Art and the two others would stand at the magazine and comic book racks pretending to leaf through *Tales of the Crypt Keeper* or *Mad Magazine*, while one of them slipped the latest girlie magazine or *True Detective* under his jacket.

Art was onto them. He'd simply add the price of the magazine to the bill. Everyone just played along with the game. Once I saw Art wink at Manny and say, "Look, Burtchick, anyone catches you with a girlie magazine, you didn't get it in my store. You hear me, big shot?"

He turned to look right at me when he said it. "What's wrong with you?" he seemed to be saying. Why are you hanging around with these Nogoodnicks?"

That's what I'd been asking myself every day for the past three weeks. But then, whenever they talked about girls, I'd remember exactly why.

When the temperature was above freezing the guys would stand in front of Art's smoking Lucky's or Dunhill filter tips and boasting about copping a feel off some girl at a make out party, or a back row hand job in the balcony of the Park Theater.

I was all ears—especially when they identified the girls by name. Manny said that he and Cindy Levine had a hot session under the boardwalk on 116th Street one night last summer. I felt a sharp pang of resentment. How did he ever get to her?

I'd had dreams about Cindy since sixth grade. Tanned olive skin, dark brown eyes, and jet black curly hair, she was the most exotic looking girl in our class. At school she wore tight, straight, wool skirts, form-fitting Orlon sweaters, and black penny loafers with white ribbed socks. Nobody seemed to know much about her— which only added to her mystique. I'd heard that her parents were part Gypsy and that she had a history of dating older guys.

Cindy wasn't like any of the other girls I knew. She wasn't the least bit interested in the clique or in what the popular girls thought of her. She never bothered to even show up at the Beth El dances or at make out parties.

In my grade school fantasies, I imagined Cindy and I were kindred spirits. Together we shunned all the popular kids. I also dreamed that we went out on coke dates, made out under the boardwalk, studied together in her room, and talked passionately about jazz and the books we were both reading. Every time someone in the clique made fun of her, I'd come to her defense—usually by squaring off in the schoolyard with one of the guys and beating the crap out of him right in front of Cindy and everyone else.

I'd always wanted to approach Cindy and tell her how I felt. But every time I was around her, I got dry mouth. If I tried to speak, nothing came out. In time, I convinced myself that she was simply out of my league. By junior high, I'd even convinced myself that she was beyond all of our reaches. That is, until I heard Manny's story.

Weeks afterwards, I was still tormented by the image of the two of them lying on an army blanket, going at it hot and heavy under the boardwalk. I was too scared to ask him how far they went. Part of me wanted to know, and part of me wanted to avoid the anger and self-loathing I'd feel if my fears were confirmed.

It perplexed me that girls like Cindy and the smart, rich girls from the Five Towns fell for guys like Manny—guys who didn't give a damn about them. But that's what I was here to find out, wasn't it? I decided it was time to join up. If they'd have me, that is.

I launched my campaign by trying to persuade my father to buy me a leather jacket.

"Why do you want to look like those hoodlums?" my mother asked.

She didn't get it. But my father did. I know he didn't approve, but he never nagged at me the way my mother did. He'd grown up in the streets, and he knew how important this was to me. So, he proposed a compromise. He'd get me the jacket if I agreed to work two Sundays a month at the pharmacy to help pay for it.

To my father the notion of working for your allowance was almost a given. So far I'd managed to avoid it, mostly because of my mother's intervention. Now, I had no choice but to agree.

My job at Neiman's was to deliver prescriptions on my bicycle. I hated it. To avoid having to pedal for blocks against the cutting ocean wind, I did everything I could to make myself useful around the store. I soda jerked, worked in the stockroom, even sold cosmetics to the women. But when I did have to deliver a prescription, I'd go out of my way to make sure I didn't ride past Art's. What would those guys think if they saw me riding a bicycle? Especially now that Manny was driving them around town in his father's DeSoto coupe.

Once I got the leather jacket, I started wearing tight Levi's and boots, and styling my hair in a DA and pompadour. In the schoolyard, in classes, and at lunch I was always stealing glances at the popular girls—hoping they'd notice my new look. So far though, nothing had changed. As usual, it only made me try harder.

I tried to imitate the things the guys did. But none of it felt right. I was lousy at pool because I couldn't get the hang of how to hold the cue stick. And I couldn't bluff convincingly at poker because my eyes and grimaces always gave me away.

If you expect to fail, that's usually what happens. I'd learned at least that much as an athlete. In jock lingo, you "choked" or "took the big apple" if you didn't come through under pressure.

When I was younger, I had a tendency to tighten up whenever I knew people were watching me. I remember blowing two potentially game-winning foul shots in a Jewish Community League game. I was so rattled by the crowd that I lost my concentration. That's exactly the kind of thing that would happen in Manny's basement. Just by razzing me, the guys could goad me into scratching a pool shot or misplaying a poker hand.

But it was all just child's play compared to the hazing I'd endure when I finally committed myself to joining the group.

First, I had to swipe a *True Detective* from Art's without getting caught. That wasn't the hard part, though. Art had been in business for so long that he knew my cousins, grandfather, mother, and aunt by their first names. To him, I was the nice kid in the group— the one who he once said was "too decent to cheat and steal."

I suspected he knew what I'd done, but he never called me on it, which made me feel even worse. In fact, the minute I was out the door I wanted to go right back in and hand the magazine to him. But it was too late.

Stealing the magazine was just the beginning. It wasn't long before all five of them were egging me on. Manny offered me a few reefers. All it did was make me dizzy. Shapiro challenged me to steal a pretzel from Gino's candy store under the El. Goldman bet me a buck I couldn't swipe a dozen Trojans and Ramses from the pharmacy stockroom. I did it all. But when Larry Rabin told me to pinch my father's French deck, I was too embarrassed to admit that I didn't know what a French deck was.

"Everyone's father has a French deck," Manny said. "Look in his dresser drawer. It'll be under the socks or underwear."

That night, Peter Desimone told me what a French deck was.

"No way," I said. "Not my father."

Turns out that Manny was right. I found it in the bedroom dresser. How in the world did he know?

When I first saw the blurred black-and-white images on those playing cards, I felt lightheaded, almost punchy. Waves of pleasure surged through me. I was giddy. My stomach felt all fluttery. I was amazed that my father actually possessed stuff like this. I wondered if my mother knew about it. For days afterward, I snuck back into their bedroom to peek at those pictures. I couldn't get the images out of my head. I had wet dreams every night.

When I brought the deck to the rec room, Manny used it as an occasion to choreograph a circle jerk. He ordered everyone to strip down to his socks while he held up the cards. I hated this ritual. It was so public. I dreaded every second. I wondered what this had to do with learning how to impress girls.

Still, it was all new territory for me. The more approval I got from the group, the more reckless I became. I even felt a secret thrill whenever I got away with those little transgressions.

Acting on my own, I brought a palm sized roulette wheel to school, and I began to take bets at lunch and recess. It wasn't long before knots of seventh and eight grade boys would be huddled around me as I knelt down next to the handball court wall and spun the wheel. To my surprise, the guys from the clique even participated. Winning the pot didn't mean a thing to me. What I loved was being the center of attention.

Crippled verbs

It was mid February and I was spending almost every night hanging around with the group. As a result, my midterm grades were conspicuously lower than they had been in the fall. I was also starting to get into trouble. In early March, a teacher on recess duty caught me running the roulette game. I was sure that Mr. Sanders would give me after school detention or else suspend me from classes. But I had a clean record, so I got a month's probation and a warning to keep my nose clean.

When my parents found out, my mother of course wanted to ground me. But my father intervened.

"Let him make his own mistakes, Stell," he said. "He'll learn the hard way—just like I did."

It didn't take long for that prediction to come true. In early March, the softball coach, Mr. Barrows, caught me smoking in the boys' john. My punishment was to take ten laps around the school building—at recess, with everybody watching.

Barrows was determined to make an example out of me. I was in good shape, I figured. I'd been running on the beach all summer. Maybe I could do this. The junior high was a city block long, and several blocks deep. It was freezing cold, and after a single lap the pain in my lungs was so sharp I couldn't catch my breath. With everybody watching and Barrows riding behind me on a bicycle, I made it through a lap and a half before I almost collapsed from fatigue.

It was another warning signal. But this one got my attention.

full of the verb "to be"

Getting caught was a good excuse for me to quit smoking. I was relieved, in fact, that someone had finally stopped me. Still, I wish it would have been anyone except Coach Barrows. Softball tryouts were less than two weeks away. I was worried that he'd hold this against me. But even if he didn't, I knew I had to start setting some boundaries. The one thing that was more important than the group's approval was playing ball.

Over the past few months, I'd gradually become aware that I'd lost sight of my original intent. Nothing we'd done lately had anything to do with girls. So what was I sticking around for?

The other thing that brought me to my senses was a plan Manny and Stuie had hatched a week after I got caught smoking. They planned to hot wire a car and take us all on a joy ride in the Riis Park parking lot right before Memorial Day weekend. It was something I wanted absolutely no part in. Stealing a car was a hell of a lot different from swiping dirty magazines and pretzel sticks.

Manny sensed that not everyone was enthusiastic about this caper. So to make certain that none of us had an excuse, one night he fished a penknife out of his shirt pocket.

"Blood brothers," he said. He held the gleaming blade up.

You had to hand it to him. He knew just how to control us.

We passed the knife around the circle, and one-by-one we jabbed our thumbs with the blade until droplets of blood bubbled up to the skin's surface. We pressed our thumbs together and the pact was sealed.

I pretended to go along with it—at least for the moment. Why risk it now? Memorial Day was almost a month away. When the time came, I'd find a way out.

In early April, Mike Rubin and I had already started playing catch outdoors. We hadn't seen much of one another that year, but

I knew Mike had to be struggling in school as much as I was. Playing softball would be a safe haven for us both. It seemed urgent that we make the team.

All of the home games would be played in the schoolyard—on a concrete surface. To simulate those conditions we spent hours after school and on weekends hitting fungos and ground balls to one another on the still-frozen turf at Riis Park. We worked out no matter how cold the weather was.

As tryouts got closer, I kept wondering if Barrows would still have it in for me. But I needn't have worried. Mike and I were the only two from the sixth grade team who came out for seventh grade softball.

I knew going in that the team didn't have the budget to travel. We had to settle instead for playing a home "exhibition" schedule against every team in the Peninsula League. Evidently, this was small potatoes to the guys in the clique. That's why they didn't bother coming out for the team. They were gearing up, Pearlman told me, for the big prize—PAL (Police Athletic League) tryouts in June.

What was the deal with those guys anyway? I wondered if they were even going to invite me to their workouts and practices. Last year, I was team captain. Now, I was back to being a nonentity. Their attitude infuriated me. I'd told myself that I'd do everything in my power to make them regret this.

Under normal conditions, Rubin and I would have had to sweat it out just to make the seventh grade team. But all the best players from the surrounding neighborhoods were guys that Barrows couldn't count on. Some had after school jobs; others just wanted to hang out with their gangs. The two of us had experience; and we wanted to play. Besides, we never missed a practice.

I couldn't have asked for a better situation. Most of the guys who Barrows was forced to recruit were inexperienced and relatively unskilled. He couldn't afford to lose Mike or me—not if he wanted to field a decent team. So, in spite of my obvious limitations, he let me play shortstop.

In time, Barrows did manage to convince some of the better neighborhood players to join up. To get back at the clique, I implored Zeidner and Brownstein to help us out. I was ecstatic when they said yes.

Since our games didn't count in the league standings, there would be very little pressure on us to win. But that's not how Barrows saw it. He was lobbying for more money and support, and he wanted to convince the head honchos that the softball team deserved to compete in the Peninsula League. So all spring, he never let up on us. To him, every game mattered.

Every team is a reflection of its coach's attitude. Because Barrows had something to prove, we all did. That season then, we evolved into a scrappy, determined bunch. We ambushed a lot of good teams. In fact, by the end, we won more games than even Barrows had expected.

The whole situation worked to my advantage. I liked being on a team of underdogs. Plus, I knew I didn't have to keep proving myself every game. For the first time I could relax and concentrate on playing.

There were games that spring when I volunteered to move over to second base just so Ronnie Zeidner could play short. But for the most part I continued to work hard at becoming better at the position. I practiced in between games and carefully studied Pee Wee Reese, Alvin Dark, and Phil Rizzuto, the three great New York shortstops. By the end of the season, I'd become a pretty decent middle infielder.

Softball had taken up so much time that I spent fewer and fewer evenings with Manny's group. With ball games and practices to occupy me, I began to see them in a different light. They seemed aimless and irresponsible. No goals or commitments. Clearly, I was ready to cut my ties with them.

I was contemplating just how to break the news to the group

when, just before Memorial Day weekend, Manny informed us that the car heist was a go. It would happen on Friday evening. I was cornered. I'd forgotten about it, and now there was no time to think up an excuse. Ok, maybe I owed them this one last commitment. I didn't want it to look like I was chickening out or being disloyal. After all, they did take me in when no one else would have me.

By the time I found out that Stuie had stolen Myron Kerns's Cadillac, I was in the back seat sandwiched between Rabin and Shapiro, with Goldman practically sitting on my lap. They'd all been drinking and getting high all afternoon. You could smell it on their breath.

As soon as we got to the Riis Park parking lot Manny floored the gas pedal, and within seconds we were going almost a hundred miles an hour. I was terrified. I was sure we were going to die. That's when we heard the sirens. The cops were right on our tail.

Big surprise, right? What were those guys thinking when they hotwired Kerns's Caddy? He was on the town board, for Christ sake. What's more, he knew my father from the Temple Men's Club. How could I have ever been so stupid? I deserved whatever I was going to get.

Squad cars came at us from all directions. You'd have thought we'd kidnapped someone, or robbed a bank. Manny hit the brakes hard, and we all pitched forward. The cops jumped out of their cars, pointed their guns at the sky, and began shooting straight up. It was a scare tactic. I don't know if I was more frightened or relieved to see them.

The desk sergeant booked and finger printed us at the precinct station. Then two cops put us all in a cell while the sergeant called our parents. Over the next hour, someone from each family showed up to make bail. But no one came to get me. After they'd all left, I was alone. When I yelled for help, the sergeant came down and informed me that my father had indeed paid the bail bond. But he'd requested that I be held overnight. It was just like him to do something like that.

All night my stomach didn't stop churning. My mind couldn't stop racing. It wasn't fair. I got suckered into this, and those guys were home, sleeping in their own beds. I imagined all the worst scenarios. What if this goes on my record? How about college? Will it be in the *Wave?* Suppose Barrows finds out? Will he let me play again?

The next morning, my father came to get me. Once we were in the car I braced myself for the lecture. He certainly wasn't happy about this, but all he said was that since I was only an accessory to a misdemeanor, the charges would probably be waved. Myron Kerns wouldn't press charges, he said, so long as the six families agreed to make sure that we never met together again as a group. I wondered just how much of this deal had been brokered by my father?

For the rest of the ride home, neither of us said anything. But I was doing a lot of thinking. It was probably just as hard for my father to let me sit in jail overnight as it was for me to endure the punishment.

I never saw any of those guys again. But I did find out later that Manny's parents had sent him away—to an upstate military academy. Stuie Issacs transferred to Andover, a rich kid's prep school in Massachusetts. Larry Ramis was sent to a junior high for delinquent students. And Goldman was killed the next fall in a motorcycle accident. I never found out what became of Shapiro, and I didn't try.

I had already begun to move on.

◆

_ 6.

If you were a competitive athlete, your fate was in the hands of three formidable coaches: Patrolman Joe Bleutrich ran the PAL basketball and baseball teams; Tom Sullivan, the junior high Phys Ed and Hygiene teacher, coached the VFW (Veterans of Foreign Wars) baseball and Peninsula League football teams; and Jack Kerchman was the high school football and baseball coach.

Each coach had a singular trademark. And each asserted his authority in a different way. Ex-players referred to them as "Rockaway's Holy Trinity." Bleutrich "the Father," was inscrutable and reserved; Sullivan, "the Son," was a ruthless bigot; and Kerchman, "the Holy Ghost, " the most powerful and feared of the three, was a disciplinarian and a tyrant. Each one was in cahoots with the other two. So, if you made the PAL and VFW teams you had a lot better chance of being chosen for the high school varsity. Which was, of course, every jock wannbe's dream.

I was a baseball player, so I'd have to contend with *all three.* That is, if I was lucky enough to get that far. The only other alternatives were to transfer to a private school, or else give up my dream of playing high school baseball, neither of which was a viable option.

I was hoping that PAL tryouts would be held on the Riis Park diamonds. I'd virtually grown up on those fields. I knew where every pothole and pebble was. And Riis Park was only a mile from our house. Maybe I could convince my father to come out and watch. Instead, Bleutrich chose the high school baseball field—almost five miles away from where I lived.

Far Rockaway was the only high school on the peninsula. It was also one of the few city schools to have its own football/baseball field. That alone gave it some prestige. Even though I'd never set foot on the field, in my imagination it already was hallowed ground. In the past five years, ever since Kerchman started coaching football and baseball, Far Rockaway had gained a reputation as one of the top sports schools in the city—which of course only added to its mystique. All of us aspirants had dreamed of one day playing on that field.

Located a few blocks up from the El in Bayswater, the high school was a sprawling three-story white brick building with several annexes. The imposing structure was lodged between a lower-middle-class neighborhood to the west and a cluster of abandoned houses and weed lots to the east.

The playing field was surrounded on three sides by a twenty-foot-high chain link fence. The first things you saw when you walked through the gate were the football bleachers, the goal posts, and the huge factory-like building looming in the background. As I crossed that threshold, I felt lost and panicky, like I did on the first day of junior high.

I became even more flustered when I spotted small gatherings of adults and kids in the third base bleachers: family members and friends of the neighborhood guys who were trying out. It reminded me that no one was here to support me.

At breakfast that morning my mother had diplomatically informed me that my father wouldn't be able to get out of work in time for the tryouts. She assured me that he really wanted to be there. But her tone of voice betrayed her disappointment. I'm sure it was true, but I still felt like I'd been deserted. I was also miffed that my mother didn't volunteer to take his place.

But that was a minor letdown compared to what I'd soon be up against. All the best baseball players on the Rockaway peninsula had shown up. Fifty of us would compete for fourteen roster spots. And a half dozen were shortstops.

As a rule, a team's most versatile infielder is the shortstop. The good ones are acrobatic enough to make the pivot on the double play, they can range far into the hole to their left and right, and they have strong enough arms to throw runners out at first. On most every team from sandlot to the pros, the shortstop is the unofficial infield captain. They're also expected to be super alert, and they're responsible for covering second on steals and third on bunts, as well as for being the cut-off man on anything that's hit to the outfield.

As withdrawn as I am in social situations, I've never been a passive ball player. I like to take charge. On the field, I thrive on being right in the middle of things. In that regard, I'm most at home at shortstop. My main assets are my intelligence, my ability to antic-ipate, and a strong accurate arm. Because I could size up the hitters, I always knew where to position myself. I'd watch where they stood in the box and observe their stances and mechanics. Did they upper-cut or hit down on the ball? Did they have an inside/out or outside/in swing? I also paid close attention to the catcher's signals and to the location of his glove. Before every pitch, I'd shade the hitters accord-ingly, depending on whether the catcher's target was up and in, low and away, low and in, or high and away.

Still, I knew that I didn't have the size or quickness to compete with Sammy Silverman, Bobby Frankel, or Larry Moshan, the first three shortstops I watched that day. Add to that mix Mandel and Zeidner—each of whom had grown almost a half a foot since sixth grade—and there already were five shortstops who were better than I was. Still, what else could I do but sit it out and wait my turn.

I'd been observing coach Bleutrich all afternoon, looking to see what I could do to hook his attention. He was a tall distinguished looking man, maybe mid forties, with salt and pepper hair, sharply chiseled features, and slightly stooped shoulders. He was very taciturn, even restrained. He spoke softly and respectfully to his fellow coaches and to all of us kids. Definitely a Gary Cooper type.

You could see why his former players referred to him as "the Father." Bleutrich's demeanor reminded me a bit of my grandfather Hymie. Like my grandfather, he had an air of quiet dignity about him. He seemed at ease with himself. My hunch was that you could trust this coach to keep his word.

I managed to make it through infield tryouts without distinguishing or embarrassing myself. I handled each ground ball cleanly, my throws to first were right on the money, and I even turned the pivot neatly on the double play. But I knew I was playing mostly for myself. I didn't stand a chance of making the team—even as a reserve infielder.

After my turn then, I sat alone in the bleachers, brooding about what a long summer it was going to be—working five days a week at the pharmacy, having no social life to speak of, and dreading having to start eighth grade with nothing to look forward to but another year of anonymity. I tried to resign myself to that inevitability. I'd made the best showing I could under the circumstances. Still, I couldn't shake off my disappointment.

Hitting tryouts were the last hurdle of the day. I'd never been much of a hitter, so things weren't going to get any better for me. After each batter took his turn, I'd watch Bleutrich take him aside and quietly inform him of his fate. You could tell by the body language and the looks on faces who'd made the cut. By the time I came up to bat, I already knew who'd made the team and who hadn't.

Brownstein and Zeidner were shoo-ins. So was Lee. I was also pretty certain that the three Bayswater guys—Silverman, Frankel, and Moshan—would also make it. They were all good enough, but I bet it didn't hurt that they were starters on Bleutrich's PAL basketball team.

I was secretly pleased that not one guy from the clique was chosen. Not even Louie Mandel. But I was mildly surprised that Bleutrich kept Barry Aronson, an awkward, rangy kid who lived five blocks from my house. Barry was only a sub on the sixth grade softball team, but he was one of the best players on our synagogue's basketball team. Who knows, maybe Bleutrich was doing a little advance recruiting for next winter.

The big shock was that Mike Rubin had made the first cut. As soon as I saw the look of joy on his face, I felt a manic surge of envy. It had occurred to me more than once that I probably would have had better chance if I'd tried out for third base. But that would have meant having to compete with Mike again—a scenario I didn't want to repeat.

After I finished hitting, I trudged over to the third base bleachers where Bleutrich was standing, writing the final notes on his clipboard. I swallowed hard when he gave me the news. He was kind about it, but he still told me in no uncertain terms that I didn't have the reflexes to be a middle infielder. Nor, he added, did I hit well enough to play the outfield. No surprises there.

I knew all along that it was coming. But now it was real, final. The prospect of not playing ball this summer was too excruciating to contemplate. My face was flushed with shame, and my ears were still ringing when I looked up and spotted a cadre of guys—Rubin among them—celebrating outside the gate. I wished I could just slip away without having to face the music. Then, in a split second, I knew *cliche* exactly what I had to do. Why hadn't I thought of it before?

The only decent pitcher I'd seen all day was Lee Adnepos, a slender, wiry left-hander who'd just moved into our neighborhood. Lee was even shorter than I was. But he looked like someone had taught him how to pitch. He had a smooth three-quarter overhand delivery, a nice, easy leg kick, and a fluid, graceful follow-through. He even had a toe plate on his right shoe.

Whenever Lee threw a fastball in the strike zone, the hitters either whiffed or topped the ball off the end of the bat. So far as I could tell, his only weakness was erratic control. And that was because he'd sometimes get bored and lose his concentration. All day, I'd wondered where the other good pitchers were. Bleutrich must have a few other studs lined up. Probably, they'd show up tomorrow after the first round of cuts.

This would be a desperate gambit, I knew. But it was my only shot.

I waited until everyone had drifted away. While Bleutrich was packing up the bats and balls, I walked right up behind him. When he turned, he was a little startled to see me still standing there.

"Coach," I said, trying to keep my voice from cracking. "I know how to pitch."

Actually, it was more of a fib than an outright lie. I was thinking about those marathon stickball games in Mike Rubin's driveway, the winter afternoons when I'd pitch to Mike and Peter in the P.S. 114 gym, and the times I used to throw batting practice to my kid brother in the backyard. And what about the schoolyard pickup games? I could always throw strikes, so in time I became the designated batting practice pitcher. In reality, I'd probably put in more time pitching than I had at shortstop. Yet until this moment I'd never thought of myself as a pitcher.

Bleutrich looked away while I held my breath. I could sense that he was thinking about it.

He turned slowly back toward me, shaking his head up and down like he was having a private conversation with himself. He was probably wondering if this short, chubby, unathletic-looking kid was for real.

Finally, he said. "I can use a batting practice pitcher."

I exhaled. Maybe the coach had seen the same thing today as I had. Maybe there really were no other pitchers waiting in the wings. If that was so, aside from Lee and Zeidner, who was also Bleutrich's best shortstop, there wasn't much to choose from. Besides, when you thought about it, what could he lose by taking on a batting practice pitcher? Especially one who volunteers.

For a second, I wished my father had been there to witness this. He'd have been proud of my gumption.

"Show up tomorrow morning," Bleutrich said.

I left tryouts feeling vindicated. So, okay, I was only a batting practice pitcher. But Mandel and those guys didn't even get that far. Perhaps, I'd learned something from Manny's boys, after all. A year ago, I'd have never had the balls to do this.

The next day, Bleutrich gave me an old faded uniform with patches on the knees of both pant legs. For a minute I felt like an impostor. I had six days to make myself into a reasonable facsimile of a pitcher. The coach told me to come back in a week for the first practice. In the meantime, he said, work on throwing strikes. Right. As if he even had to tell me that.

At thirteen, I was what baseball coaches called a "shlepper"—a slightly awkward but not entirely inept athlete. I knew I'd never be one of the top baseball players. I'd seen a lot of games, and I could spot the good jocks in an instant. They have an effortless grace, an ease and fluidity that infuses every gesture. I'd never have that kind of raw ability. Still, I was driven to play ball.

That summer then, I literally taught myself how to pitch. I read dozens of how-to books and I scrutinized the mechanics and flaws of the major league hitters I watched on TV and in person. I went to Ebbets Field and sat directly behind the plate—the best angle for studying pitchers' habits and delivery. And I took pages and pages of notes.

Preacher Roe was tall and lanky, all arms and legs. He had a big sweeping motion and high leg kick that shielded the ball from the batter's vision. Don Newcombe was built like a lumberjack. He had a ninety-mile-an-hour fastball and a perpetual scowl designed to intimidate opposing hitters. Carl Erskine was the pitcher I identified with most. He had a slender build—narrow shoulders and a tapered waist. He looked more like a distance runner than a pitcher. But he had a sneaky fastball and a wicked overhand sinker that induced hitters to beat the ball into the ground. I noticed too that he threw all his pitches, including the change up, with the same motion. What made him so effective was that the hitters couldn't pick up the ball's rotation until it was right on top of them.

Moreover, I liked his cunning and resilience. In a *Sporting News* interview, an opposing manager said that unless you got to him right away, you were in for a long day. But even when he got roughed up in the early innings, I noticed that Erskine rarely lost his composure. Usually, he'd settle down by the third inning. Just like the article said, he'd get stronger as the game went on. That summer, I studied him more carefully than the others.

When workouts began, Bleutrich kept his word. He started me off as a batting practice pitcher. There were other pitchers ahead of me besides Lee. They all threw harder than I did. It didn't take much to do that. But none of them were very savvy. Nor did they seem interested in learning anything about the craft of pitching. Lee and I were the only pitchers who practiced in between scrimmages. It wasn't long then, before Bleutrich began giving me more innings in the intra-squad and preseason games.

There were brief moments when pitching seemed to come naturally to me. If I concentrated hard enough, I could throw strikes, change speeds, and make the ball sink or break sharply away from the batter. I even had a knack for sizing up a lot of hitters' weaknesses. I could tell what a particular batter's blind spots were just by studying his habits and mannerisms.

As a pitcher, my inhibitions and self doubts seemed to dissolve. Whenever I was out there on the mound, I felt as self-assured as I did when I was sitting in the stands at Ebbets Field, explaining the ins and outs of the game to my cronies.

Every new inning and batter was a challenge. On the mound, all of my senses were open. I could feel the warm breeze on my cheeks, hear the muffled noise of the crowd, my teammates' chatter, and the other team's barbs. None of it distracted me. In fact, it made me bear down harder.

Even the little gestures and rituals felt natural: tossing the spongy resin bag nonchalantly to the ground and watching the swirl of dust kick up, inhaling a baseball's pungent scent, and rubbing up its smooth, slick surface. I also loved the feeling of wrapping my thumb and middle fingers around the ball's raised seams, searching for the right grip on the curve, fastball, sinker, or change up. Most of all, I relished the cat and mouse game that went on between pitcher and hitter—me deciding what pitches to throw, the hitter trying to read my mind.

I didn't throw hard enough to have what coaches call a live arm. To build my strength and endurance, each morning I got up early and ran on the beach—wearing army boots and a rubber jacket. I soon began to think of myself as a pitcher. During the day, I pedaled my bike harder when I delivered prescriptions. After work, I'd go down into our cool, damp cellar and lift weights. Even in the hottest weather, I emulated the big leaguers by draping a satin warm up jacket across my right shoulder. Whenever anyone made a sarcastic remark or questioned me about it, I'd explain that it was to keep my pitching arm warm between ballgames.

In the evenings, I set up a regular practice routine. First, I cut a twelve-inch hole (the size of home plate) in a bed sheet, and hung it on the backyard clothesline. Then every night, until it got dark, I threw hundreds of rubber covered baseballs at the target. I got those balls by trading my Topps and Bowman bubble gum cards with Arnold Berkowitz, who worked at the local batting range.

By mid July I could throw four out of every five pitches through the bed sheet hole. By the end of the summer I could throw three of five with a blindfold on. Some evenings Alan stood in front of the garage door with a bat in his hand while I pitched shaved tennis balls to him. By trimming the ball's fuzz, you could make it break and dip crazily.

One night when I was pitching to my brother, the four guys in the clique happened to walk past my house. They were on their way to a party up the street, but when they spotted Alan and me they slowed down long enough to make a couple of snide cracks about playing their own "night games." I didn't respond, but I was thinking, "Keep it up guys. Someday, you and your stuck-up girlfriends'll be paying a half a buck to watch me play."

The more I worked at pitching, the more instinctive it felt. By midsummer it was as natural to me as reading a book. I was convinced that with the right guidance and coaching I could get a lot better at this.

In the early season games Bleutrich was hesitant to use me. You couldn't blame him. I was inexperienced, and I still couldn't throw very hard. In fact, my ex–high school teammate, Andrew Makrides, to this day, still ribs me about it.

"You had three speeds, Mike," Andrew has said, "slow, slower, slowest. And your sinker was a dying quail. You were lucky that the pitcher's mound was sixty feet, six inches from home, because if someone ever moved it back a half a foot, your pitches would have bounced in the dirt six inches before they got to the plate."

Nevertheless, I continued to pitch well and with confidence in all the practice and intra-squad games. And I'd looked pretty good whenever I got a few innings in preseason exhibitions. But no one could predict how I'd fare in a league game. A lot of players look great in practice and then get rattled when the games really count.

For the first few weeks Bleutrich experimented with Ronnie Zeidner as his second pitcher. Zeidner was even better than Lee. He was also our best hitter and shortstop. It's hard to pitch and play shortstop. There's a big difference between throwing a hundred plus pitches from sixty feet six inches away, and making a half dozen throws from shortstop. Not to mention the different mind-set that each position requires.

After the first few games we could all sense that we had the talent and chemistry to contend for the borough championship. Bleutrich also knew that our strongest lineup was with Lee (or someone else) pitching and Zeidner at short, especially when we played the better teams.

As we approached the halfway point in the season, I'd only pitched a few innings of middle relief—mostly in games that were blowouts. But none of the other pitchers were especially effective, including Burt Levy, another kid from our neighborhood. Burt was big and husky, and he could throw good heat. But he had a tendency to get spooked with men on base.

I was getting antsy to show Bleutrich what I could do. Let's face it, he was going to have to pitch me sooner or later. We must have been thinking the same thing, because right at the beginning of the second round he took me aside after practice and told me to just be patient. He'd work me in as a second starter once the schedule got heavy.

A good coach has to be part psychologist, part tactician. Coaches always want their players to be on edge. That's why they rarely tip their hand when it comes to who plays and who sits. There's a fine line between keeping a bench warmer's spirit alive and breaking his spirit. No doubt, there was a certain amount of expediency in Bleutrich's promise to me. Just the fact that he took the trouble to inform me settled me down. And it gave me even more incentive to prove that his confidence was justified.

Just as he'd promised, Bleutrich started me in the next game. It was the vote of confidence I was looking for. It's an old cliché, but when opportunity meets preparation good things happen. That day I pitched five shutout innings before I got tired. I left with a six run lead and two men on base. Levy relieved me, and I sat on the bench chewing my nails to the quick, hoping he wouldn't blow my lead. Burt gave up four runs before he got out of the inning. Zeidner pitched the seventh and set them down one, two, three. We were lucky to win the game. Unkind as it sounds, Burt's failure to come through worked in my favor. It made me look even better in Bleutrich's eyes.

By early August I'd improved so much that I even took Bleutrich by surprise. At the end of the league season Lee and I were each pitching every other game. To chart my progress I recorded my game stats in a spiral notebook—along with the notes I'd made on opposing hitters and pitchers. After each game I wrote a detailed description of what I was thinking and feeling before, during, and after each inning. I specified what pitches and strategies had worked and hadn't worked. And I described in detail the adjustments I planned to make next time. I even noted what I ate before the game and how much sleep I got the night before.

I enjoyed writing in my notebook almost as much as I relished pitching the actual games. When I think back, my happiest childhood moments seemed to involve either writing or playing baseball.

everything is so spelled out. So little is left for the reader.

Our team moved through the rest of the season and the playoff elimination round without a loss. In the borough championships we would face the 102nd precinct from Richmond Hill in a best two out of three playoff. The first two games would be played on successive days on each team's home field. The third, if necessary, was scheduled for the following weekend at a neutral site, Franklin K. Lane High School, in Jamaica.

To everyone's surprise, especially mine, Bleutrich started me in the first game. It was just as well that he didn't tell me in advance, because I'd have had too much time to dwell on it. All during warm ups I noticed that Lee sat on the bench scowling at me, as if to say, "What the hell are you doing out there? This game is mine."

I tried to block the image out of my mind, but I was so shaken that I kept losing my concentration. I gave up three early runs before settling down in the third inning. I was angry at myself for losing my

[handwritten note: so many words like this, why don't you let the reader figure that out.]

focus in such a big game. Once I regained my confidence I didn't give up another run. Luckily, we rallied and won it 5-3.

I was glad that I'd come through for Bleutrich. But I was a little disappointed that that no one from my family showed up to watch. My most pressing concern, though, was Lee. He was ticked off. Never even said "Nice game" on the bus ride back. What could he be thinking? About me, and about Bleutrich? Was he doubting his ability? Even I believed that he hadn't gotten a fair shake. After all, he'd carried us for the first half of the summer. It reminded me of the tense situation with Mike Rubin back in sixth grade. After the game, I saw Bleutrich take Lee aside and put his arm around his shoulder.

Lee was scheduled to start the next game, at home. Normally we'd talk about how to pitch to the opposing hitters. But during warm ups he went out of his way to avoid me. Can't say as I blame *[handwritten note: cliche]* him. Had I been in his place, I probably would have acted the same way.

When the game started I was sitting on the bench charting Lee's pitches. I could see right away that he was still unnerved by yesterday's events. He was wild and inconsistent all day. He put men on base every inning. More times than not, we managed to bail him out. But we finally lost 5-4 on a seventh inning bases loaded walk. You could feel that one coming for the entire game.

I had to admire Bleutrich, though. He didn't take Lee out, even though we might have won the game had he elected to let Zeidner pitch the last few innings.

Bleutrich had six days to decide who would pitch the rubber game. It felt so strange to be on this end of the transaction. As much as I wanted it, and as much as I wanted us to win, I'd have almost preferred it if Bleutrich chose Lee instead of me. I didn't want that weight sitting on my shoulder again.

All week, though, I had a hunch that it would be me.

"Worry about yourself, not the next guy," my father counseled.

He was right. I needed to focus on *my* game plan. If I worried about Lee's feelings, I'd be sabotaging my own chances. On Saturday, right after infield practice, Bleutrich handed me the ball. By now I was getting a vague sense of where all this was headed. Coaches used you not because they wanted to give you a fair chance but because they thought you could help them win games.

During warm ups I didn't dare look at the bench for fear that I'd see Lee. But when I spotted my father and brother in the stands, I became even more distracted. As a result, I gave up a run in each of the first two innings. We lost the game 2-1. I gave up only five hits, and I struck out ten batters—the most strikeouts I'd ever gotten in a game. Every pitch I threw had something on it. But that was the problem. The ball was moving so much that I didn't have my usual control. I gave up five walks, two to leadoff hitters who eventually came around to score. If I were a pitching coach, my first piece of advice to a new pitcher would always be, "Never walk the first batter of an inning. It'll always come back to bite you in the ass."

But even with the final loss, I'd succeeded way beyond my original expectations. Despite some concentration lapses, I'd pitched my two best games right at the end when it really counted. And I finished both games. It proved I could stand up to the pressure. Yet, I didn't want to get too hyped about it. It was only a first step. VFW tryouts were the next hurdle.

That same summer, 1953, the Dodgers beat the second place Milwaukee Braves by thirteen games. Their 105-49 record was the best in team history—and their 208 home runs were the second highest total in baseball history. It was the fifth consecutive season they'd led the league in home runs; and for the eighth consecutive year they were first in stolen bases. If that wasn't enough, Brooklyn compiled a 285-team batting average; Carl Furillo won the batting title with a 344 average, and four other players hit over 300. And yet in the World

Series the Yankees beat the Dodgers in six games. It was the fifth consecutive year that the Yankees had won the world championship, and the seventh time in a row they'd beaten the Dodgers. According to the press, the Dodgers' 0-7 Series record was a major embarrassment. Until they beat the Yankees in the World Series they'd continue to be judged as also-rans and under-achievers.

It was an unfortunate coincidence that such a talented, determined team was peaking at the same time that the Yankee teams of that era were winning one championship after another. Any other decade, Brooklyn would have already won several championships. As the game was teaching me, the world worked in strange ways. *cliché*

Regardless of their track record in the World Series, or perhaps even because of it, my bond with the Dodgers got stronger and more intense. Like me, they still had something to strive for, something left to prove.

◆

_ Z.

Before eighth grade had even begun, I was thinking about
coach Sullivan and next June's tryouts. My plan for the school year
was to stay focused on that goal. I'd work at the pharmacy after
school, and I'd keep in shape by lifting weights and running on the
beach. And to atone for last spring's lousy grades, I'd spend more
time studying. I also promised myself that I was done brownnosing
the guys in the clique.

On paper, it was a perfectly good scheme, so long, that is, as I
could avoid all other distractions. But there was as much chance of
that happening as there was of my father becoming a millionaire.
What I'd neglected to factor in, of course, were girls and sex.

Over the summer, I turned thirteen. My voice got deeper,
and hair started to sprout on my chest and face. I still hadn't shed
all my baby fat, but I'd grown at least a half inch. Clearly, the hormones were starting to take over. When I wasn't playing ball, girls
and sex were constantly on my mind. No matter how hard I tried, I
couldn't hide from all those erotic thoughts and stirrings.

Now that I was back in school, everywhere I turned—at lunch,
in class, at recess, on the bus—there was an unrelenting barrage of

gossip about who was making it with whom. All of a sudden, even zit-faced losers like Sandy Kalish and Jerry Rosenbaum were starting to brag about getting "serious nookie." Who from, God only knows.

On the bus one day I overheard Frank Pearlman telling the other guys in the clique that Rosenbaum's and Kalish's faces looked like "close-ups of the moon." I winced. A piece of me identified with those two guys. Whatever else I might be on the ball field, to the guys in the clique I was the same social outcast that I'd always been.

As much bragging as I heard, it seemed unlikely that many eighth graders were "going all the way." The only hard evidence of this was the newborn babies that some of the greasers' girlfriends had delivered over the summer. Still, if the rumors were true—and how would you ever know, anyway?—the class studs like Chuck Weiner, Dickie Stern, and Sammy Black were making it with the fast seventh grade girls. Even if it was all smoke and mirrors, it couldn't help but affect me.

At school I continued to have sexual fantasies about Cindy Levine. And she continued to act like I didn't exist. So I retreated into fantasy and voyeurism. That fall, I discovered *Playboy*, a brand new men's magazine that featured color photos of half-naked women. The first issue had a full-color nude picture of Marilyn Monroe. I also rooted out my father's French deck when he wasn't home. Plus, I was still swiping Ramses and Trojans from the pharmacy stockroom—in the unlikely event I'd ever get to show them off to fellow pretenders. And like every other horny eighth grader, I thumbed through a dog-eared copy of *Love without Fear*, seeking out the descriptions of sexual intercourse—as disappointingly clinical as they were. Nothing, it seemed, could satisfy my curiosity and fascination.

As far back as grade school, I'd had a crush on Diana McCaffery, my next-door neighbor. When we were kids, we used to play hide-and-seek and ring-a-levio in my backyard. But after she started Catholic school in seventh grade, I'd catch a glimpse of her only from time to time on her way to school.

I couldn't help but notice that Diana's figure had changed dramatically. Only a year ago she was a skinny, tomboyish girl with blonde pigtails. The guys in the clique used to make fun of her behind her back, calling her "the carpenter's daughter; flat as a board."

Almost overnight, however, she'd developed pear shaped, *nice description* pointy breasts. And when she started wearing tight skirts and stockings, I'd sit out on the front stoop watching her walk up the block on her way to the bus stop. I couldn't stop staring at her curved hips and perfectly rounded rear end. I began to imagine what she looked like without any clothes on. To my surprise, it wasn't long before I'd get to find out. *not necessary*

One warm night in mid September, I was studying upstairs in the spare bedroom. I was just finishing up when I saw the light go on in Diana's room. Our houses were separated only by a narrow alley, and on that unseasonably mild evening her window was wide open. Diana, wearing a pink terrycloth bathrobe, was pacing the room barefoot, drying her long blonde hair with a towel. My heart-beat quickened, and my pulse began to race. I just stood there, *pulse raced.* frozen in place, staring out the window.

I flicked the light off and knelt down in front of the window, hoping she wouldn't notice that the room was suddenly dark— *yuck* and praying that no one in my family would come in and catch me spying.

As she undid her sash, I held my breath and bit down on my thumb. Then with a causal shrug of her shoulders, the robe slid to the floor. An urgent, pulsing sensation started to well up in my groin. It spread to the pit of my stomach and traveled up through my chest.

For a long, slow moment, Diana stood in the center of the room facing my window. She was completely naked. Was she smiling at me, or did I just imagine it? Did she know I was spying on her?

She pivoted and slowly walked over to the light switch. An instant before she got there, she turned her head back toward the window. Maybe she did know, and she wanted to give me the full show.

The knot in my throat choked off my saliva, my cheeks and ears burned, and my entire body thrummed with excitement. I felt like I was in the grip of an invisible force. I knelt there, chin in hands, elbows on the windowsill, transfixed by what I was seeing. I was intoxicated and, at the same time, powerless. Diana was fully exposed; and yet it felt like *she* was the one in charge. All she had to do was flick the light switch and the show was over.

I wanted to stop time and etch that image into my memory— so I could call it up any time I wanted to.

For weeks, I couldn't get those images off my mind. At least the Catholic kids could confess to the priests. Who could I confess to? My rabbi, who I hardly knew? Certainly not guys my own age. I was afraid to talk to my father. He'd never brought sex up to me before. My mother wasn't an option either. I was too concerned that she'd think I was some kind of pervert or weirdo.

I tried to put Diana in the back of my mind. But even if I wanted to stop thinking about sex, I was reminded of it every day in school and on the bus—and every time I went to Miss Mencken's third period Art class.

We started hearing the scuttlebutt about Miss Mencken back in seventh grade. Everyone agreed that she was a head-turner: petite, trim, in her mid twenties, with long, reddish blonde hair, Kelly green eyes, and soft, clear skin, with just a hint of freckles at the bridge of her nose. Each day she wore eyeliner, a tight wool sweater, and a knee-length straight skirt. Sometimes we'd spot her in the halls between classes. Whenever she talked to Mr. Adler, the handsome Social Studies teacher that the eighth grade girls were ga-ga over, Miss Mencken would arch her back ever so slightly and nervously twist her hair around her index and middle fingers.

Sammy Black, the class blabbermouth, claimed that Adler and Mencken were making it after school in Adler's classroom. Sammy also said that he'd copped a look up Miss Mencken's dress one day during free hour. He was passing the Art room, and she was sitting at her desk facing the door with her legs crossed. "Miss Mencken's skirt was riding up so high on her thighs" Sammy said, "that I could see her underpants."

"Yeah, what color were they?" Pearlman chided.

All the guys in the clique tried to play it cool—acting like it was no big deal. But the second the bell rang in second period Social Studies, all four of them, with me in pursuit, jumped up and ran down the hall. We were hoping to catch a glimpse of Miss Mencken before she draped her long blue paint-spattered smock over her clothes. That's how pathetic we were. *why do you have to say that?*

Since the incident in kindergarten, I'd always dreaded Art class. But not this one. I looked forward to the times when Miss Mencken would walk around the room and look at our work. When she'd lean over my right shoulder, her left breast would brush lightly against my arm. The first time it felt like a mild electric shock. Sometimes, she'd take my hand and guide the crayon over the drawing paper. Her gentle touch and the scent of her perfume and shampoo made me light-headed and giddy. My throat constricted, my mouth got dry, and I'd begin to break out in a sweat. For the rest of the hour, I was too goofy with lust to concentrate on drawing.

As a last resort I went back to books, looking for anything that could explain these unceasing desires and confusions. But nothing in the public library had the answers I was looking for. The books and magazines that might have offered some clues were sequestered away in a special section that was forbidden to anyone under eighteen.

So I remained in a kind of limbo, sometimes thinking I was just an ordinary kid with a large imagination and overactive hormones, other times believing that I was one of the few boys my age who didn't have a handle on these things. The more confused I became, the more curious I was to pursue this fascination, which was already becoming a minor obsession.

The most popular girls our own age were already dating high school guys. And so most of the eighth grade boys had to go out with seventh grade girls. I'd pretty much resigned myself to being dateless until one evening in late September when I happened to run into Art's daughter, Karen, at her father's candy store. I was buying a pack of Lucky's for my mother, and Karen was filling in while her father was over at Sam Cahmi's deli, schmoozing with the horse handicappers.

I remembered Karen from the days when I hung around the candy store with Manny's gang. She was in sixth grade, working behind the counter after school—making tuna and egg salad sandwiches, and egg creams and black-and-white ice cream sodas.

I knew she had a crush on me. Sometimes after she got off work Karen would hang around and then walk with me up to my street. Then there'd be this awkward silence right before I'd turn to head home. It was like she was waiting for me to ask her out or put a move on her.

Back then, though, I didn't pay much attention to her. She was like all the other sixth grade girls—childish and giggly. And I wasn't at all attracted to her. I thought she was carrying around too much baby fat. But who was I to talk? Whenever I looked in the mirror, I saw a short, chubby kid with freckles and a crooked nose.

Now, a year later, here we were back in her father's store. Karen was dicing onions and green peppers for the sandwiches. I couldn't put my finger on it, but now that she was a year older she looked more alluring somehow. Was it her eye shadow? The ponytail? Her form-fitting sweater? Had she lost weight?

Karen wasn't plain looking or pretty. She had the kind of baby face that an aunt or grandmother would call "sweet." I didn't feel the same kind of overpowering desire for her that I did for Cindy Levine or some of the popular girls. Yet I'd been hearing stories about Karen since seventh grade. She and Connie Tarpoff used to hang around with Chuck Weiner and Dickie Stern, two arrogant rich guys from Neponsit who were reputed to be heavy hitters with younger girls. I couldn't help but wonder.

The story making the rounds these days was that Karen gave that creep Sammy Black a hand job in the back of the store one night after Art had closed up. Sammy bragged about it to everyone who'd listen. He also boasted that Karen had "a great set of knockers," and that he'd already gotten to third base with her. I'd always disliked that jerk. Now I hated him even more.

Karen must have sensed that I was staring at her, because she came right up to me and started making small talk about school, classes, and summer vacation. I didn't hesitate. I sat down at the counter and ordered an egg cream. While I was watching her work, I imagined Karen and that putz Sammy going at it in the back room. Something inside me started to stir. She'd given me an opening, and this time I decided to go for it. So I asked her out for Friday night. She didn't wait for me to suggest a movie or bowling or even a party.

"My dad doesn't close up till eleven on weekends," she said. "Come over to my house around seven."

She'd caught me off guard. Manny used to say that girls want it as much as we do. We just have to give them an excuse to do it. Could it really be this easy? I started imagining the possibilities.

It was only Monday, and I had all week to think about it. By Wednesday I was already wavering. What would I do if she came on to me? Should I bring a condom? I daydreamed about it in school, at home, while I was studying, and before sleep. It was the kind of free-floating anxiety I'd feel before a baseball tryout, or right at the moment when I'd have to ask someone to dance. By Thursday, I was wishing that Manny was around to give me a pep talk.

Friday night I was so nervous that I must have combed my hair a dozen times. I'd already slapped half a bottle of Canoe on my face. By the time I got to Karen's house, my blue oxford shirt was soaked with sweat and my palms were so clammy I couldn't grip the doorknob. When she answered the door, she was wearing a short pleated skirt and a forest green turtleneck jersey that fit so tight her nipples were straining against the fabric. I felt a spasm deep in my belly—like a fist tightening.

We'd never been alone together. Neither of us knew what to say, and we were getting more jittery by the minute. Karen made the first move when she put "Secret Love" on the hi-fi. The one thing I didn't want to do was slow dance. I was afraid that she'd find out what a klutz I was, and it would ruin everything. Still, how could I say no?

I was counting the seconds until the end of the song, worrying the whole time that I'd step on her toes. But Karen didn't seem to notice or care. Halfway though the song, she pulled me so close I could feel her warm breath on my cheek. She gently laid her head on my shoulder and ran her hands up and down my back. I could smell the residue of shampoo in her hair. Then she put both hands on my butt and pulled me closer, pressing me right up against her pelvic bone. Was she testing her power, trying to see if I had a hard-on? Once she knew it, she ground her hips even harder and began to moan softly. By now, I wasn't even aware of the music.

I felt light-headed and dizzy like when Miss Mencken would lean over my shoulder in Art class. I closed my eyes and the image that kicked in was of Diana undressing in front of my window. The next thing I remember was lying on Karen's bed, the two of us French kissing. There was nothing I could—or wanted to do—to stop her. Every time I rolled over and brushed her nipple with my elbow, she'd moan, very softly. The more pliant she was, the more aroused I became. We groped around on the bed and, with a lot of help from her, I wrestled Karen's turtleneck over her head and then somehow I got her bra unhooked. When her breasts floated free, I sat up, wide eyed, mouth agape. I started rubbing my palm very tentatively across her bare nipples.

"Oh, that feels good," she said.

I was speechless. I couldn't believe this was happening: no girl had ever let me go this far. Now I was the one in control. It was like standing on the mound knowing that no matter what pitch I threw, I had the hitters eating out of my hand.

I kept stroking Karen's breasts, first the right, then the left. I had no idea what I was doing or what to do next. But Karen didn't stop me. Then she rolled over and sat up. She kneeled down and began to stroke my crotch. She was in charge again. Or maybe she'd been in charge the whole time. I started to get scared. I'd heard enough stories and imagined enough times what it was like to get to second base or third base. But this was uncharted territory.

I felt my stomach contract as she slowly unzipped my fly and slid her hand under my Jockeys. As soon as she touched my penis, I froze: I had this awful flashback of the six of us guys standing with our pants down in Manny's basement, trying to jerk off in front of his French deck. I fought the image off and tried to call up the memory of Diana or Miss Mencken. I even tried to picture one of the models in *Playboy* who turned me on. When Diana's image came back into focus, I felt a surge of relief.

But then everything got even weirder. I heard Manny's voice whispering, "Don't choke Burtchick, this bimbo's a sure thing." It was like he was right there in the room with us. As if by instinct, I took hold of Karen's shoulders and slowly guided her back down on the bed until she was lying flat on her back directly beneath me.

I could see by the look in her eyes that I'd taken her by surprise. Hell, I'd taken myself by surprise. But, other than giving me a funny look, she didn't offer any resistance. I sat up on my knees and slid my hand beneath her skirt, then pushed the skirt up over her waist and slowly worked my fingers under the elastic bands of her cotton panties. I held my breath and my throat tightened as my fingers worked their way ever so slowly down the inside of her thigh.

All of a sudden, her whole body went rigid.

"Please don't," she whimpered. Did I do something wrong?

I didn't know whether to stop or keep going. Manny always used to tell us, "Listen to everything they say and just agree. But remember, with girls 'no' always means 'yes.'"

Karen kept saying, with more urgency now, "Please don't, please stop."

I was starting to get spooked. What kind of signal she was giving me?

I was losing my erection, but still I kept going, inching my hand ever so tentatively down Karen's thigh until I brushed my fingers across her pubic mound. She caught her breath and gasped. So did I. This time, she didn't attempt to stop me. I closed my eyes and tried to relax into the moment. As I kept stroking her pubic mound, she was shaking her head from side to side. Her eyes were closed and she was sighing, "Yes, yes, yes." I'd never possessed this much leverage before. She was thrashing around, legs splayed, her long dark hair falling over her eyes. It was the most extraordinary sight I'd ever seen. I knew it was time.

Just as I as was easing myself down between her legs, I flashed on an image of Art in his white, three cornered paper hat and apron. He was standing behind the soda fountain, waving to us and calling out, "Have a good time, you two."

Then, I went completely soft.

Everything was a blur after that. I don't remember either of us putting our clothes back on. But somehow we ended up in the living room, watching TV. My mind was racing, my insides were churning, and yet my body felt numb. I couldn't sort any of it out. How can you be so turned on one minute and so weirded out the next?

We tried to make small talk, but it was useless. She looked dazed, and I felt mortified. What was she thinking? Would she tell her girlfriends about this? I wanted to apologize or ask her how she felt. Anything to ease my confusion. But I couldn't think of anything to say that wouldn't make me sound like I was retarded. So I mumbled something like, "I'll see you at the store," and I ducked out the door as fast as I could.

For days, I kept mulling over the scene, looking for clues—anything that would help me get a handle on what had happened. What made me stop? Had it all happened too fast? For me? For both of us?

I wanted to call Karen back and apologize. But Manny would have said that was uncool. The more I thought about it, the more mixed-up I became. What's worse is that there was nobody I could talk to about it.

But this much I did know. I did not want to repeat this failure any time soon, with Karen or anyone else. It was too humiliating. The only thing I wanted right now was to get back on safe ground.

what's obvious

It was early October, thank God, and the '53 World Series was just beginning. Each afternoon, I'd catch the early bus home from school to see the games. It was hard to watch the Dodgers go down again, but it kept my mind off what had just happened. And I wanted it to stay that way—at least until I sorted everything out.

When the Series ended, I compulsively cataloged and recatalogued my baseball card collection. Then I stored it in my father's empty cigar boxes and slid the boxes under my bed. At night and on weekends I sweet-talked my brother into playing marathon competitions of All Star Baseball, a popular board game. And when it turned cold, I read all the hot stove league gossip I could dig up from *Baseball Digest*, the newspapers, and *The Sporting News*.

Right before Halloween, I began going to the public library again, this time to look for books on pitching. While I was browsing in the baseball section, I found *The Southpaw*. At first, I mistook it for a guidebook on how to pitch. The librarian who shelved it probably thought the same thing. But it turned out to be a coming of age novel narrated in the first person by Henry Wiggen, a rookie pitcher for the New York Mammoths, an invented amalgamation of the 1940s Giants and Yankees. I couldn't have stumbled over it at a more opportune time. I became so engrossed in the story that I took the novel home and stayed up half the night reading it.

To Henry, baseball was a sacred calling and he treated it with a disciple's reverence and respect. Naturally his dedication struck a chord in me. For the moment, it helped put my world back in focus. VFW tryouts were coming up in the spring, and I wanted to be ready for coach Sullivan.

◆

_ 8.

We all knew about Tom Sullivan's reputation for hazing Belle Harbor Jews. If you were lucky, the guys in the clique said, you might not get him for Guidance or Hygiene, the two classes he taught. Yet in spite of the scary rumors, I was strangely excited when I found out that next term I'd be in both of Sullivan's classes. This way, maybe I could learn something that would give me an advantage with him when VFW tryouts rolled around in June. I needed to somehow convince Sullivan that I was different from all the other Belle Harbor kids.

"Big Tom," as the greasers called him, was in his mid to late thirties—a broad shouldered, thick necked, World War Two vet. Every day he wore the same outfit: a white or light blue oxford shirt and a rep tie, dark brown or navy blue wool pants with cuffs, and spit shined brown wingtips. He had a prominent jaw, thinning sandy blonde hair, and a Marine style butch crew cut. And it was no surprise that he ran his classes just like a platoon leader.

Teachers, parents, and coaches have their favorites and their scapegoats. It was clear from day one that Sullivan favored the toughest kids in the class, the Irish Catholic and Italian guys from the surrounding neighborhoods, several of whom were on his

Peninsula League football team. And it was equally obvious that he had a thinly veiled contempt for the rest of us.

For the first few weeks I watched as Sullivan singled out the most insecure and easily intimidated kids from my neighborhood. As soon as he sensed their fear, he upped the ante. Whenever guys like Elliot Reiss or Danny Klein screwed up even the slightest bit during Phys Ed, he made them take extra push-ups and run laps. He also called on them repeatedly in Hygiene class. Just as Ira and Billy had said, Sullivan would snidely refer to those two guys as "candy ass sugar babies." We all knew that was his euphemism for "Belle Harbor Jews."

I hated it when he deliberately picked on guys like Reiss and Klein. But I knew I couldn't ally myself with the likes of them. So I steered clear of the victims and made a conscious effort to buddy up to the guys from Arverne and Hammels.

Every once in a while he'd single out Burt Levy, Mike Rubin, or me and call us sugar babies. My strategy was not to talk back to him and not to flinch whenever he picked on me. Let him play whatever games he wanted to. He'd see what I was made of when tryouts rolled around.

If I didn't get to pitch for the VFW team, there was virtually no chance of making the high school varsity. So in early March I decided to pass up eighth grade softball. It wasn't an easy decision. Coach Barrows had given me a chance last year, and now I was letting him down. But, like my father said, I needed to think about myself. If I played softball, I'd fall behind the guys who were gearing up for VFW tryouts.

By late April I was practicing outdoors with my old PAL teammates, Mike Rubin, Rob Brownstein, Ronnie Zeidner, and Burt Levy. Lee was even talking to me again. Things were back to normal— whatever "normal" meant at that age.

By Memorial Day weekend I was back into my old routine: going to Ebbets, studying big league hitters and pitchers, running on the beach every day, throwing hundreds of baseballs through the hole in the sheet, and pitching to Rubin and my kid brother. By the time tryouts came around, I was as ready for Sullivan as I'd ever be.

Say what you will about Sullivan, he knew how to whip a team into shape—and fast. He didn't waste any time with motivational speeches. By the end of the first session, infielders and catchers were already turning double plays, fielding bunts, and covering bases on steals. Outfielders were attempting to throw runners out on the bases and learning to hit the right cut-off man on relays. There was so much simultaneous activity, you couldn't relax or think straight. Which is exactly what Sullivan had in mind.

When infield and outfield drills were over Sullivan would stand at the plate with a bat in his hand, while a backup catcher fed him one baseball after another. If a hit and run was on, the pitcher and catcher had to decide right on the spot whether to throw a pitchout or try to make the hitter bite on something just out of the strike zone. On a bunt or a grounder to the right side of the infield the pitcher had to get over to first in time to take the throw. If you screwed up, you did it again until you got it right.

The last activity of the day was "situation" batting practice where Sullivan would set up simulated game situations for the hitters and pitchers. Each pitcher would pitch the equivalent of three innings to a rotating group of hitters.

By the end of the first day I'd acquitted myself pretty well. But I knew I hadn't exactly dazzled Sullivan with my brilliance. Therefore, it wasn't a complete surprise when after the first round of cuts, he picked Lee, Rob Brownstein, and Ronnie, plus two of the Wavecrest guys—Larry Moshan and Bob Milner. He also added Ducky Warshauer, an outfielder from Laurelton, and Bubba Murphy, a third baseman from Broad Channel. You couldn't really second-guess any of those picks. They were the seven most talented players at tryouts.

Still, I was a little disappointed that I wasn't in the first group. Especially after seeing the coaches' final two choices: Frankie Ortiz and Hughie Whalen, neither of whom I'd ever heard of. Rubin, Levy, and I—along with about a dozen others—were told to come back next Saturday morning for final tryouts.

Naturally, I couldn't sleep all week. Yet, I felt strangely optimistic about my chances. You could see by the way he ran tryouts that Sullivan was big on preparation and knowledge of the game—two of my strongest assets. One thing still bothered me, though. Rubin, Levy, and me were all Belle Harbor Jews. Was that a good or bad sign?

I got my first clue that something was up when Sullivan stopped me after our Hygiene final and told me to meet him on Saturday morning ten minutes before tryouts. What could he possibly want with me?

Sullivan's office, if you could call it that, was a steam-heated compartment above the St. Francis de Sales gym. Amidst the banging and hissing of the old pipes, he told me in no uncertain terms that if I wanted to make this team I'd have to convince him that a Belle Harbor sugar baby had what it took to play ball for him. I'd anticipated he'd be testing me sooner or later, I just hadn't expected it to happen so soon.

Tryouts were held on the St. Francis de Sales field, right behind the church. I was out in the bullpen when I heard Sullivan yell out my name. The bastard didn't even give me a chance to warm up. Just as I was running in to the mound, I heard Sullivan ordering Burt Levy to get loose and Mike Rubin to grab a bat. Then he gave me ten warm-up tosses and told Rubin to get in the batter's box.

So there I was on the mound of the church field staring down at Mike, who stood sixty feet, six inches away nervously taking his practice cuts. So many thoughts were racing through my mind. I'd been preparing for this moment for the last nine months. I didn't want to blow my only shot. Last year's team almost made it to the state finals at Cooperstown. They got eliminated in Westchester County—one game away from the regionals. With the talent Sullivan had assembled, there was no telling how far this year's team could go. Then there was Coach Kerchman. Sooner or later, he'd be scouting this team, looking for next year's rookies.

But what about Rubin? We'd played on every team from sixth grade to PAL. This would be his last chance to make the VFW team. Next year we'd all have to try out for American Legion ball, a tougher, more competitive league.

Goddamn it. Why did it always have to come down to bullshit like this? Why can't it just be about your ability to play?

But I knew I couldn't let it get to me, like it did last season with Lee. I had to get the Rubin dilemma out of my mind. I needed to calm down and start thinking about what I was doing. And fast.

Over the years, Rubin had seen my entire repertoire of pitches. And, of course, he knew exactly how I thought. But I was aware of every one of his weaknesses. And I had the ball. Within seconds, I knew just how I'd work him.

Rubin had an open stance and he always stood deep in the box, a few inches off the plate. Hughie Whalen, the catcher, went into his crouch and signaled for a high inside fastball. That's how much he knew. Up and in was right in Rubin's kitchen. High inside fastballs were just what I didn't want to throw. If I threw him low-breaking balls away, my stock-in-trade, he was finished. Kaput. But if I deliberately pitched him too fat, Big Tom would know it. Then I'd be history too.

While I was trying to figure out what to do, Sullivan called time-out and ordered Frankie Ortiz to be the runner at third. This was not a good sign. Ortiz was one of Sullivan's football goons. He was a bruiser from the Arverne projects, and he could hurt you. That's when Sullivan shouted out. "Game situation, ladies," and he called for a suicide squeeze. It's a risky play, and it's meant to work like this: as soon as I go into my windup, Ortiz will break for home and Rubin will square around to bunt. My job is to make certain Rubin doesn't bunt the ball in fair territory.

Instead of tossing me the ball, Sullivan swaggered out to the mound. As he slapped the grass stained baseball into my glove, he deliberately sprayed black, bitter tobacco juice across the bridge of my nose. Then he motioned Whalen, his other football thug, to the mound.

Sullivan and I were inches apart. I could feel his breath on my right cheek. His nose was red and swollen, and slanted to the right, broken three times in his college football days. Just as Whalen arrived, Coach rasped, "Steinberg, when Ortiz breaks from third, throw it at his head."

He meant the batter, Rubin. Why would I want to throw a baseball at my friend's head? It wasn't the right strategy. It was another one of Big Tom's stupid tests of courage.

"At his head, coach?" I said, stalling for time.

Sullivan gave me his that's-the-way-it's-done-around-here look.

It wasn't like I didn't know what he was doing. Everyone knew that if you wanted to play ball for Big Tom you did what you were told and you kept your mouth shut. So why was I being such a smart-ass? It wasn't like me. Why was I so willing to risk it all, right here, right now?

I tried to calm myself down, remind myself what the costs were. Just cool it. Try and think it through, I said under my breath. Pretend to go along with Big Tom's program. The whole time, though, I could feel the knot in my stomach twist and tighten.

Sullivan glared at the third base bleachers where the final ten guys fidgeted nervously, waiting for their chance to bat. Then he looked back at me. With his cap pulled low, the coach's steel blue pig eyes seemed all the more penetrating. He smiled. The lower part of his jaw was distorted from taking too many football hits without a facemask. So the smile came off looking like a mocking leer, which rattled me even more. I could feel my palms getting clammy; my armpits were already drenched with perspiration.

He looked at the guys waiting in the bleachers and said loud enough for everyone to hear, "Steinberg, let's show this wet nosed bunch of rookies how the game is played."

Then he grabbed his crotch with his left hand. It was the old comrade routine. He was giving me a chance to look like a leader by pretending we were buddies. We weren't. Big Tom and I didn't operate in the same universe. He was a bull-yock Irishman from Hell's Kitchen, a high school juvi who learned to fight in the streets. His platoon had fought in the Pacific, and the pride still showed in his eyes. To him, guys like Rubin and me were too privileged, and he resented us for it.

I turned to glance at Rubin. He looked like a Thanksgiving turkey on the block. I was embarrassed for him. Maybe the wind was just blowing at his sweatpants, the stiff ocean breeze we get on the Long Island south shore. Then again, maybe his knees really were shaking.

"Let's get the goddamned show on the road," Sullivan muttered. I thought about quitting. But what if Kerchman found out? The two coaches were like an Australian tag team. "Bad cop, bad cop," I once heard an ex-player say. But everyone here would have sold his own mother into slavery if it meant that Sullivan would put in a good word with Kerchman. That's why those two bastards could jerk us around like this.

Whalen trotted back behind the plate and Sullivan turned to leave. To him this kind of stuff was routine. I wanted to refuse, but I kept reminding myself that this is my only chance to make the team, to maybe pitch at Cooperstown. In my mind's eye, I could see my dad, brother, and Kerchman sitting in the stands at Doubleday Field.

I tried to buy some time, thinking maybe I could reason with Sullivan. Convince him there was another way to do this. I was red-in-the-face pissed, hoping it looked like windburn.

"You want me to stop the bunt, right?" I said. It came out sounding too timid.

He turned. What the hell was I saying? Nobody second-guesses the coach. Sullivan walked back to the mound and spat another wad of chew on the ground, making sure to splatter some on my new spikes. He looked at Whalen, then at Ortiz. Then he turned to me and shook his head from side to side.

"Thaaat's right, Steinberg," he said, stretching out the words. "You stop the bunt. Now, let's please execute the fucking play, shall we?" He muttered to himself through clenched teeth as he ambled back toward the bleachers.

It was out of my mouth before I knew it. More assertive this time. "Suppose I hit him in the head?"

Sullivan's own head swung around like a tetherball, making that last tight twist at the top of the pole.

"Don't worry, it's not a vital organ. Pitch."

I think Big Tom knew that he was undermining his credibility by arguing with a piss-ant kid. So he turned and silenced everyone's murmurs with a long glare. As if rehearsed, the seven guys behind me started to grumble, distancing themselves from me and Sullivan's wrath. Whalen stood behind the plate, looking at the ground, his mask pushed back on top of his head.

"Pitch the fuckin' ball," Whalen yelled.

"Do what coach tell you man," spat Ortiz from third.

To those guys, especially, the coach was George God. If he told them to take a dump at home plate, they'd get diarrhea. But me? I'm like Gary Cooper in *High Noon*. Everyone's watching, no one's volunteering to help.

Then I noticed Mike, still frozen in his batter's crouch. He looked like a mannequin with bulging eyes. Before I could think, the words slipped out.

"It's the wrong play, Coach."

It was my voice, all right, but it couldn't have been me who said it. I'd never have the guts to say anything like that. Not to Sullivan's face, anyway.

Dead silence. You could hear the breeze whistling through the wire mesh of the backstop. At first, Sullivan was too surprised to even curse me out. But after a long moment, he turned and strode up to Rubin, who was still frozen in the batter's box.

Like all of us, Rubin was jackrabbit scared of the coach. And just like a rabbit about to be prey, he was riveted to the ground.

"Goddamn it," Sullivan ripped off his cap, exposing his jet-black crew cut and sunburned forehead. He spoke like rolling thunder, enunciating every word.

"WHAT DID HE SAY, RUBIN?"

It was a calculated ploy. I'd seen it before, in the streets. Coach was going to punish me by humiliating my friend.

Rubin managed weakly; "Uh, wrong—wrong play. Coach?"

Louder then, like a Marine D.I. "NOBODY IN THE STANDS CAN HEAR YOU, RUBIN."

"WRONG PLAY, COACH."

My stomach turned over watching Sullivan humiliate Mike just for the amusement of the guys in the bleachers. And Big Tom knew it. Knew it oh so well.

Still advancing, Sullivan took it to the grandstand.

"ALL YOU LADIES, SAY IT!"

The accusing chorus rained down.

"WRONG PLAY, COACH."

"AGAIN."

"WRONG PLAY, COACH."

Then he ran out to the mound yelling, "YOU, TOO, STEINBERG, YOU SAY IT."

He was hopping up and down like someone had pranked him with a hotfoot. Adrenaline overcame me then, and before Sullivan could order another round I let the words tumble out in a single breath.

"If I throw a pitchout chest high in the left-hand batter's box, Whalen takes two steps to his right and he has a clear shot at Ortiz."

By this time, I was so shook up I had no idea if it was the right play or not. I was just trying to call Sullivan's bluff by parroting what Coach Bleutrich had taught me last summer.

Sullivan squared himself and casually put his cap back on. He was trying to regain his composure. He'd let a snot nosed junior high school kid get to him, and now he had to regain control.

My stomach was in knots, Rubin's eyes looked like marbles, and the whole team was hungry to see what would happen next.

Softly now: "That's enough, Steinberg."

Then to Rubin: "Get back in the box. Let's do the play."

And to be sure there was no misunderstanding, he took it right back to me: "*My play*," he said deliberately. "*My play, my way.*"

He was giving me a second chance. Why didn't I just fake it? I had good control. I'd brushed off plenty of hitters before. Maybe deep down I believed that Sullivan was right about me. Maybe I didn't have the balls it took to play for him.

I wanted to give in, get it over with. So I said, "I can't do it."

Sullivan slammed his cap to the ground, and in one honest, reckless moment, it all came out: "You fucking Belle Harbor Jews are all alike. No goddamn guts," he yelled. "You're a disgrace to your own people."

Nobody moved. The wind whipped a funnel of dust through the hard clay infield.

So that's what this was all about. It was no secret that Big Tom was a bigot. But it still came as a shock. He was a coach, a teacher. Some of the guys, I'm sure, had thought the same thing, but we were teammates and they'd never say it to my face. Even in my worst moments I believed that this stuff was for the anti-Semites from the sticks, the ones who say "Jew York."

There was no chance Sullivan would apologize. He'd used tactics like this before—to get us mad, to fire us up. If I wanted be a real putz, I could report him to the league's advisory board. My father knew some of the officers. But I knew I wouldn't do it, because if I turned him in, it would confirm what he already thought of me, and I didn't want to give him the satisfaction. Besides, I still needed him. And in some odd way I must have sensed that he needed me. If I said or did the right thing, I could still bail him out. For that moment, then, we were yoked to each other, like Sidney Poitier and Tony Curtis in that movie *The Defiant Ones*.

I think Sullivan believed that somehow I had made him say

what he said. He was angry at *me* for making *him* look bad. So to cover his own ass, he had to make it seem like it was my fault.

"Get out of my sight, Steinberg," he snapped. "You make me wanna puke."

He motioned toward the bullpen. "Levy, get your butt in here and pitch."

To my mind, Burt was more timid than either Mike or me. But, it was all part of Big Tom's design.

Sullivan grunted; the cords of his muscular neck wound tight. Just as he reached to take the ball, something snapped inside of me. I pulled my hand back. Then an eerie calm began to wash over me. My stomach stopped churning, my chest didn't feel as if it was about to burst, and my neck wasn't burning. I could tell that Sullivan sensed something was going on, but he wasn't sure what it was. Neither was I. Not yet, anyway.

"I'm not leaving, Coach," I said.

Yeah, he sensed it all right. But he misread it. He waved Levy away. Maybe this was Sullivan's obtuse way of atoning for the Jew remark, by allowing me to stay on *his* pitcher's mound.

"Get back in the box, Rubin," he snapped.

"No Coach," I said

"What?"

"You grab a bat, Coach."

A frozen moment. Was I really doing this?

Sullivan looked at me, then he looked at the guys in the bleachers and laughed out loud. We all knew he was going to do it. He ripped off his windbreaker and took a couple of practice cuts, his biceps rippling. He bowed at the waist when muffled cheers rose up from the third base side. Did it ever occur to Big Tom that they might be cheering against him? Or that maybe they were just morbidly curious to see what would happen? Anyhow, he was smiling that crooked ass grin of his. The players in the bleachers spilled into foul territory, inching closer to the backstop.

He stepped into the box and took a few swings.

why do you have to say that

Ok Coach, I'm thinking. You're gonna get just what you asked for.

I was ready to play me some chin music. Chin music, where the ball whistles as it buzzes just underneath the batter's throat. Before I went into my windup, Whalen took two steps up the first base line. He was sure I was going to throw the pitch-out. Can't blame him. It's what he would have done. It's what anyone in his right mind would have done. Sullivan must have thought so too, that's why he was still grinning.

It was the smirk that did it. Screw chin music, I'm gonna' take his fucking head off. *Nice*

As I brought both arms over my head, I saw Ortiz streaking from third toward home. In that split second I realized that this really was happening. When Big Tom squared to bunt, I zeroed in on the black line on the inside corner of the plate. Calm down, I told myself. Brush him back. Just let him know you're here.

That's what my head was saying, but when I started my motion I lifted my eyes from the plate and locked them on the bill of Sullivan's cap. That shit-eating grin was still on his face. I pushed hard off the rubber, and cut loose. I watched the ball tailing in, in, in, right toward Sullivan's head. But he didn't back off, not even an inch. Maybe he didn't believe I could throw hard enough to hurt him.

I yelled, "HEAD'S UP," tucked my chin into my chest and shut my eyes. I heard a dull thud. I opened my eyes just in time to see his cap fly off his head. And as I watched him crumble, feet splayed in the dirt, I felt sick to my stomach.

Stunned players surrounded the fallen Sullivan, not knowing what to do. With leaden strides, I joined them, growing a little more lucid. Rubin shot me a "Man, you are dead meat" look, and I thought about suspension from school. Jail even. But the coach sat up. Jesus, was he lucky. Was I lucky. I must have clipped him right on the bill of the cap. Why was I so surprised? It was the target I was aiming at.

Sighs escaped as one breath. Legs and arms unraveled. Players backed away. Slowly, Big Tom lifted himself up and brushed the dirt off the seat of his pants. He shook his head like a wet cocker spaniel

don't need

who'd just taken a dip in the ocean. Then he wobbled to the bleachers, looking like a young girl testing out her mother's high-heeled shoes.

Before I could collect my thoughts, Sullivan's voice boomed out: "All right, here we go again. Ortiz, hustle back to third, Rubin, up to bat, Steinberg, get your butt back on the hill. Suicide squeeze, same play as before. This time I know we will get it right, won't we ladies?"

He'd caught me by surprise again. I should have known that he'd have to get the last word. But I couldn't—wouldn't—jump through his hoops. Not this time. I resigned myself to my fate. I took a deep breath, bowed my head, and slowly walked back toward the mound—all the time knowing exactly where I was headed. When I got to the rubber, I kept going. At second base, I pushed off the bag with my right foot and started to sprint. I was unbuttoning my shirt, and as I passed our center fielder, Ducky Warshauer, I tossed my cap and uniform jersey right at him. Ducky stared at me like I'd just gone Section Eight. When I stepped onto the concrete walkway outside the locker room, I heard the metallic clack, clack, clack of my spikes on the concrete floor. I opened the door and inhaled the familiar perfume of chlorine, Oil of Wintergreen, and stale sweat socks. For a moment I thought about going back out there; instead I headed straight for the shower and pushed the lever as far to the right as it would go. As the needle spray bit into my shoulders, I watched the steam rise up to surround me.

Walking home, I replayed the whole scenario. I did it, I told myself, because he provoked me. What else could I have done? It was a knee-jerk response.

All weekend, I brooded about the incident. Should I take what was left of my uniform to his office? Nope, all that would do is let him know he'd won. Ok, I'll wait for him to ask for it. But what if he doesn't? Will I lose my nerve and give in?

Sunday night, seven thirty, he called me at home. Ten minutes later I was back in that stifling office, the steam pipes hissing and banging away. Sullivan was sitting at his desk, head down, shuffling papers. He made me wait for about two minutes. Didn't even look up. When he knew I couldn't take the tension any longer, he said matter-of-factly—as if nothing had ever happened—"I'll see you at practice on Saturday."

Without taking his eyes off his papers, he handed me a paper bag with my cap and jersey inside and said, "Get your nasty butt out of here, kid. I got work to do."

Of course I went back. That's what you do when you're fourteen and your identity is wrapped up in being a ballplayer. I had a pretty good season too. Rubin also made the team, but he sat the bench for most of the summer.

We didn't win the state title, but we did make it to the final game in Cooperstown. We got bombed that day, but my father and brother got to see me pitch a few good relief innings at Doubleday Field.

While I was on the mound that summer I'd hear Sullivan razzing us from the bench. I always listened closely, curious to see how far he'd push me. But whatever else he yelled, I never heard him say "Jew boy" or "candy ass sugar baby" again.

I'd survived Sullivan. The last hurdle would be Coach Kerchman. And, as I later found out, Big Tom did indeed invite Kerchman to scout me that summer. He just never took the trouble to tell *me* about it.

◆

_9.

All summer I'd been looking forward to high school with mixed anticipation. The competition for teams, grades, and recognition would be a lot tougher. But how could it be worse than junior high? Maybe high school would be a fresh start. I was cautiously pinning my hopes on two long shots: making the varsity baseball team and the school newspaper staff.

The first setback came a week before school began. All incoming freshmen were notified that the entire school would be going on double session. The freshman class would attend school in the afternoon, while the sophomores, juniors, and seniors went in the morning.

It meant that all freshmen were excluded from participation in every after school organization, including cheerleading and all five sports—football, baseball, basketball, tennis, and swimming. We'd even miss out on the hazing rituals that would certify us as bona fide high school freshmen.

It was another crushing disappointment. The newspaper and baseball would be on hold for at least another year. The only consolation was that I'd have more time to prepare for Kerchman.

All the jock wanna-bes in the neighborhood knew the Kerchman stories by heart. We'd been privy to them as far back as seventh grade. In his first three years at the high school "Mr. K" had become a local legend. Since he arrived in the fall of '51, the football team had won two Queens championships, and the baseball team had gotten as far as the city championship semifinals. During that time, people in the Rockaways—kids, parents, teachers, local merchants, and newspaper reporters—began to take notice. As I'd learned for myself back in sixth grade, winning teams have a way of galvanizing communities, especially in New York, where neighborhoods are marked according to who commands the "turf."

If you believed the buzz on the playgrounds, Mr. K was an obsessed man. Max Bernstein, a reserve end on the football team, regaled us with stories about the coach's fiery locker room speeches. The way Max told it, before each new season Kerchman would gather the team around him in the boy's shower and give them a spiel about his old college days at Syracuse, where under coach Biggie Munn he was a one-hundred-sixty-pound offensive guard and defensive tackle. Kerchman also made it a point to let everyone know that just after the war he'd had a tryout with the New York football Giants, and that he'd made it to the last cut. He always finished up by saying that he did it all "on a little talent, a big heart, and a whole lot of guts."

Like Tom Sullivan, Mr. K had a reputation for hazing his Jewish players, the difference being that Kerchman himself was a Jew. The story goes that because he grew up in poverty he believed, like Sullivan did, that the Jewish boys from suburban neighborhoods like Neponsit and Belle Harbor were too soft. But where Sullivan was a flat-out bigot, Kerchman was convinced in his own perverse way that it was his mission to toughen us up.

On the first day of football tryouts, Max said, Kerchman always made the same speech—about the time his Army platoon liberated a concentration camp at the end of World War Two. It was designed to let the Jewish players know just how important he thought it was for them to shape-up. Max also said that at the first practice of each new season Mr. K would order the Jewish boys to scrimmage without helmets and shoulder pads.

Exaggerated or not, those rumors were enough to convince Ronnie Zeidner's and Rob Brownstein's parents to send them to Poly Prep and Woodmere Academy, two private schools that were not above bending the rules when it came to recruiting top athletes. The Kerchman stories spooked me too, but boarding school was not an option. Either I played for him, or I didn't play at all.

By the time school started, then, I was anxious to get my first look at this pugnacious coach. So, the weekend after classes began I collared Ira and Billy, my old Ebbets comrades, and off we went to the first home football game.

"You're not gonna like what you see," Ira said, as we walked from the bus stop to the high school.

"The guy's an animal," Billy added.

On game days, the atmosphere outside the high school field was like a carnival. Vendors hawked everything from hot dogs, popcorn, and peanuts, to red and blue "Rockaway High" pennants and pom-poms, to souvenirs etched with representations of the school mascot, a miniature seahorse. In the bleachers, students and parents chanted "Let's go Seahorses," while the cheerleaders bounced up and down in their white wool sweaters and short scarlet and blue pleated skirts. There was a hushed moment just before the football team sprinted out on the field. Most of the guys on the team were only a few years older than me. But in their scarlet helmets and full gear the red and white clad players looked like Roman gladiators. Though I didn't care much for football, I couldn't help but think about how exhilarated I would feel to charge out of the locker room with the rest of the team, while everyone in the stands—parents, teachers, local bigwigs, and students—were all on their feet applauding and yelling.

Once we settled in, I scanned the field and spotted Kerchman standing in front of the team bench on the opposite sideline. He was in his late thirties, maybe 5' 8", and heavyset, wearing a chocolate brown porkpie hat and a rumpled tweed topcoat. You could hear him yelling above the band and the crowd noise. During the game he'd sometimes hurl his hat to the ground and scream obscenities at a player who screwed up. He reacted to missed blocks, fumbles, broken plays—whatever derailed the game plan he'd engineered in his head. A couple of times I saw him grab offending players by the shoulder pads and shake them until their heads bobbed like they were on a swivel. In the middle of the second quarter he grabbed Stuie Schneider, a Jewish halfback, by the jersey and cuffed him with vicious open-handed helmet slaps.

Billy was right. Why would anyone in his right mind want to play for such a monster? Then, I spotted the pitcher's mound just to the right of the south goal posts. In less than an instant, I'd floated free of the razz-ma-tazz. In my daydream fantasy I imagined myself standing on that mound in a Rockaway High uniform. My parents, brother, friends, and a make-believe girlfriend were all in the stands watching. The cheerleaders were chanting my name as I toed the rubber, went into my windup, and got ready to snap off a sharp, dipping sinker.

After the game Billy and Ira declared that they'd seen enough, thank you very much. But I wasn't done observing this contentious coach. His ferocious intensity frightened and fascinated me. So I went back alone to the rest of the home games.

In November I announced to Ira and Billy that I was going to try out for baseball next year. They told me I was crazy to even think about it. But they didn't understand. It wasn't a matter of simply wanting to play ball. I'd long since convinced myself that I *had* to make this team.

Ever since their resurgence, I'd linked my fortunes with the Dodgers. For the past two seasons Brooklyn had made it back to the

World Series. Despite losing again to the Yankees, I thought it was a hopeful sign. But in September of '54 the team faltered down the stretch and finished second behind the Giants.

I told all my tormentors that the Dodgers simply had had an off year. Snider, Reese, Hodges, and Furillo had less than outstanding seasons. The always dependable Roy Campanella injured his hand and hit only 207. Plus, the smooth fielding third baseman Billy Cox and longtime ace lefty Preacher Roe were nearing the end of their careers.

What did them in, though, was the collapse of the pitching staff. Don Newcombe, just back from the service, won only nine games. Carl Erskine had arm problems and finished 18-15. My only comfort was that for the first time since 1948 the Yankees didn't win the American League pennant.

Like most self-proclaimed baseball experts, I predicted that Cleveland would beat the Giants handily. After all, the Indians had won 111 games during the regular season—the second highest total in baseball history. Early Wynn, Bob Lemon, Mike Garcia, and an aging Bob Feller formed the best starting staff in baseball. And Ray Narleski and Don Mossi were among the league's top relief pitchers.

But the Giants stunned everyone by sweeping the Indians in four straight. Their success, coupled with the Dodgers' setback, seemed like another disastrous omen. First the double session, now this.

The split session had forced us all back on the same old alliances and rivalries we'd formed since grade school. At first I felt like I was back in sixth grade, marking time and waiting for my real life to begin.

Mornings, the guys in the clique reverted to playing pickup basketball in Pearlman's driveway. When the clique was a man or two short, I'd sometimes get a last minute invitation to come over and fill in. And while the weather was still mild, I'd get up a stickball game with Mike Rubin.

In the meantime, I revived my old friendship with Peter Desimone. In the last couple of years Peter had evolved into even more of a hipster than he used to be. He frequented the downtown coffee houses, attending readings by Allen Ginsberg and Jack Kerouac—"Zen Buddhists," Peter said, who were writing "some pretty far-out stuff."

I'd always been aware of how different Peter was from the rest of us. In the five years I'd known him, I never saw him attend a dance, mixer, or a sports event. But he was part of a small coterie, a group of faux Bohemians that included Sarah and Rita, the year-book editors who'd rejected my Holden Caulfield knockoff two years ago. On weekends, they'd go down to the Village Gate or the Vanguard where they'd listen to "hard boppers" like Miles Davis, Dizzie Gillespie, and a "super hip piano player" with the exotic name of Thelonius Monk. There were times when I would have loved to tag along with them. But with those two girls around, I didn't have the nerve to invite myself.

It was all so confusing. I desperately wanted to be an insider, but I didn't fit with the clique or with Peter's avant-garde crowd. Where, then, did I belong?

Right after Halloween I started gathering information about all the after school organizations. Among those I quickly crossed off my list were the automotive, chess, rifle, math, visual aid, and science clubs. I also wasn't drawn to Hebrew culture, photography, language, and modern dance—all of which would have been relatively easy to join. The one that gave me some pause was the creative writing club. That was until I found out that Rita and Sarah were in charge.

The organizations I wanted to belong to were the yearbook (*The Dolphin*) and the newspaper (*The Chat*) editorial staffs, plus, Arista (the honor society), the G.O. council, and the senior play committee. To get into any of those you had to be invited or nominated. But how would that happen if nobody knew who I was?

With summer league baseball still so far off, music became my temporary refuge. By Thanksgiving I was tuning in again to Jazzbo Collins's late night show. I convinced myself that by listening to jazz I was cultivating an esoteric taste. In school I'd casually refer to "Miles," "Diz," "Bird," and "Monk," the way I used to mention baseball players.

On Saturday mornings I'd listen to Martin Block's *Make Believe Ballroom* on WNEW. That's where I discovered Sinatra, Tony Bennett, and Nat "King" Cole. It was also my first exposure to Cole Porter, Rogers and Hart, the Gershwins, and Johnny Mercer. Their songs conjured up visions of a cosmopolitan, "uptown" milieu, so opposed in values and style to the downtown Bohemian lifestyle. At different times, in different moods, I was attracted to one or the other—sometimes to both simultaneously.

But when it came right down to it, jazz and standards were aimed more at well-heeled adults and Ivy League college types than at adolescents like me.

On a Friday night in late November, I was lying in bed half listening to Jazzbo Collins. The only light in the room was the orange-yellow glow on the dial of my plastic Philco. During a commercial break, I turned the dial, randomly scanning other stations. When I hit 1010 WINS, I perked up. The music coming out of the tiny speaker was unlike anything I'd heard. It wasn't pop and it wasn't jazz. Above the four-part harmony, a lead singer was crooning in a plaintive, almost pleading baritone. He sounded like an adolescent boy lamenting a lost or unattainable love. The music—piano, drums, and upright base—and the harmonies were simplistic. The lyrics were corny, even trite. But they seemed so familiar, so personal— the kinds of embarrassing things you'd always wanted to say to a girl you had a crush on.

The song was "Earth Angel" by The Penguins. The program was *Alan Freed's Moondog Show*. Freed, who sounded like a hyper used car salesman, kept calling the music rock and roll, a term I'd never heard before.

For weeks afterward I gathered all the information about this music that I could. Some disc jockeys called it R&B, others referred to it as doo-wop or "neighborhood street-corner" music. The music was an urban hybrid form derived from traditional black American blues. But clearly it was aimed at middle-class white teenagers like me. Even then I knew that rock and roll had something to do with girls and sex. I could sense that this music could open up whole new vistas to me.

The State Diner was *the* gathering place for most of the school's shakers and movers. I'd been so removed from the social scene that on Friday night of final's week I decided to go to the diner and see it all for myself. I couldn't bring myself to go alone, so I invited Mike Rubin to come along.

The diner was located in Far Rockaway on Beach Channel Drive and Bayswater Avenue, just beneath the El station. The parking lot was packed with choppers, hot rods, and assorted junkers from all over town. I could see silhouettes moving behind the drawn window blinds, and above the rumble of the Manhattan E-train, muffled strains of jukebox tunes drifted out into the lot. As Mike and I stepped into the alcove we inhaled the aroma of French fries and greasy hamburgers sizzling on the open grill. To the left was a pull-out cigarette machine, to the right, bubble shaped pie and cake containers sat on the Formica counter right next to the glass encased menu that offered BLTs, grilled cheese sandwiches, burgers, fries, tuna and egg salad sandwiches, malts, egg creams, cokes, shakes, and the all-night special—two eggs any style with hash browns and toast.

Directly behind the counter were the stainless steel mixers and the sputtering grill; to the right, rows of red upholstered booths with red Formica tabletops. Each tabletop had an accordion shaped "Seeburg" jukebox that sat right next to the window, right between the creamers and the condiment trays. Above the noisy chatter and the clink of silverware and plates, jukeboxes blared out songs like Sinatra's "Young at Heart," "Sh-Boom" by the Crewcuts, the Hill-toppers' "Till Then," and "The Little Shoemaker" by the Gaylords.

If you were a freshman, you knew to sit in the back. As soon as we spotted an open table, we threaded our way down the narrow aisle. Peering through the haze of smoke, we squeezed past the sweaty crush of guys and girls who stood between the booths and the counter preening and showing off.

Before we were even seated, the waitress appeared. She was wearing a shapeless pale yellow dress, a smudged white apron, and scuffed gym shoes. She tapped her pencil, snapped her gum, and scribbled down our orders. Then she sashayed away.

seems out of place in his writing

Mike and I looked around the long, narrow room to see who was with who. The diner's fixed hierarchy reminded me of the junior high school bus. The greasers and hoods still acted the same way. They flicked their cigarette butts on the floor and draped their muddy boots across the tables. One of them yelled to a passing waitress, "Hey cupcake, I need a refill over here." Others made loud, crude remarks to the girls who were with them. But no one in the diner even bothered to turn around and stare at them. Somewhere between eighth grade and freshman year, they'd lost their aura.

Two tables in front of them were the preppies; current and future class officers, newspaper and yearbook editors, and honor society leaders. I also recognized some of the popular girls from grade school and junior high.

The old clique—Mandel, Klein, Nathanson, and Pearlman—sat between the greasers and the preppies. It was odd not to see them being the center of attention. Still, it was just a matter of time before they'd be the preppies' heirs apparent.

But not even the preppies were the top dogs here. The acknowledged royalty—the varsity athletes and cheerleaders—always held court at the three booths closest to the front door. Football heroes like "Moose" Imbrianni, Leon Cholakis, and Angelo Labrizzi all wore standard jock threads; red and blue letter jackets with tan leather sleeves, V-necked sweaters with white undershirts, tight jeans, and black Converse high-top sneakers. The cheerleaders were dressed in tight skirts and form-fitting blouses. Each one was wearing her boyfriend's oversized white cardigan letter sweater.

All evening, I noticed that everyone in the diner would periodically glance over at the front tables. But the athletes and cheerleaders never let on that they were aware they were being scrutinized.

By the time we left I was almost dizzy with envy. On the bus ride home I closed my eyes and inhaled deeply. I knew I'd never be satisfied until I was a part of that exalted group.

On a chilly March afternoon I cut seventh period Biology to go watch baseball practice. It had been on my mind for weeks.

The workouts were closed to anyone who wasn't affiliated with the team, so I stood outside the field huddled in a windbreaker, straining to see through the chain link fence. My heart leapt the second I saw the team's uniforms. They were exact replicas of the Brooklyn Dodger's uniforms. In place of the traditional blue scripted *Dodgers* was the word *Rockaway*, and stitched just beneath the high school's name were small red felt numbers. I knew immediately where those uniforms came from. In August of '51 the Dodgers had little red numbers placed on all their uniforms—in anticipation of the team's appearance in the World Series. But that was before Bobby Thomson hit "the shot heard 'round the world." Everyone knows the rest of that story.

It took a little digging for me to find out how the high school got those uniforms. In the fall of '51, the school's administration decided that Far Rockaway would have to cancel its '52 baseball season because they couldn't afford uniforms and equipment. The rumor goes that the Dodger brass donated the tainted uniforms to the high school. Everyone made out on that one. The Dodger organization took public credit for its philanthropic gesture, and the high school team got to keep on playing.

As I stood outside the ball field that cold afternoon, I promised myself that I'd endure whatever hardships it would take to earn one of those uniforms.

I stayed sharp that summer by pitching in the Rockaway Beach Teener League—a loosely organized conglomerate of local teams whose talent at best was pretty uneven. I was the number two starter on my team, but I knew I'd need to challenge myself by pitching against higher caliber teams.

The Coney Island league fielded some of the best teams in the city, developing some of the best high school players in the city—including Lafayette's great pitcher Sandy Koufax, Manual Training's Joe Pepitone, Frank and Joe Torre from St. Francis Prep, and Tommy Davis, the former basketball and baseball star from Boy's High. Koufax, of course, became a Dodger Hall of Famer; Pepitone had a colorful and turbulent career with the Yankees; Tommy Davis played with the Los Angeles Dodgers; Frank Torre was with the Milwaukee Braves, and his brother Joe played for years with the Cardinals and Phils before becoming a Yankee manager.

In midseason I managed to catch on as a backup starter with one of the more average teams in the league. I didn't get to pitch a lot, but when I did get an inning or two I could see how tough this level of competition was. Almost every player in the league was a starter on his high school team. Even my mediocre team was a notch better than any I'd ever played on. That summer I earned every out that I got.

Always the salesman, my father continually preached to us that "It's not what you know, but who you know." One of his pinochle partners was Al Seidman, an attorney who back in his college days pitched for the University of Michigan and later in the low minor leagues. My father asked Al to give me some pitching advice. Al agreed, and in midsummer I began working out with him in his backyard.

Al was a grey haired, distinguished looking man in his late forties. He had a little bit of a paunch, but he possessed all the loose-limbed mannerisms of an ex-pitcher. A gentle, soft-spoken man, he reminded me of my grandfather Hymie and of coach Bleutrich. After a while, I even started calling him "Uncle Al."

Al tutored me with great patience. To him, pitching was an art and a craft; he had a firm grasp of the "inner game" that goes on between pitcher and batter. Al also knew that I didn't have the size or power to dominate hitters. But he recognized my intelligence and willingness to work hard. In post-workout conversations, he'd dope out specific strategies to help me outthink the hitters.

"There's a fine line between throwing a pitch over the plate and making a pitch look like a strike," he said. "You want it to look like a strike for as long as you can. By the time the hitter commits, the ball's already a hair outside the strike zone."

I'd always had an intuitive grasp of baseball strategy. And what I didn't know, I'd learned from studying big league players and managers. Most everything Al told me made sense. He saw that I had a good sinker, so he kept reminding me to keep the ball between the batter's belt buckle and his knees. He also taught me how to throw the curveball at three different speeds to three different locations. I'd figured some of this out on my own, the hard way. But his confirmation gave me even more permission to trust my instincts.

The other person my father schmoozed that summer was Gail Sloane, our neighbor from across the street. Gail was an attractive woman in her mid thirties. She had strawberry blond hair and an hourglass figure. Some of the kids on the block bragged about hiding in the bushes and spying on her when she sunbathed in the backyard.

It turns out that Gail worked in the administrative office at P.S. 198, the new junior high where Kerchman taught Guidance and

First Aid. Every so often I'd heard rumors that the coach had a thing for her.

Maybe talking to Gail about me was my father's way of compensating for missing so many of my games. But I was uncomfortable with the idea. It was not the way I wanted to make my first impression on a coach who already believed that boys from my neighborhood were too privileged.

◆

My grandfather, Hymie (pictured here circa late 1940s), was my earliest mentor and a horse racing aficionado. By taking me to the track, he opened for me a whole new world of excitement and adventure.

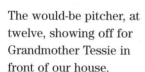

The would-be pitcher, at twelve, showing off for Grandmother Tessie in front of our house.

This was taken in my backyard when I was ten or eleven years old and just beginning to imagine myself as a baseball player.

My first baseball uniform, bought for me by my father when I was twelve.

This is me at thirteen wearing my P. A. L. (Police Athletic League) uniform. It was the first competitive team I ever pitched for.

A rare photo-op for me my junior year, 1956. I was a rookie sports reporter for *The Chat* (the high school newspaper). The two girls in the picture are the cheer leading co-captains. Maybe my luck was about to change, after all.

RIGHT: I'm fifteen here, pictured with Carole Wertheimer, my first confidante and platonic girl-friend—another mentor of sorts.

BELOW: The Village Vanguard on Seventh Avenue near Sheridan Square in the spring of 1957. A high school friend took me here when I was sixteen and she was fifteen. For years afterwards, I went back to this fabled club to see the likes of Monk, Coltrane, Miles Davis, Cannonball Adderley, Mingus, Dizzie Gillespie—the great jazz players of that era.

Grove Day Camp – 1957

ABOVE: Group photo taken at Grove Day Camp in 1957—the summer of my transformation. No longer a chubby, unpopular out-cast, I'm at the far right striking my best "I know I am a very cool guy" pose. My co-counselor and summer advisor about matters of girls and sex is at the far left.

RIGHT: That same summer, 1957, I found this photo taped up above the lockers in the girl's locker room. Shot by my soon-to-be first girlfriend, it's one of the most flattering pictures taken of me during my high school years. I swiped it to remind myself that for a brief moment at seventeen I really did look this good.

American Legion team photo taken the summer of 1957. We went all the way to the state finals that summer. I'm in the second row, far left, holding a baseball and showing off.

The banner from my first *Chat* sports column and my best "Joe College" pose.

SPORT SHORTS

By Mike Steinberg

The girls in the clique.

Me in the spring of 1958, wearing my high school baseball uniform—an authentic hand-me-down Brooklyn Dodger uniform donated to the high school by the Dodgers in 1951, right after they lost the playoff to the Giants. I'd wanted this uniform since my sophomore year. Getting one of these from Coach Kerchman meant that I'd finally arrived as a ball player.

ABOVE: Senior Prom photo taken at the Shore Club in Atlantic Beach, Long Island, June, 1958. Another symbol of having arrived. The couple pictured in the middle was the only one that stayed together. They're still married today. The rest of us all broke up within a year.

LEFT: My future wife Carole Berk and I went to the same high school. When she proudly showed this photo of her new boyfriend to a friend, the friend commented, "Yech! He's so ugly. Why would you want to go out with him?"

Myself, Coach Kerchman, and my brother Alan posing at our high school's one-hundredth anniversary reunion in 1998. My brother is wearing the high school uniform jersey that he swiped after his team won the city championship in 1964, still the only city championship that any of Kerchman's baseball teams ever won.

_ 10.

On the first day of my sophomore year, I was sitting in home-room when Mrs. Klinger handed me a note. "Be at my office 3 o'clock sharp." It was signed by Kerchman. I had to read it twice before I could even react. How did he even know who I was?

The rest of the day was a blur. I couldn't hold a conversation, I picked at my lunch, and every time I opened a book my thoughts drifted. By three my stomach was in knots.

Kerchman's "office" was across from the boiler room, deep in the bowels of the ancient brick building. To get there you had to walk past the showers and through the boys' locker room. I opened the stairwell door and inhaled the steam from the shower. Above the hum and buzz of locker room small talk, I heard the clackety-clack-clack of aluminum cleats hitting the cement floor. To my right was the bank of lockers reserved for Angelo Labrizzi, Mickey Imbrianni, and Leon Cholakis, the football players whom I'd been idolizing from afar at the diner.

Football, of course, would never be my sport; but playing var-sity baseball offered some of the same privileges. I'd already wit-nessed it for myself. Parents and friends actually paid a half a buck to watch you play; cheerleaders chanted your name ("Steinberg, Steinberg, he's our man"), and they kicked their bare legs so high you could see their red silk panties. But the biggest ego-trip of all was when everybody watched with envy whenever a varsity athlete left sixth period Math or Econ to go to a road game.

I tried to push those thoughts out of my mind as I tapped timidly on Kerchman's door.

"It's open," a booming voice said.

The room was a ten-foot-square box, a glorified cubby-hole, smelling of Wintergreen, Merthiolate, and stale sweat socks. The chipped, brown cement floor was coated with dust and rotted out orange peels. On all four sides, makeshift two-by-four equipment bays overflowed with old scuffed helmets, broken shoulder pads, torn jerseys and pants. Muddy cleats and deflated footballs were piled haphazardly on top of one another.

Mr. K stood under a bare light bulb wearing a blue baseball hat, white sweat socks, and a jock strap. He was holding his sweatpants and chewing a plug of tobacco. "You're Steinberg, right?" He said my name, "Stein-berg," enunciating and stretching out both syllables.

"I don't beat around the bush, Stein-berg, You're here for one reason and one reason only. Because Gail Sloane told me you were a reliable kid. What I'm looking for, Stein-berg, is an assistant football manager. And I'm willing to take a chance on you."

So that was it. I'd forgotten about Gail. For a second I was angry at my father. But I was more annoyed at myself for not stopping him when I had the chance. I wanted to run out of the room and find a place to cry. Assistant football managers were glorified water boys; they did all the shit work, everything from being stretcher bearers to toting the equipment. I was numb with humiliation.

Sensing my disappointment, Kerchman waited a beat.

"Gail also tells me you're a pitcher," he muttered, as he slipped into his sweatpants.

Another tense beat. I tried to compose myself.

Finally, he said, "In February, you'll get your chance to show me what you've got."

And to make certain there was no misunderstanding, he added, "Just like everyone else."

He paused again, deliberately waiting. "So what's it going to be, Stein-berg?"

It had all happened too fast. I couldn't think straight. In a trembling, uncertain voice, I told him I'd think about it and let him know tomorrow.

When I brought it up at dinner, I was tempted to tell my father, "See, I told you so." But I held back. After I explained the situation, he told me exactly what I predicted he'd say: that I was the only one who could make the decision. My mother's advice, which was to politely decline the offer and concentrate on my classes, was just as predictable.

What did she mean, "politely decline?" Did she have any idea who Kerchman was? Then, my brother weighed in. He said, "Tell the coach to shove it." Not a lot of help there.

All night I lay awake debating with myself. If I took the offer, would it diminish me in Kerchman's eyes? Would he write me off as a pitcher? Suppose I took this job and didn't complain? Would it give me an edge at baseball tryouts?

The next day in sixth period Econ everyone seethed with jealousy when Harold Zimmerman left early for football practice. That's when I knew I was going to take Kerchman up on it.

When I told him, his only comment was "Good, now that we've got that settled, report to Krause, the head manager, on the double."

Without even a "Glad to have you aboard" he pointed at the equipment bays. "Get some sweats and cleats," he added. "And as soon as practice ends, clean up this room. Get everything stacked up in the right bins, and mop the floor. Let's get this place shaped up."

On his way out the door he said, "And make sure we've got enough Merthiolate, cotton swabs, gauze, and tape. First game's in a week, and when we step out on that field, I want us looking sharp and ready.

"We set the example, Stein-berg," he added. "If we do our jobs, the players will do theirs. You understand me, son?"

It was as if he knew all along that I was going to say yes. I thought about what my kid brother had said. I imagined myself telling Kerchman to take the job and shove it. But I knew what the consequences of that would be.

You've been here before, I told myself. This guy's just like Sullivan. He's testing you, trying to see how much you can take.

Kerchman interrupted my reverie to give me a parting shot.

"Chop-chop, Stein-berg," he said. "Let's get the show on the road."

While my fortunes were in decline, the Dodgers' luck it seems was about to change for the better. There was a palpable sense of urgency about the '55 season. Everyone knew that the only way they'd get the critics and fans off their back was to win the pennant and beat the Yankees in the World Series. But to do it, they'd have to overcome some big obstacles, one of which was that the Dodgers were an aging team. Their average age was thirty-two, relatively old by major league baseball standards. Robinson and Reese were thirty-seven, and Furillo and Campanella were thirty-four. How many more chances would they get?

The Dodgers answered the critics by winning twenty of their first twenty-two games. By mid August they were fifteen and a half games ahead of the second place Braves, hardly a shabby team themselves. Still, the lead wasn't big enough to satisfy the congenital pessimist in me. Until they won a World Series, the '51 collapse would always linger in the back of every Dodger fan's mind.

But this wasn't '51. They clinched the pennant in early September and eventually won it by thirteen and half games.

Campanella came back from last season's injury to win his third MVP award; Snider had his best year, hitting 42 homers, driving in 136 runs, and batting over 300; Newcombe won twenty games and hit 381. The other starting pitchers, Erskine, Billy Loes, Johnny Podres, and Roger Craig, all had winning records; and the bullpen of Clem Labine, Don Bessant, and the rookie Ed Roebuck was the most formidable in the league. It was a typical Dodger scenario, following last season's failure with a gritty comeback. It's almost as if they'd staged the whole thing just to prove they could do it again.

The Dodgers weren't the only team in New York with something to prove. After winning five world championships in a row, the Yanks had finished second to the Cleveland Indians last season. Now two of their most dependable pitchers were gone; Allie Reynolds had retired, and Vic Raschi was traded to the Cardinals. They'd added Bob Turley, "Moose" Skowron, and Elston Howard—their first black player. But it would be years before those three would emerge as stars. Mickey Mantle, Whitey Ford, Billy Martin, and Yogi Berra were still the heart of the team.

The '55 Yankees had struggled all season. In the end, it took an eight-game winning streak in September for them to finish a few games in front of the Indians and Red Sox. Heading into the Series, it looked like the Dodgers might finally have the edge.

But that illusion was quickly dispelled. The first two games were played at the Stadium, and the Yanks won both. At the time, no team had ever lost the first two games of a World Series and come back to win. So when the Series shifted back to Brooklyn, it looked like it would be a replay of the past five encounters.

Athletes and coaches are always pontificating about "defining moments." For the Dodgers, this most certainly was one of them. If they lost again, they would forever be remembered as the team that couldn't win the big games. Perhaps they sensed what the stakes were, because they played all three of their home games as if they were possessed. They won them all. But with a chance to wrap the Series up at the Stadium, they lost the sixth game.

Same analogy.
but not potent.
or poignant
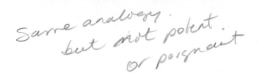

Déjà vu. Nothing's changed, I thought. Somehow, they'd find a way to lose again. Would chronic failure become my m.o. as well? It was a chilling thought.

Losing game six set up another dramatic seventh game. In the bottom of the sixth inning, the Dodgers were ahead 2-0. Gil Hodges had driven in both runs, and Johnny Podres was pitching beautifully. Was it another occasion for false hope? I paced back and forth in front of the TV on every pitch.

When the Yankees got the first two men on base, it looked like the momentum was about to shift back to them. Yogi Berra, the Yankees' most reliable clutch hitter, was at bat. He reached for an outside change-up and lifted a twisting pop fly that was headed for the left field foul line. As soon as Berra hit the ball, Gil McDougal, the runner at second, started for third. Sandy Amoros, the Dodger left fielder, had a long way to run. Just when it looked like Berra's pop fly might drop in for a hit, Amoros reached down with his right hand and made a shoestring catch. Then he wheeled around and doubled McDougal up before he could get back to second base. The play killed off a potential Yankee rally and ultimately changed the course of the game.

From that moment on, you could sense that the Dodgers had a chance to win. I stood in front of the TV holding my breath as Pee Wee Reese threw Elston Howard out at first for the last out of the game. The final score stood at 2-0.

It was a fitting redemption. The Yankees had always seemed so invincible. It was also a confirmation of the Dodgers' resilience. A lot of teams would have faded into oblivion after blowing that thirteen and half game lead in '51.

The Dodgers' turnaround gave me a shot of renewed hope. Like them, I knew I'd have to pay my dues. *This I find weak.*

Working for Kerchman that fall would be the first test. In addition to doing the coach's dirty work, I had to put up with a lot of crap from the senior managers and star players. It was even more humiliating than I'd anticipated. "Moose" Imbrianni sent me on a fool's errand to fetch a bucket of steam; I earnestly searched for a rabbit's foot for Leon Cholakis; and I came up with a pair of fuzzy dice for Angelo Labrizzi's convertible. Before games I taped ankles, treated minor injuries and sprains, and inflated the footballs. At half-time I cut the lemons and oranges. During games I'd scrape mud off of players' cleats, carry water buckets and equipment, and help injured guys off the field. After the games ended I stayed to clean out the locker room.

The worst jobs were being a water boy and stretcher bearer. It was bad enough that I had to run out there in front of thousands of people during the timeouts, but it was humiliating to have to listen to the taunts and jeers of my classmates. Whenever I heard "Hey water boy, I'm thirsty, bring the bucket over here," or "Man down on the fifty," or "Hey medic, get the stretcher," I wanted to run off the field and just keep going. *So much more interesting with dialogue*

When I wasn't at practice I deliberately avoided Peter and Mike. I was too embarrassed to face them. As often as I could, I took the public bus to school, and I stayed away from dances and neighborhood parties. I thought constantly about quitting, but I was already in too deep. If I quit now, I could kiss my baseball dreams goodbye.

In late October, two other sophomores and I applied for a single internship on *The Chat* sports staff. I'd been waiting a year for this opportunity, and I was determined to get this position. To test our competence, Daniel Roth, the editor, asked us to write up the results of the first home football game. The best of the three, he said, stood a chance of getting printed in the next issue.

I've always loved having the inside dope on things. As a student manager, I was privy to information that the other two aspirants didn't have access to. So along with the game highlights, I wove in some pointed anecdotes about the star players, I explained a few of Kerchman's game strategies, and I added some of my own sideline and locker room observations.

Even I could tell that the piece had more authenticity and pizzazz than the typical generic story. Luckily for me, Roth wasn't a stickler for the conventional "who, what, where, when, and why" news report. He praised me, in fact, for making the story so personal and idiosyncratic. Naturally, I was thrilled when it appeared.

Two other stories followed, and by mid fall Roth had expanded my assignments. He asked me to do an exclusive interview/profile of Kerchman; and when football season was over he selected me to cover the basketball games in the winter.

My stories began to attract some attention—mostly from the sports nuts. I'd avoided them in school because they were so uncool, but it moved me a notch higher in the pecking order, if only in my own mind. And I couldn't deny that I enjoyed seeing my name in print again. Especially now, when I was so embarrassed by my other role.

Thought I hated the degrading football jobs, watching Kerchman in action continued to engage me. In his pregame pep talks he invoked the names of past Far Rockaway football heroes, and he preached impassioned sermons on the value of courage, character, loyalty, and team play. His scrimmages were grueling tests of fortitude and stamina. When players didn't follow orders, he'd single them out for public ridicule. His favorite victim, it seemed, was poor Stuie Schneider, our best halfback.

At one practice session, it was getting late and everyone's butts were dragging. On a drop-back pass play, Stuie brush blocked Harold Zimmerman, the oncoming defensive tackle. Harold and Stuie were good friends. Neither wanted to injure the other, especially in a meaningless scrimmage. But Kerchman was on to them. He stopped play and walked right up to them. He sighed and rolled his eyes—clearly playing to the crowd.

"Let's see what you've learned this year Schneider," he said.

Without pads or a helmet, the coach took a three-point stance on the defensive line and came charging right at Stuie. My encounter with Sullivan had put me wise to this tactic. We all held our collective breath. As scared as Stuie was, he knew what the stakes were. So he stayed low, dug his cleats into the turf, and proceeded to knock Kerchman right on his butt. Everyone, I bet, was inwardly cheering. We all looked down at the ground and pawed the dirt with our cleats, waiting to see what the coach would do. I was pretty sure what was coming next. Stuie had played right into Kerchman's hands. Did coaches talk to each other about stuff like this? Or was it just business as usual to them?

Just as I'd thought, Mr. K got up and clapped Stuie warmly on the shoulder pads.

"That's the way to hit son," he said.

Then he turned to the rest of the squad. "This is football, not cheerleading practice," he said. "You make the man pay."

It didn't take long to grasp what Kerchman was trying to teach us. In a late season game against St. Francis Prep, Stevie Berman, our star quarterback, was picking their secondary apart with his passing game. When we lined up offensively, their guys tried to unnerve Stevie by calling him "dirty Jew," and "kike," and chanting in unison, "the Jews killed Christ, the Jews killed Christ." We'd heard it all before—in the streets and on the playgrounds. It only made our linemen block harder.

By the end of the first quarter we were ahead by three touchdowns, and everyone could sense a fight brewing. Sure enough, on the next offensive series their nose tackle deliberately broke Stevie's leg as he lay pinned at the bottom of a pile-up. It's a chicken-shit maneuver because it's so easy to execute. Before the ref can unscramble the pile-up, you just grab the guy's leg and twist.

There's a kind of perverse, unspoken ethic at work here. It's agreed upon that taunts and racial slurs are part of the game. But when you deliberately take out an opposing player, especially the quarterback, it's a declaration of war. As hard-nosed as Kerchman was, he'd never allow one of his own players to pull a stunt like that. But now that it had happened, he knew what had to be done.

As we carried Stevie off on a stretcher, Mr. K squeezed his hand and said, "Don't you worry pal, we'll get them back for this." As if that was going to do Stevie any good.

Leon Cholakis, our 275-pound, all-city tackle lived for moments like this. I winced at the thought, but we all knew what was coming. Cholakis had been waiting all game for Coach to turn him loose. Kerchman nodded in Leon's direction, and on the first play of the next offensive series, Cholakis hurled himself full-force on their prone quarterback. Even on the far sidelines, you could hear the guy's collarbone snap. It was a clean break. When they carried the guy off, I had to turn my head away. The refs of course tossed Leon out of the game.

By now, things had gotten way out of hand. The crowd was yelling obscenities at us, students were throwing glass bottles out on the field, and fistfights were breaking out all over the bleachers. The South Arverne Boys Club, a Rockaway street gang, was mobilizing behind the stands in preparation for a sure rumble.

I wondered how we were going to get out of there alive. But Kerchman was way ahead of me. He quickly dispatched Krause and me to the locker room.

"Krause, find out how we can get the hell out of here the back way," he said. "Then, report back to me."

"Stein-berg, as soon as we know where to go, alert the bus driver where to pull up. Then let Krause know. Wait for us. We'll be there in five minutes."

By the time the St. Francis fans had spilled out on the field— some of them brandishing rusty tire irons and duct taped zip guns— our team had already snuck out through the basement boiler room door. We made it to the bus before anyone could figure out where we'd gone.

On the ride back to school I felt nauseous and dizzy. But a piece of me was grateful to Kerchman for protecting us. And for having the presence to get us out of there.

By the end of '55, rock and roll had become part of most every urban teenager's identity. It validated our deepest passions and anxieties. For me, in particular, it was a retreat from all the ongoing disappointments and frustrations.

Vocal groups like the Moonglows, the Platters, and the Flamingos were expanding and refining the doo-wop sound—crooning songs about unfulfilled longing and unrequited love (our teenage anthem). At the same time, Chuck Berry, Little Richard, and Fats Domino were raising the stakes. Songs like "No Particular Place to Go," "Maybelline," "Blueberry Hill," "Rip it Up," and "Havin' Me Some Fun Tonight" lyricized our yearnings and curiosities about sex and lust.

In response, parents, the media, politicians, teachers, and spiritual leaders actively campaigned against the music, calling it "lewd," "anarchistic," "scandalous," "offensive," and "distasteful." Which of course only increased the music's currency with us. Rock and roll had given teenagers a voice and a common language. We were beginning to think of it as our own personal music.

Alan Freed was now the most visible disc jockey in the country. Teenagers lined up for hours to buy tickets to Freed's live stage shows at the Brooklyn Fox and Paramount. The first time I went, I watched with envy as kids my own age danced in the aisles, screamed, and sang along while Chuck Berry did the "duck walk," or Jerry Lee Lewis set his piano on fire. When the teenage heartthrob acts like Pat Boone were on, the girls shrieked at the top of their voices and jumped up and down in their seats, skirts flying above their knees. I could feel my whole body pulsing with desire. They looked exactly like the wholesome, pony-tailed girls in my classes—the pretty, popular ones I'd been day dreaming about since junior high—the girls who only let you get to first or second base.

Even at basement make-out parties, I'd never seen anything as openly uninhibited as this was. For the first time it dawned on me that those girls had the same kinds of desires as I did. Watching them gyrate to the beat of the music reminded me of the erotic jolt I felt at football games whenever the cheerleaders and boosters screamed and jumped up down as they rooted the team on.

Now more than ever, I wanted to be a part of the State Diner jock clique.

At the season-ending banquet in December, Kerchman announced the names of the players who'd won individual awards. It was no surprise that Cholakis won the John Kelly Award, the gold medal that traditionally went to the team's inspirational leader and most valuable player. But when I walked up to the podium, I could see that Kerchman was holding a varsity letter in his hand. As he handed it to me, he shook my hand and said, "Nice job, son, see you in the spring."

It would have been a breach of decorum for me to wear a varsity football letter. But Kerchman's gesture disarmed me, and my baseball hopes soared.

◆

_ 11.

On February fifteenth, more than 100 jittery dreamers turned out for baseball tryouts in the dingy, grey high school gym. No surprise there. Far Rockaway was the only high school on the peninsula, which meant that Kerchman always had his pick of the best athletes. More than 250 had tried out for football last fall.

On the first day Kerchman announced that he had ten spots to fill. Two would be pitchers. Then tryouts began. Standing less than twenty yards away, Mr. K swatted rubber-covered batting-range baseballs at would-be infielders. When he ripped a hard grounder, the rubber-coated ball would skip off the basketball court's polished wooden surface and spin crazily across the floor. If the fielder missed the ball, it would rocket into the gym's brick wall with a loud "thwack," then ricochet back. The terrified rookies, myself among them, watched from the oval running track above the gym, while Imbrianni, Hausig, Berman, and Gartner—the veterans who'd already survived this ritual—got to stand right behind the coach, horsing around and heckling the newcomers. While I watched the drill, I couldn't help but wonder what kind of ordeal Kerchman had devised for the new pitchers.

We were the last group to tryout. Kerchman placed eight of us in a line across the width of the basketball floor. We each had our own catcher and one varsity hitter to pitch to. There were no nets or batting cages to separate us. No pitching screens to protect us. Kerchman and his veterans stood in safety, up on the running track, and when he blew his whistle all the pitchers simultaneously threw to the hitters. It was rough enough trying to concentrate on throwing strikes to varsity hitters, but as soon as you let go with a pitch, line drives and ground balls went whizzing past you. It was a scene right out of a Keystone Kops movie.

The drill, of course, was designed to unnerve us. Our job was to screen out everything else and concentrate on each pitch we threw.

That night, my arm was so sore that I slept with a heating pad wrapped around it. Every hour or so I'd get up and wander around the house, wondering if I should even bother going back the next day. But when the sun rose I was eager to get right back at it.

By the last day my arm throbbed with pain every time I threw a pitch. I had no zip left. I was sure I'd never make the cut. I tried to prepare myself for the worst. At home and in school I brooded and moped around, continually reassuring myself that I'd done the best I could under the circumstances. I slept in fits and starts. Late at night, a persistent voice would wake me up. "Who would you be without baseball?" it said. "If you don't make it, what will become of you?"

Two days later Kerchman posted the final squad list. One spot was sure to go to Mark Silverstone, a cocky, Jewish left-hander from Neponsit. I disliked him, yet I envied his arrogance. The first time I went over to his house he pulled a copy of Machiavelli's *The Prince* off his bookshelf and pointed with pride to a sentence that read, "It's better to be feared than loved." It couldn't have epitomized our differences better. Was he serving me some sort of notice?

A former prep school kid with a chip on his shoulder, Mark was handsome, a good athlete, a ladies' man, and an honor student.

Silverstone kissed no one's ass. He was a lot like Kerchman in that way. Either you dealt with him on his terms or he simply ignored you.

My hands were shaking as I scanned the alphabetically listed names. Right below "Silverstone" was "Steinberg." At first I thought there must be another Steinberg, and when I read my first name I was too stunned to even speak. My first impulse was to telephone everyone I knew.

I was still a little wobbly when I went over to the equipment cage to pick up my uniform. I could barely wait to hold that Dodger jersey in my hands. Lenny Stromeyer, the student manager, scanned his list and abruptly informed me that "batting practice pitchers don't get uniforms." Nor, he said, did they travel to road games with the rest of the team. Then came the kicker: "At home games," Lenny said, "your job is to stand at the entrance behind the backstop and chase the foul balls that are hit out of the park."

He was openly gloating—letting me know in no uncertain terms who had more status than who around here. But who the hell was fat Lenny to be telling me this stuff? My gut burned. A batting practice pitcher? A ball chaser? I wanted to march right into Kerchman's office and protest. But I had to remind myself that he'd cut at least three or four pitchers who clearly had more talent than I did. I wondered what that was all about.

On the bus ride home I kept telling myself that at least I'd made the team. I remembered my PAL season and how surprised Bleutrich was by my progress. Maybe the same thing would happen again.

When I pitched outdoor batting practice Kerchman was always egging me on.

"That's the way to do it, Stein-berg. Nothing fancy, just throw it right down the pipe," he'd say.

At first, I mistook his remarks for encouragement. But they were nothing of the sort. This was his way of reminding me of my role—that is, to be cannon fodder for the hitters. It was the varsity players' confidence he was concerned with, not mine.

In the beginning, most of the veterans teased me because I wore my old VFW uniform at practice.

"Are you with this team, rook?" our catcher, Mike Hausig, yelled out.

"Hey water boy, toss a big fat one up here," Imbrianni said.

"What's VFW stand for, anyway?" Frannie Cooper asked. A beer bellied pitcher, Cooper was the team's self-appointed buffoon. Before I could reply, he looked at the rest of the guys and said, "Personally, I think VFW means 'Virgins fuck wimps.'" Then he laughed.

Just wait till these assholes have to hit against me. Two years of summer league had taught me that big, free-swinging sluggers—like Imbrianni, Hausig, and Cooper—were usually the most impatient hitters. They wanted to crank everything out of the park. So, when Mr. K wasn't watching, every half dozen pitches or so, I'd sneak in an off-speed slider or a sinking curveball.

Just as I'd figured, most of the big hitters over-swung and either topped the ball or popped it up. But it still didn't stop them from ribbing me.

"Man, can't you throw any harder than that?" Imbrianni said. "The fuckin' ball takes forever to get up to the plate," Hausig said. To mask his frustration, Imbrianni added, "Yeah, I just got too tired of waiting."

It's exactly what I wanted. Maybe it would get Kerchman's attention, even if it was just to chew me out for not being a pitching machine. But when I looked to Mr. K for some kind of acknowledgment, he'd say things to the hitters, like "What's with you guys? If you let a little pissant like Stein-berg here make you look like a monkey, what's gonna happen when you face a really good pitcher?"

I knew what he was doing, but I hated to have to stand there in front of the whole team and take it.

Then there were those afternoons when I'd have to stay late and pitch batting practice to the rest of the scrubs. And I dreaded the miserable Saturday mornings in March when the stiff ocean breezes blew winter's last snow flurries across still frozen turf. The rest of the team would sit huddled in parkas, while me and Henry Koslan, another scrubbie, threw batting practice. An added indignity was having to listen to the varsity players complain about how hard Mr. K was driving them. Those guys didn't know how good they had it.

By midseason I was feeling so demoralized that I had to do a heavy psych job on myself just to get to practice. The team was good, I rationalized. They're on the way to winning the league championship. Imbrianni was leading the borough in hitting and Stevie Berman and Jack Gartner, both still juniors, were two of the best pitchers in the Public School Athletic League. Even Mr. K's protégé, Silverstone, only got to pitch the last few innings of a blowout.

It's only your first year, I kept telling myself. Remember how long it took the Dodgers to get there. Just hang on and wait your turn.

The worst of it, though, was chasing those goddamn foul balls, while my classmates in the stands ragged on me. It was just like the humiliation I felt as a water boy or stretcher bearer. Couldn't Kerchman at least have spared me that indignity?

By season's end, I was just putting in time. We won our last five games and cruised into the playoffs. But just when it seemed we might go all the way, in the borough finals, Berman had his only off game of the season. Bryant High eliminated us 4-1. Silverstone told me that on the gloomy bus ride home Kerchman really reamed the guys out—told them that they played like girls. For once, I was happy not to have been there.

The season ended, as always, with the awards banquet. The local media, school bigwigs, and our families all attended. Just as everyone predicted, Imbrianni, a four-year letterman in two sports, won the top prize, the John Kelly Award. I got a minor letter, as expected, and I watched with envy when each member of the "big team"—including that bastard Silverstone—received his varsity R.

For the past three years, summer break had been anything but a vacation. And this year promised to be no different. As soon as school let out, I was running my two miles a day and working out with weights. I was going to Dodger games, playing American Legion and Teener League ball, delivering prescriptions for the pharmacy, and working in a canning factory, lifting heavy boxes of pineapples and peaches. I hated those long, boring days, doing the same repetitious jobs. And on the nights we didn't play ball, I was too tired to even hang out at Art's.

"Is it worth it?" I'd ask myself over and over again. Wasn't vacation a time for having fun? For hanging around at the beach, pursuing a summer romance, going to sleep away camp?

I wanted to blame my family's circumstances for my hardships. My parents couldn't afford to send me to camp or give me much of an allowance, so I had to work at menial jobs I didn't like. The real truth was that I was terrified of looking foolish in front of the other kids on the beach, and of feeling like an outcast at parties. So, I retreated into the familiar world of baseball, the one place where I could walk the walk and talk the talk.

One day I made the mistake of whining to my mother.

"Somehow, you manage to find time to play ball," she said.

I had to scramble to find a rebuttal.

"If I don't practice, how will I ever make the team?"

"That's your problem," she said. "Instead of enjoying yourself, you worry too much about impressing those dreadful coaches."

She was right. I'd been so driven to make one team or another that I'd sacrificed just about everything else.

Over the past few months, I'd started to feel a little bit better about myself. Last year I'd grown a couple of inches, bulked up, and even lost a lot of my baby fat. When I looked in the mirror, I no longer saw a short, chubby, homely kid. Maybe it was time to start coming out of my shell.

What first drew me out was a series of unexpected postcards from Ronnie Zeidner and Rob Brownstein. I'd envied those guys from as far back as sixth grade. They had it all: money, popularity, and athletic ability. Both were already starting on the varsity baseball and basketball teams at Poly Prep and Woodmere Academy. And I'd recently heard that they were part of an exclusive crowd of guys who were hosting wild parties in their parents' plush Manhattan apartments.

Ever since I'd read *The Catcher in the Rye* I'd been ambivalent about that whole milieu. Like Holden Caulfied, I'd always resented the spoiled rich guys he calls "phony bastards"—the preppies who paraded their entitlement. Yet, I couldn't help but wonder what it was like to be a part of that scene. Lately I'd even been thinking about someday attending Columbia, so I could hobnob with the Ivy League types and urbane Barnard coeds. It was a universe that seemed so far beyond my means.

I was reminded of all this when I started receiving those postcards. Both guys were junior counselors at a sleep-away camp in the Adirondacks. On the front of the cards were color photos of rustic-looking cabins surrounded by impossibly blue lakes and abundant woods. Scribbled on the back were descriptions of lazy afternoon swims and moonlit canoe rides over to the girls' camp, where Ronnie and Rob would romance their counterparts. Or so they claimed.

If that wasn't enough to fire my imagination, the lyrics to summer love songs like "In the Still of the Night," "You're a Thousand Miles Away," and "The Great Pretender" were continual reminders of what I longed for and didn't have. Even thirteen-year-old Frankie Lymon was crooning about why fools fall in love.

It had been two years since my mortifying encounter with Karen. Since then, I'd dated only one girl, Carole Wertheimer; and she was strictly a platonic friend.

We'd known each other since our Hebrew school days. Our parents were officers in the Temple. Initially they tried to play matchmaker, but that only made the two of us more self-conscious.

We each had a secret crush on the other, but, neither of us wanted to risk declaring our real feelings for fear that the other wouldn't reciprocate.

So we settled into a routine where Carole would listen to my litany of complaints about girls. I tried to do the same for her whenever she asked for advice on boys. God knows I was no authority on that subject. Lately I'd been whining so much about not being able to get a date that Carole offered to set me up with Donna Kaufman, a girl who used to baby-sit for her kid brother. When I cross-examined Carole, all she'd tell me is "You'll like her. She's different."

Thinking about a blind date is like preparing to pitch against a team you've never faced. You rehearse your repertoire; you worry about how you'll match up; and you wonder if you'll be able to get it together enough to keep your composure. In both instances you have to be prepared for your game plan to go wrong and be ready to make split second adjustments—all of which came a lot easier to me when I was pitching than when I was dealing with girls.

As it turned out, Donna was just as Carole had predicted. She was attractive in a Bohemian sort of way—dark disheveled long hair, no makeup, and a little portly. She wore all black and liked jazz, modern art, and poetry. Her demeanor attracted and intimidated me. In some ways, she reminded me of Sarah and Rita, the old yearbook editors. It's too bad Peter Desimone wasn't interested in girls; Donna would have been a perfect match for him.

I didn't want to get off on the wrong foot, so I took Carole's advice. I spent the evening asking Donna about herself. But I wasn't doing it only because I was coached. Donna was fascinating in her own right. She was almost two years younger than me, but she seemed more mature than most of the girls who were my own age. Listening to her, I could tell that she went her own way and didn't cozy up to any of the popular kids in junior high. She was a more cerebral but less glamorous version of my fantasy goddess, Cindy Levine.

For someone so young, she was awfully opinionated. She was adamant about letting me know that she wasn't a sports fan or a follower of rock and roll. Rock and roll was, as she phrased it, "juvenile music." And about baseball, she said, "Why does it matter that a team of professional athletes wins or loses a game?"

Donna also disapproved of my obsession with being popular. One time when I was complaining about the snobbishness of the clique, she called my bluff.

"Why do you want to impress people you don't respect or have anything in common with?" she asked.

I didn't like being put down, but she did force me to examine myself more honestly. In her way, Donna suggested that I might be a more interesting guy if I worried less about baseball and popularity and began paying attention to more important things.

To the casual fan the '56 baseball season was business as usual. The Dodgers and Yankees won their respective pennant races. For the fifth time in nine years, they played each other in the World Series. The Yankees won it in seven games, the highlight of course being Don Larsen's perfect game—still the only one in Series history.

More disturbing were the rumors that the Dodgers might soon be leaving Brooklyn. As far back as a year before, Dodger owner Walter O'Malley had publicly hinted that if the city didn't provide the team with a new stadium, he would consider moving the Dodgers out of New York. Giant owner Horace Stoneham quickly followed suit. He was quoted as saying that if the Dodgers left Brooklyn, he'd move the Giants elsewhere as well.

The two owners had been complaining for years that their ballparks were old and in disrepair, that the neighborhoods around Ebbets and the Polo Grounds were deteriorating, that attendance had been decreasing steadily, and that they were losing money—an all too familiar owner's litany, as the following four decades would demonstrate.

To back up his threat, O'Malley sold Ebbets Field to a developer in the summer of '55. This past season he scheduled seven Dodger "home" games in Jersey City. And in December he sold Jackie Robinson's contract to, of all teams, the Giants.

I was too absorbed in my own struggles to understand the implications of these transactions. But in some obscure corner of my mind, I sensed that both the Dodgers' fate and my own were about to be irrevocably altered.

I'm personally tired of this analogy.

I wasn't planning on being an assistant football manager in the fall. But on the first day of practice Kerchman cornered me in the boys' john. Without so much as a "Hello, did you have a good summer?" he informed me that this year I'd be the liaison between him, the players, and the head manager. How he even knew I was in the bathroom is a mystery to me.

"Look at this as a promotion, Stein-berg," he said, while I stood at the latrine fumbling with my zipper.

This was the first time Kerchman had ever sought me out for anything. If I had any hope of pitching in the spring, there was no way I could turn him down.

That season, my junior year, I had a much easier time of it. Mostly I worked with the head manager, Krause, and I delegated all the grunt work to the assistant managers. On game days I stood behind the bench and kept the stats.

I found that I liked being behind the scenes managing things. Plus, my "promotion" included an unexpected perk. My charge was to write up the highlights of each game and phone my "story" in to several newspaper sports desks.

Five of them, the *World Telegraph and Sun, Journal American, Daily News,* and *Daily Mirror,* ran composite summaries of the games. But the *New York Times, Herald Tribune,* and *Long Island Press* not only printed my game summaries almost verbatim, but a couple of times they even gave me a byline.

The first time I saw my name in the New York papers I ran out and bought three copies of each one. I clipped the articles and pasted them into a scrapbook alongside my sixth grade columns. Soon after the first two stories appeared, the editor of our local paper, *The Wave*, asked me to write a 600-word weekly article on the remaining six games.

I took full advantage of the moment. On the long bus ride to school I boasted to anyone who'd listen that I was a "stringer" for the *Times* and *Herald Tribune*, which of course was a slight exaggeration—in the same way that making it past first base with a girl could be construed as having sex.

At the football banquet I got another major letter that I couldn't wear. But this year I was determined to pitch enough innings to earn my varsity baseball letter. For months I'd been envisioning myself sitting at the State Diner jock table, bantering with the other letter winners and their cheerleader girlfriends. As soon as we were back from Christmas break, then, I started throwing indoors with Bob Milner, our second-string catcher.

Things in school were also beginning to look up. My grades were good, especially in English and History; I'd started thinking about what colleges I'd apply to; I began studying for the junior boards; I was writing sports features for *The Chat;* and at the end of the term I was accepted into an advanced Journalism class—a class I'd set my sights on since I was a freshman.

Over a hundred students applied for admission, and only twenty-two were selected. Earl Jagust, who taught the class, was one of the most popular and quirky teachers in the school. Jagust, it so happens, was also *The Chat's* faculty advisor.

Between baseball and Jagust's class, I finally had something to hope for. But now that the stakes were raised, I had a lot more to lose as well.

That fall Donna and I saw each other every weekend. By this time our roles had become even more clearly defined. Donna had taken it upon herself to become my intellectual and cultural guru. And, to my benefit, I was a willing accomplice. On alternate weekends she'd escort me downtown to the Village jazz clubs and coffee houses I'd been so curious to see. At the Village Vanguard one Friday night, I sat transfixed, watching Thelonius Monk, his eyes closed, head tilted back, riffing off the melody line of "Straight, No Chaser." That same night we saw John Coltrane play an extended solo as if he was in a trance. Another time, at the Village Gate, we watched Miles Davis, his eyes bulging, cheeks puffed out, blowing into that shiny gold horn that he tilted straight up to the ceiling, as if to defy the gods. We also saw Gillespie and Coleman Hawkins and the Adderley brothers jamming after hours. In live performance, jazz was far more captivating than I'd ever imagined.

One Saturday night we stumbled out of a jazz club at three A.M.—both of us drunk with elation, our nerve ends still tingling. The only sensation I could compare it to is the unconscious rhythm I'd drift into when I was pitching well. I described for Donna in detail what it was like to be in that "zone." It's what jazz musicians call "the groove," I told her. I don't think she bought my analogy. It was the baseball comparison that put her off.

Her campaign to educate me included excursions to Upper East Side "art house" theaters where we saw foreign films like *The Virgin Spring* and *The Seventh Seal*, which I admit went completely over my head. We went to avant-garde plays like the revival of *The Threepenny Opera*. Yet, when I suggested we see *My Fair Lady*, Donna turned up her nose. Maybe the Pygmalion story or, in our case, the reverse Pygmalion story, was too close to home for her.

There was no denying that Donna was a snob. That was part of her appeal. But we were kindred spirits in other ways. Both of us wanted a more exotic existence than the one we were given. For her, it was the Bohemian scene; for me it was becoming a baseball star. Also like me, Donna didn't talk much about her family. Neither her mother nor her father had a college education. She never invited me to her house, I think because she was ashamed of them.

It was clear when I met her that Donna was already reinventing herself. But I was still groping, still uncertain of who I was. It was inevitable that we'd eventually part company. I didn't expect it to be so sudden, though. It happened shortly before baseball tryouts began. She told me that she couldn't bring herself to accept this obsession or my need for recognition.

But I wasn't ready to give up either one—no matter how gauche or childish they seemed to her.

◆

_ 12.

At tryouts in February I practiced with the veterans, easily made the cut, and even got an old hand-me-down uniform. It wasn't the Dodger uniform I'd hoped for, but at least I was a legitimate member of the team.

I knew I had to wait my turn behind Berman, Gartner, and now Silverstone. But I hadn't counted on Andrew Makrides or Steve Coan. Both were sophomores, and both were big and strong and threw hard. I sensed I was being passed over, but I pitched batting practice, kept my mouth shut, and waited for my turn to come.

By the end of the preseason, my patience had run out. I was in the bullpen rehearsing what I was going to say to Mr. K when he called me in to pitch the last three innings of our final preseason game. I wasn't expecting it. Coach, it seemed, had an instinct for knowing just how far he could go with me. I knew if I didn't show him something special, I might never get another chance.

Naturally, I started out tight; my concentration was way off. I walked the first man, got the next on a force play, then gave up a hard-hit double on a sinker that hung. Second and third and one out. I watched Kerchman carefully, looking for a signal of some kind. But he was going to make me pitch my way out of this—or else suffer the damage.

I had to make a fast mental adjustment. So I gambled and

walked the next man intentionally. I saw the look on Kerchman's face. Loading the bases was a risky move, even though it set up a double play situation. But there was another reason I did it. I was buying time for myself. It was the only way I'd get myself to settle down.

After the intentional pass, I slowed my pace and began pitching more deliberately. I remembered Al Seidman's advice. I repeated it over and over like a reproachful mantra: "Mix up your pitches. Change speeds. Keep the ball down. Make 'em hit your pitch." On a two-two count I threw a low, outside breaking ball that the batter reached for and hit into an inning-ending double play—second to short to first.

That's all it took. Once I got my confidence back, it was like pitching summer league ball. I got through the next two innings without giving up a hit. Even throwing less than my best, I was convinced that I was ready to pitch at this level. But what mattered was that Kerchman believed it too. I knew I'd have to wait a while longer to find that out.

I got my first clue when the league season began. We had another strong team. As expected, Berman and Gartner pitched the important games. Silverstone got an occasional start, and he was first man out of the bullpen. But in the blowouts Makrides and Coan always got to finish. I sat in the bullpen and never even got a call to warm up. It was like I'd never pitched those three preseason innings. To Kerchman I was still invisible.

During the bus trips home, everyone horsed around. Typically after a winning game on the bus home, we'd all be listening to rock and roll on WABC or WINS. The music was cranked up to the threshold of pain, and guys were croaking lyrics from "Don't Be Cruel" or "Why Do Fools Fall in Love," while others poked their heads out the window, whistling and shouting stupid come-ons to the girls in the street.

Those bus rides were ordeals. There was no place to hide. Harder still was when Kerchman passed the scuffed-up game ball around, which we'd all sign for the winning pitcher. I burned with envy when Silverstone, Makrides, or Coan got one of those balls. And once we reached the high school, I'd have to watch my teammates receiving kudos from the cadre of parents, girlfriends, classmates and, of course, the cheerleaders.

As soon as I got off the bus I'd sneak off under the cover of darkness. All the way home, I'd admonish myself for not having the guts to quit. Then I'd start thinking about what it would feel like to hold one of those game winning baseballs in my hand.

Whenever baseball went badly, I'd usually pull away from everyone and sulk. I'd walk around school in a perpetual funk and berate myself for allowing those moods to ruin my enjoyment of everything else. But lately I noticed that my sulks didn't seem to last as long as they used to. I think it was because my social life was picking up. Part of it had to do with the way I looked. I'd been shaving for over a year, and in the last six months I'd grown to what would be my full height, 5' 7½". Plus, all those summers of lifting weights and running had gradually transformed me from a rotund, flabby kid to a solid looking, well-proportioned athlete. Buoyed by the physical changes, in mid-spring I began dating Ellen Wiseman, another girl Carole had fixed me up with.

At the same time, I was starting to plan for college. I'd taken the junior boards and had set up a series of campus visits for early fall. I'd narrowed my choices down to four schools—Syracuse, Boston University, Trinity, and Columbia. Mostly, I was flying blind. I didn't even know if I could afford to go away to college. But my parents encouraged me to apply, on the chance that my grades would be high enough to qualify me for a loan or scholarship.

I picked Trinity College in Hartford because it was a "Little Ivy," and because the son of one of my father's pinochle partners went there. Boston University and Syracuse were my "safe" schools. Both, I'd heard, had good journalism programs. I didn't have much of a chance of getting into Columbia, but I wanted to try for it anyway—because, well, it was Columbia.

On top of all the changes and new distractions, the one thing that consistently took my mind off of Kerchman and baseball was Mr. Jagust's Journalism class.

Jagust and Kerchman were polar opposites. Where Kerchman looked and acted like a prizefighter, Jagust had a slim, wiry physique, disheveled sandy blonde hair, a Boston Blackie mustache, pale skin, and a baby face. His aspiration was to become a college teacher. He even dressed the part—corduroy sport jackets with plaid shirts and black wool ties. He had an impish smile and a wry, sardonic wit that always kept you off balance. On first impression, he looked like the shy, skinny kid in the Charles Atlas ads, the kind of guy that a bruiser like Kerchman would have intimidated by kicking sand in his face.

But Jagust was no pushover. From the start, you could see that he wasn't going to be the typical, by the book English teacher. In fact, the first thing he did to shake us up was to seat us in reverse alphabetical order, starting with the Zs and finishing with the As. For our first assignment, he told us to look up at the ceiling and observe what seemed to be human footprints. Then, at home we had to write a 500-word essay speculating on how those footprints got there.

The next day, we all read a short excerpt from our pieces. The guesses ran from space aliens to student pranks. Just before the bell rang, Jagust reached behind his desk and produced a long pole with an old leather boot attached to it. Maybe he was trying to loosen us up, give us permission to use our ingenuity. Maybe it was a way of poking fun at all the silly assignments we'd suffered through in school. Whatever his intent, he sure as hell got our attention.

Jagust also had a personal agenda. For the first few minutes of every class he'd recite a witty, biting monologue. Sometimes tongue-in-cheek, sometimes deadpan, he'd rail against the absurdities of the school's lock-step curriculum. Or he'd tell us pointed anecdotes that were designed to expose the petty-mindedness of school officials.

Everyone, the deadbeats included, was drawn to him. Even when he was directing his sarcasm at you, it was clear that Jagust was on your side. He was always challenging you to stretch your imagination, think for yourself, and question all first assumptions—yours and everyone else's. Moreover, he didn't make us compete against one another. Whether you were talented or unimaginative, he'd keep encouraging you—but only if you made an effort to do the work.

Because it was a required English course, we had to do all the common readings and grammar exercises that every other English class did. We read the four required books: *A Tale of Two Cities*, *Macbeth*, *Giants in Earth*, and *The Good Earth*. We took the tests, wrote the 500-word themes, and did the weekly grammar exercises. But half of our final grade was based on our term project—a four-page newspaper.

This wasn't just any newspaper. We'd have to choose one of the four required books to work from, and then come up with a series of news stories, feature columns, interviews, illustrations, photographs, editorials, and reviews—some of them written in the voices and personas of different characters in the book.

I immediately chose Peter Desimone to be my partner. I knew he had an imagination, a talent for drawing, and a nose for doing research. If you got him going, he'd dig up every shred of information that was out there.

Both of us were fascinated by the French Revolution, so we picked *A Tale of Two Cities* to work from. Together we decided to split the writing and research. I volunteered to do the layout and all of the feature writing. Peter would write the "hard news" stories, do the extra library work, and take care of the illustrations.

We had our run-ins, but the one thing we agreed on was that we'd use as many contemporary parallels as we could. So we dreamed up far-fetched analogies between the French Revolution and McCarthyism; we found ways of invoking jazz innovators like Charlie Parker and Miles Davis, and movie anti-heroes like Brando and James Dean. We even used the Elvis phenomenon as a way of illustrating different forms of rebellion.

For all of its demands, the project allowed our imaginations to roam at the same time that it taught us how to integrate our knowledge of the world with historical events and research. It's still the most absorbing project I've ever done in a classroom.

You know you've crossed the line from desire to obsession when your longings infuse your every thought or action. By midseason I was so distraught that I couldn't get a night's sleep, concentrate on any class except Journalism, or even drum up the desire to socialize with anyone I knew. During the games I found myself silently rooting against my own team. I'd sit on the bench or in the bullpen and hope that we'd get blown out, just so Kerchman would give me a few innings. At night I dreamed up scenarios where I'd be up at bat and Kerchman would be pitching. He'd throw me a fat one down the middle, daring me to hit it, and I'd rip a line drive right at his nuts. There were days when I was angry enough to walk into his office and confront him. But what could I say that wouldn't make me sound whiny? If I complained, I was certain he'd order me to turn in my uniform. So just to spite him, I decided to hang on and finish out the season. When I quit, I wanted it to be on my terms, not his.

With three games left, the team clinched the Queens championship. Everyone of course was revved up on the bus ride home. And when we arrived back at school, the cheerleaders and a crowd of screaming boosters and adults were as usual waiting to greet us. I slipped quietly into the darkness as soon as I could get away.

didn't matter, character didn't matter, work ethic didn't matter. In coaches' minds, the only thing that counts is winning games. But how do you win games if you never get your ass off the bench?

I walked home from the bus stop in a daze. Kerchman knew how badly I wanted this. That was his lever over me. He knew he could string me along. I'd already put up with it for two years. Deep down, I had been hoping all along that he was testing my resolve, toughening me up for game competition. But this time he'd gone too far. Two years before, when Sullivan pushed me to my limit, I retaliated. Now, I didn't even have the heart to fight back. All I could do was to cut my losses and try never again to let myself get into this kind of bind—with him or anyone else.

I thought about how life would be without Kerchman. No more five-hour practices and sitting on the bench; no more getting home at nine o'clock at night too tired to do my homework or to go hang out at Art's candy store. It was the perfect time to tell him to take the uniform and stick it up his ass. Still, there was only one more week to get through. Why give that bastard the satisfaction? If I could just stick it out, I'd have all summer to put this bullshit behind me.

Right about this same time, my grandfather Hymie had the second of two consecutive heart attacks. When he recovered he seemed weak and lethargic. But he still insisted on going to the track. There were more and more days when he skipped the flats and slept all afternoon so he'd have enough energy to go to Roosevelt at night.

By now, the old racing crowd had broken up. Hymie was going to the track with Jimmy Sparrow, a retarded kid he'd been kind to when he still had the pharmacy. And just so he'd have company, sometimes he'd even take crazy Shep, the shell-shocked war vet, or old Hilda Bells, who he was still loaning money to. On occasion, he'd even go alone.

My mother was concerned about him driving by himself. So once a week, usually on a Friday night, she'd give me fifty dollars, ostensibly to bet for her and Ruthie. But really it was a bribe to get me to go along with Hymie to the track. She didn't have to buy me off, though. I was all too willing to be his accomplice again.

It had been almost seven years since I'd spent any real time with Hymie. He was approaching seventy, and he seemed frail and tired. But the minute we got to the track, he was as animated as ever. This was his arena. This was what he lived for.

As I watched him dope out his choices, it struck me that even after fifty years he wasn't the least bit jaded about the horses. In fact, he took in the whole spectacle with the wonder and awe of a child who is seeing it for the first time. It reminded me of the enchantment I felt whenever I went to Ebbets Field, and the rush of exhilaration I experienced when I watched my father and his cronies on those summer Sundays. Isn't this what made me want to become a ball player in the first place?

As the semester came to an end, I was so caught up in my class project that I wasn't even thinking about how it would affect my chances to become sports editor. That is, until the last week, when Jagust invited *The Chat*'s editorial board into our classroom. He introduced each one and then asked them to read our grades aloud. It seemed like a needlessly perverse gesture.

Jagust's minions were haughty and condescending. Some of them even giggled as they read the grades. Annoying as it was, the whole scene reminded me of how badly I wanted to be sports editor. I even imagined that I could be up there reading out the grades next year.

A week before school ended, I was sitting in class brooding about Kerchman, when without any warning Jagust announced the names of next year's editorial staff. It happened so fast that I didn't even have time to get nervous. Out of the welter of names, the only one I heard was my own. "Thank you, God," I mumbled under my breath. At that point, I don't think I could have endured another setback.

While the new editors were congratulating each other, I sat quietly in my seat. Why wasn't I beside myself with elation? I'd wanted this job ever since I'd started high school. Yet all I could think about was how demoralizing it would be to write stories about my former coach's and teammates' achievements. My second thought was that maybe this would be my way of exacting some revenge. Neither were very appealing prospects.

The final league game, top of the sixth. I was sitting on the bench thinking "only six more outs and I can finally pack it in." Kerchman had one wrinkle left though, and I should have seen it coming. We were winning by six runs when he called me in to pitch. I wanted to say, "You pitch the fucking innings." But I'd been waiting so long for this opportunity.

I packed two years of frustration and rage into those two innings. If this was going to be it for me, I wanted to show that peckerhead what a mistake he'd made by passing me over. So I bore down and concentrated like it was the last game of the World Series. I snapped off curve balls and sinkers; I changed speeds and mixed locations. I got all six hitters in a row, easy outs.

It was exhilarating to be out there. I wanted those two innings to last forever. When it was over, I was so high that I craved the varsity letter more than ever. I had goddamn earned it. Once I got it, I could walk away from the whole thing. Clean break, nothing more to prove to him—or to myself.

As it turned out, we were eliminated again in the borough finals, by the same team, Bryant, and the same pitcher, Don Large, who'd beaten us the previous year. For the first time since I'd joined the team, Kerchman didn't yell at us on the trip home or make a locker room speech. He just went into his office and cracked the door.

I was relieved—and strangely elated—that this awful season was over. I couldn't wait to turn in my uniform and get the hell out of there. But when I passed by his office, Mr K was still sitting in his chair staring at the wall. It was more than just a playoff defeat to him. He was losing two All-City pitchers and two All-Queens seniors from a squad that had won three straight league championships. Next year he'd be starting again from scratch. It was absolutely nuts, but my first impulse was to feel sorry for *him*.

The mood at the banquet was subdued. Still, it was a prestigious event. Kerchman had invited two previous Kelly Award winners to make the customary inspirational speeches. When I listened to them delivering the old rah-rah, I remembered how good it felt to pitch those last few innings. Mike Hausig won the Kelly Award, and Berman and Gartner shared the *Long Island Press* MVP trophy. Next year those guys would be gone. No matter, I'd made up my mind to pack it in.

Then, just as I expected, Koslan received his varsity letter. That sealed it. I knew I was next. When Kerchman shook my hand and handed me a minor letter my stomach turned over and I had to bite my lower lip hard to keep from crying. My knees were so wobbly I don't know how I made it back to my seat. I couldn't recall a single detail from the rest of the evening. I didn't even wait for my father and brother to take me home. For hours I wandered around the neighborhood, hearing the same script over and over in my head. How could I have let him do this to me? Why didn't I throw the fucking letter right back in his face?

At one point, I found myself wandering barefoot on the beach, my suit pants rolled up to my knees. I took the letter out of my jacket and scaled it like a seashell into the Atlantic. I felt a pang of relief when it disappeared into the black sea. That night, and for three nights following, I didn't sleep for more than a few hours at a time. Nobody in my family could console me.

The last week of school I sat in the back of my classes hiding behind a book. I ducked into empty corridors when I saw teammates and acquaintances coming toward me. At noon I ate lunch alone in an empty classroom. And I cut out as soon as the three o'clock bell rang.

I thought about possible reasons why Kerchman might have denied me the letter. Was this a punishment of some sort? Or was it another ploy? Could he have known somehow that the minute I got the letter I'd be history? I obsessed over it for days. But it didn't matter what the reasons were. I'd have to have my head examined to go back for more. I was done with him and with baseball once and for all.

My father knew how badly I was hurting inside. He wanted me to go back and play next year, but to his credit, he didn't try to dissuade me. His silence was a dead giveaway, though. In his universe, there was no such thing as cutting your losses.

To my mother though, it was a no-brainer.

"Now you can get on with your own life," she told me.

Right, mom. And just what life would that be? Baseball was my life.

again last 3 words
don't add

_ 13.

When school ended in June, I still couldn't escape my melancholic thoughts. Five years of practice and striving and what did I have to show for it? Zilch. Bupkis. A big, fat goose egg. The question now was how to fill the void.

To keep my mind occupied, I signed up for *two* summer teams—one in the local Rec League, and the O'Connell Post American Legion squad, a hand-picked all-star team composed of the best seventeen and eighteen year olds on the peninsula. Playing Legion ball was a step up in competition from high school. If I was good enough to make this team, then why in the hell wasn't I good enough for Kerchman?

Right around that same time, I began hearing rumors again that the Dodgers might soon be leaving Brooklyn. Just the thought of it made my stomach churn. It was a double whammy—too much to absorb all at once.

In the spring of '57 the newspapers reported that Walter O'Malley had peddled the Dodgers' minor league parks in Fort Worth and Montreal for a million dollars apiece. He assured the fans and press that the money would go toward operating expenses for a proposed new ballpark—a domed stadium in downtown Brooklyn, above the Atlantic Avenue Long Island Railroad station.

At first I thought it was a P.R. stunt—a front office maneuver designed to drum up more interest in the team. Major League baseball teams didn't just up and abandon their cities, especially New York, where baseball was practically a religion.

Why would the Dodgers leave? Why now, right at the height of their success? For the past ten years Brooklyn had had one of the best records in baseball. Only two summers before they'd won their first World Series title. Wasn't this precisely what the head honchos had been aiming at for the past five decades?

And what about the millions of fans who'd suffered through the heartbreak collapse of '51? What about the succession of excruciating Series loses to the Yankees? And all of the dog seasons in the 20s, 30s and 40s—when the Dodgers were the sad-sack losers of the National League? How could the team brass ignore the fans' loyalty and devotion? I thought about Donna's warning of a year ago, when she chided me for caring so much "about a team of professional athletes."

To add still another piece of bad news to the mix, I learned from my mother that my father's sales commissions had fallen off drastically. Translation: I needed to bring in some money to help out at home. Normally I'd already be working by now. But in the last few weeks I'd been too busy sulking and feeling sorry for myself. There were mornings when I didn't even want to get out of bed.

I supposed I could fall back on Neiman's Pharmacy. But the thought of it was so demoralizing. I was too old to be pedaling my ass all over town for minimum wage and twenty-five cent tips. If I could have driven the pharmacy's car, it might have been another story. But at seventeen you can't drive inside the city limits without a supervising adult, and that would have been even more embarrassing than riding the bike.

I was still pondering what to do, when one night after Legion practice Ronnie Zeidner approached me with a curious proposition.

It seems there was a last minute opening for a senior counselor at Grove day camp. One of Zeidner's prep school buddies had just backed out because his parents were sending him on a tour of the French Riviera. There was no irony in Ronnie's voice when he told me about it.

As far back as grade school, Zeidner and Rob Brownstein were the two guys in our neighborhood who commanded the most respect. They were the best athletes in our crowd. Both came from wealthy families. Even before they went to prep school, they carried themselves with an air of assurance and poise, like characters right out of *The Catcher in the Rye* or an F. Scott Fitzgerald novel.

My main contact with them was through baseball. That was until I started receiving those camp post cards in which Ronnie and Rob boasted about their escapades with the jc's across the lake. I'd wondered at the time why they were sending them to me. When it came to girls and dating, those guys were lifetimes ahead of me.

While I was throwing hundreds of baseballs at my garage door, spending Saturdays at Ebbets Field, and playing summer league ball, the popular guys were hanging out at the beach, showing off and flirting with girls. At night they went to parties and out on movie and bowling dates. Some were already driving their parents' cars and having sex with their girlfriends—or so the rumors went.

Now that I had some free time, it slowly began to sink in. I was only a year away from college, and I'd never even been in love, and except for a brief fling with Ellen Wiseman in the spring, I'd never had a real girlfriend. What's worse was that my only sexual encounter had been an embarrassing disaster.

Zeidner's offer, then, had come along at just the right time. If I took the day camp job, I'd be around girl counselors all summer. Maybe I could make up for some of that lost time.

The first few days of camp I hung around on the fringes—just like I used to do at dances and parties. But this time I was sizing up the situation, looking for a safe opening or a welcoming invitation—neither of which were forthcoming. At the daily staff meetings I stood back and watched the coalitions form. God knows, I'd had a lot of practice being on the outside looking in.

It didn't take long to see what the pecking order was. At the top of the pyramid were the head counselors—all high school seniors. These guys all went to prep school or Five Towns high schools like Lawrence and Hewlett. Zeidner and Brownstein were easily the top ladies' men. While most of us underlings rode the camp buses to work, they took turns driving matching candy-apple red '57 Chevy convertibles that the other guys called "pussy wagons."

One step below them were the head counselors like me who attended public high schools. The jc's, all fifteen- and sixteen-year-old girls, were another notch lower, and at the bottom were the waitresses and kitchen staff—high school freshmen and sophomores. The male counselors all referred to them as "fair game."

At the top of the girls' food chain were three attractive and classy high school juniors from Woodsburg, the most exclusive village in the Five Towns. They were cheerleaders at Hewlett High, and each one had her own car. Their parents belonged to the Hewlett Yacht Club and to El Patio, a trendy Atlantic Beach cabana club.

I was immediately taken with them. Even in ratty camp T-shirts and cut-offs, blonde and well-tanned Linda Price, Joanne Morse, slender and elegant, and sexy, kinetic Julie Rabin all looked and carried themselves as if they'd just stepped out of a teen fashion magazine. Like Ronnie and Rob, they epitomized the privileged and exclusive milieu I was so ambivalent about.

I couldn't tell which of the three I was most drawn to. They were all prototypes of the unattainable girls I'd been dreaming about since grade school. That they seemed so far out of reach only added to their mystique. How could I even hope to attract their attention?

When I asked Ronnie and Rob what they knew about the three, Rob said, "Don't get your hopes up. They're strictly off limits."

I should have known better than to ask.

Zeidner and Brownstein loved to parade their entitlement. They'd acknowledge the likes of me, but only so long as I was content to remain in their orbit. If I deferred to them, then every so often they'd allow me brief glimpses into their privileged world— like those post cards, and now this job. Guys like them cultivate devotees, if only to reinforce their own perceived superiority. In my desperate state, I was all too willing to comply.

Come to think of it, I'd always had a tendency to subordinate myself to those who had more power or stature than I did. Back in sixth grade I let Elaine Hirsch and Alice Rosen humiliate me at the Beth El dance. In seventh grade I played disciple to Manny and his boys. And I let those two girls from the yearbook staff intimidate me. A year ago I allowed Donna to dictate the terms of our relationship, and for three years I'd willingly done Kerchman's bidding. The price you pay in that tradeoff is the loss of your integrity. Yet, here I was doing it again.

From the beginning of summer league I'd channeled my anger and disappointment into pitching. When you think you have nothing left to prove and nothing to lose, it's a lot easier to let go of your restraints. So in those early season Rec games I was more assertive than I'd ever been before. Whenever a hitter crowded the plate, I'd buzz the ball right under his chin. If I sensed any fear, I'd brush him back again and then snap off an outside curve ball or a low slider.

That summer I pitched better than I ever had—especially whenever I faced my now ex–high school teammate Andrew Makrides. It was well known in local jock circles that Makrides was one of the best young pitchers on the peninsula. Coaches and players talked about him as a potential big league prospect. That's why I'd always taken a special pride in out-pitching him. But this time, I had even more incentive. Next season he was certain to be one of Coach Kerchman's top three starters.

In early July, my team, the Wavecrest Democratic Club (a.k.a., "The Donkeys"), beat his team, the Guardians, 2-1, to win the first-half championship. But I didn't see it as a payback or a vindication. Andrew and I always had a mutual admiration for one other. He was one of the few guys on the high school team who'd showed me any respect.

"You were a cool customer out there, Mike," Andrew said after the game. "Who do you think you are, 'Sal the Barber'?"

He was teasing me. Sal Maglie had been an old Dodger nemesis. His nickname was "Sal the Barber" because of his penchant for "shaving" the corners of the plate, as well as for brushing hitters back. Maglie was also known as a "gamer." He was the pitcher who Leo Durocher gave the ball to whenever the Giants needed to win a big game. So I took Andrew's remark as a compliment, of sorts.

The only place where I felt aggressive and confident was out on the mound—more so now than ever before. When I was pitching well, I could erase that sorry image of myself as the short, chubby kid who the popular crowd shunned or overlooked. As a result, I relished the opportunity to surprise the skeptics who didn't think I had the goods. But put me in the middle of a social gathering—a party or a dance—and I was paralyzed with self-doubt.

I knew I'd have to reinvent myself if I were to have any chance of impressing those Woodsburg girls. I'd have to display the same kind of chutzpah and assurance that I possessed when I was pitching. And what better opportunity than now? Nobody at Grove day camp—except for Ronnie and Rob—had had any previous dealings with me. So far as those girls were concerned, I was an unknown quantity. And that's just the way I wanted to keep things for a while.

For the first few days of camp, I spent a lot of time getting to know my co-counselor, Steve Katz. Something began to spark when we started commiserating about our high school coaches. Steve was a junior on the Lawrence High basketball team, and he was still waiting for his chance to play. I was in the same bind, I said, with my baseball coach. But I didn't mention that I'd just quit the team. I didn't know this guy well enough to trust him yet.

Shortly after that, we started up what would become a daily ritual. Just before reveille each morning, we'd take off our shirts, shoot baskets on the camp's makeshift court, and make small talk. We knew we were also out there to show off—to impress the girls and let everyone know that we were jocks.

At seventeen, both of us were in the best shape of our lives. Steve was about five ten, with short blonde hair and a lithe, wiry build. He was proud of his physique—almost vain about it. I was more tentative, but I readily followed his lead.

In the previous six months I'd become much less self-conscious about my physique. My chest had filled out, my stomach was tight from doing sit-ups, and my legs were strong and firm from all those years of running on the beach.

Each morning, just after the last bus pulled in, the girl counselors, jc's, and kitchen staff all walked past us on their way to the locker room. To attract their attention, every few days we'd challenge Ronnie and Rob to a game of two-on-two. Some mornings we managed to draw a pretty good crowd of staffers and kids.

Those games quickly turned into fierce competitions—a lot of pushing and shoving and flying elbows. To Steve and me, that court became a kind of proving ground. We cast ourselves as the scrappy underdog kids from public high schools, and we were going to vindicate ourselves by taking on the privileged preppies who we envied and disdained.

It wasn't long before we became close allies. We both had similar backgrounds—not fully middle-class or blue collar poor. Lawrence High was an upscale Five Towns school, but Steve's parents lived in the low-rent district. Their house, a run-down old clapboard, was situated right across the railroad tracks that divided

Lawrence from Inwood, the only working-class village in the Five Towns.

Another thing that drew me to Steve was his swagger and savvy with girls. I also knew that he had a connection of some kind to the Woodsburg trio, because I saw all four of them get out of a car together on the first day of camp. I was dying to ask, but I didn't know how to bring it up.

I imagine he knew what I was thinking anyway, because one morning when we were shooting around Steve casually mentioned that he was going steady with Annie Lieberman, the fourth member of the Woodsburg clique. I tried to hide my excitement. Since the first day of camp, I'd been trying to find some pretense that would allow me to talk to even one of those three. Now it looked like I had a possible "in"—a direct line to these previously unapproachable girls.

For the next few days I fired one question after another at Steve. At first, I was worried that he'd think I was too much of a snoop. But the more I asked, the more forthcoming he was. According to Steve, Linda was the self-proclaimed jock of the group. In his opinion, she was something of a show-off. Joanne was "the brain, the intellectual." And Julie was what Steve called a "provocateur," a social operator.

Each day he fed me another piece of information. Linda and Joanne were dating Ivy League college guys, he said. And last summer Julie had made it a point to let all her friends know that she was going steady with the Long Beach High basketball ace, Larry Brown. Before long, I knew all about the girls' dating histories.

Steve was having a good time playing off of my curiosities. You could see that he relished his role. I wasn't sure why he was deliberately trying to demystify the three girls, and, it surprised me that he was so forthcoming about his own relationship with Annie. They'd been sleeping together on the sly, he said, for nine months.

He talked about it with an edge of pride in his voice, as if what he had going with Annie was something he took for granted. It had always confounded me that some of the most well-bred, sought after girls were suckers for guys like Steve and Manny. Their attraction seemed to derive from a practiced indifference, an attitude that said, "Don't mess with me. I'm bad." It was the kind of reckless pose I admired but was never able to bring off.

Whether it was conscious or not, I began to look at Steve as a kind of mentor. Aside from his swagger, I was drawn to his unbridled, almost childlike enthusiasm. If there was such a thing as a connoisseur of girls, he was it. He studied their mannerisms and analyzed their behavior with the same kind of passion and intensity that I brought to baseball.

As a rule, I'd been too self-conscious, too ashamed to let other guys my age know about my inexperience and my fear of girls. I didn't want to risk the sarcasm and ridicule. Whenever I'd talk to a guy about girls or sex, it almost always turned into an uncomfortable competition. Up until now, my only confidante was my friend Carole. For years I'd been looking for a guy like Steve to help guide me through my confusions.

I trusted Steve because so far he hadn't tried to use my naiveté against me. And when he discussed his own sex life, he didn't act like he was rubbing it in or trying to make me feel inferior—the way Ronnie and Rob did. My biggest worry was that I'd grant him too much power over me, the way I'd done with Manny back in junior high.

Midway through the summer, Steve and I were out shooting baskets, as usual, when the buses pulled in. It was two days before the night of the staff beach party. All week it had been troubling me that I hadn't gathered the courage to approach any of the three girls.

The early morning sun was already heating up the court. Even with our shirts off, we'd already started to break a sweat. As the staff started to shuffle by, I spotted Julie, Joanne, and Linda coming up the path. They were swinging their lunch bags and chatting away. Just as they were passing the court, they turned and looked at us. My mouth went dry. I kept on shooting baskets and talking to Steve, pretending not to notice them. When they moved up the path, I heard what sounded like a wolf whistle, followed by a chorus of high-pitched voices.

One of them said, "Pretty sexy, you guys. You oughta be in the Charles Atlas ads."

The blood rushed to my neck and face. When I turned, I saw them pointing their fingers at us and giggling. I suddenly felt exposed and shamed. It reminded me of that awful sixth grade dance.

"What was that all about?" I asked Steve.

"They think you're cute," he said. "It's their way of letting you know it."

His reply seemed too flip. Was this a set-up that the four of them planned? A way of making me look foolish?

He must have seen the look on my face, because he dropped the basketball and started to explain. He'd gotten a ride home with the girls the night before, he said, and all three pumped him for information. His story seemed way too contrived. I was becoming even more suspicious.

"They were asking me if you have a girlfriend, where you're from, where you go to school, where you live—that kind of stuff."

I wanted to believe that he was telling the truth, so I decided to test him.

"How come you didn't tell me all this before?"

"I was going to, later on."

I still wasn't buying it.

"What did you tell them?"

"That you were taken. That you had a girlfriend."

"But, it isn't true. Suppose one of them asks me?"

"What are the chances of that?" he laughed. "You're not exactly Mr. Personality, you know. You haven't said a word to any of them since camp began."

Steve shook his head, like he was scolding a kid brother for not picking up his toys.

"Look, you need to lose this attitude," he said. "They're interested in you, okay? Handle it. It's no big deal, believe me."

He paused for a long moment and grimaced. He seemed more amused by me than exasperated.

"Why me?" I said, fishing for reassurance. "They can get any guy they want."

He softened his tone. "That's just the point. I know those girls. They're convinced that every guy on the planet has the hots for them."

"I'm not following you," I said.

"They have no idea that you're afraid to talk to them. They think you're not interested."

"Look, he went on," warming to the task. "Don't flip out just because they're rich and popular. Guys like us are trophies to them. They think we're either rocks or juvenile delinquents."

I'd thought about this before, but it was reassuring to hear it from someone more practiced and confident than I was. Steve now had my full attention.

"It doesn't hurt that we're athletes, either," he offered. "They're cheerleaders. What does that tell you?"

Everything he'd said made sense. It was like I was seeing it for the first time, though. I checked the impulse to tell him how grateful I was for his advice. There I was, putting myself in the subordinate role again.

"Look," he said, "Julie didn't pick Larry Brown because of his good looks or money. You know what I'm saying?"

It's funny how just a little bit of reinforcement can shift your point of view. At the afternoon staff meeting I thought I caught all three girls staring at me and giggling again. This time, it gave me a tiny morale boost. And a glimmer of hope.

After the meeting, Steve and I hung around to devise a scheme for Saturday night's beach party. I'd been worrying all week, thinking about the humiliating dances and mixers I'd gone to. The awkward sparring, the small talk, the popular crowd pairing off with one another, while I'd invariably end up alone or with some other loser.

But Steve's plan calmed me down. He would run interference for me. The only thing I'd have to do was follow his lead.

"It'll be a two-minute hit and run," he said "Then we'll both be out of there like a cool breeze."

When I woke up the next morning, I was looking forward to the party with almost as much anticipation as if I was preparing to pitch a ball game.

That night, everyone sat around the fire, roasting marshmallows and singing "Ninety-Nine Bottles of Beer on the Wall" and a bunch of other dumb camp songs. After an hour, I started getting fidgety. Finally Steve gave me the "let's go" sign, and we started to walk over to the fire pit where the three girls had congregated. I made certain not to look over at them, but every step I took made me feel more self-conscious and uneasy. I was thankful it was so dark.

Without any small talk, Steve introduced me. Then he quickly said something about the two of us having a previous commitment. Right as we were leaving, he turned back and said, "Why don't we all get together at the picnic next Friday, right after the softball game."

I thought I saw Linda the jock nod in agreement. To sweeten the offer, Steve promised he'd invite Annie to come along. Before they could respond, he nodded in my direction and we took off.

It was his idea not to hang around at the beach party. It would go better, he said, if the girls saw me first on my own turf, doing what I did best—which was, of course, playing ball.

"Think of it as having home field advantage," he laughed.

How did Steve become so shrewd, so fearless? You had to have a lot of balls to make this work. If I'd have dreamed it up on my own, I'm sure I'd have already bailed out by now.

On Monday morning, Steve added one more wrinkle to the plan. He wanted my "phantom girlfriend" to show up at the picnic on Friday.

"It'll make you look even better," he said.

I tried to talk him out of it. But he'd been right about everything else. No matter how improbable the whole thing seemed, I decided to go along with it.

The phantom girlfriend idea took root the previous week, when I was whining about my lousy luck with girls. To gain some sympathy, I'd told Steve the story of my recently failed romance with Ellen Wiseman.

Just before Memorial Day weekend, my friend Carole had brokered another blind date for me, this time it was with Ellen, who she described as a cute, brainy sophomore from her Advanced Geometry class.

On first impression, Ellen looked like the epitome of the "sweet old-fashioned girl" that Teresa Brewer was singing about that spring. She had shoulder-length sandy-blonde hair, deep blue eyes, a pale complexion, and an angelic smile. The way she dressed made her look much too staid: flair skirts, loose cardigans, and lacy blouses, which, I later found out, hid a shapely, alluring figure. But when I met her, Ellen could have passed for a choirgirl. Not exactly my ideal. With my track record, though, I couldn't afford to be choosy.

We seemed like such an improbable match. On our first few dates, she was so demure and reserved. When I finally pressed her, I found out that Ellen was class valedictorian in junior high, she'd been an exchange student in France, and she was already aiming for a scholarship to Vassar or Wellesley.

I was ambivalent about her. She seemed too straight-laced and aloof. Yet she was enthusiastic about me. She went along with all my suggestions. I took her to a jazz club, a foreign film, and a Dodger game. She came to one of my summer league games, and she even seemed amused when I went off on one of my half-cocked rants about Kerchman, or some riff about the Dodgers. It was a heady feeling to be the one who was setting the agenda. It was what Donna must have felt like when she was running the show with me.

But it still troubled me that Ellen was so reticent to talk about anything personal. Every time I'd ask who her friends were, what kind of boys she liked, who she'd gone out with before me—she'd change the subject.

The big surprise was that when it came to making out and petting, Ellen took the lead. It disarmed me, of course, and made me reconsider all my preconceptions. Once we got started, we were grabbing each other every chance we got. I continued to feel ambivalent, though. Ellen was so much the opposite of the popular girls I was enamored of. Yet I loved the idea that she had a crush on me. For the first time, I wasn't waiting for the other shoe to drop.

It all changed on a balmy evening in June when we went to the beach to watch the fireworks display. Everything about the setting was exotic: the salty ocean aroma, beach fires burning in the distance, muted strains of music from portable radios, waves lapping on the shore, and the sporadic pop-pop-pop of the multi-colored flares that intermittently lit up the beach and the water.

One thing led to another, and we ended up on Ellen's blanket making out under the boardwalk. We started necking, then quickly moved to petting. The night, the music, the fires, the waves, the fireworks—everything fell away. I'd been dreaming about this ever since that time in junior high when I found out that Manny and Cindy were making it under the 116th Street boardwalk.

Ellen and I kept at it, but at the instant when it seemed there'd be no turning back, she jumped up, shook the sand out of her hair, and sat cross-legged, Indian style on the blanket.

"We have to talk," she said.

All I could think of was that it's happening again: the old game of who's in charge of sex. Turns out that there was a boyfriend—at

Andover—a guy she characterized as smart but unimaginative. Too preoccupied with school and college applications, she said. Even in my super-agitated state, I knew what that meant. He wasn't paying enough attention to her. That's why she was here with me.

He was from a rich family in Hewlett Bay Park. At sixteen, he was already driving his own T-Bird and traveling abroad with his parents in the summers. His future was mapped out. When he graduated from college, he'd go to med school and later take over his father's Park Avenue Orthopedic practice. They'd been going steady, it seems, for three years; and of course everyone expected them to get married after college.

Had this been a movie, it would have been a funny scene. But I was furious with her. And mad at myself for getting chumped again. My stomach was hollow. I stood up to leave. Ellen pulled me back on the blanket. She was under a lot of pressure, she said. Didn't know how to break up with this guy. Both sets of parents agreed they were made for each other, and so on.

What it came down to was that she just wasn't ready to betray the boyfriend. She was asking me in her typically indirect way if I wouldn't mind being the "other guy" just for a while, until she got her priorities straightened out. I said I'd think about it. I wasn't happy about any of it, of course. But under the circumstances, I had to admit that it was not an unreasonable request, because the truth was that neither of us had a good enough reason to cut the other one loose. We were both using each other to bolster our confidence.

When I finished the story, Steve said, "You're not in love with her, right? And you're not screwing her? Means you're in the driver's seat."

" So how come it doesn't feel that way to me?"

"She owes you big time. And don't kid yourself, she knows it. Ask her to the picnic and tell her why."

Just like that? What was I getting myself into? The whole thing was turning into an elaborate production. I told Steve I was too embarrassed to ask Ellen to do it.

"I bet you an egg cream she won't say no," he said.

Never second-guess an aficionado. Steve knew how all of this worked. Just as he'd predicted, Ellen was all too willing to participate.

The whole routine was more complicated than I'd ever imagined. All I could do was shake my head in wonder. The gamesmanship here wasn't a lot different from the kinds of tradeoffs I used to make with all three of my coaches.

What transpired on Friday was surreal. For the entire day— the game, the picnic, and the evening—I was in "the zone." The ball game itself was like a dream fantasy. Steve and I, and Ronnie and Rob were the co-captains for our respective teams. That was incentive enough to want to win the game. We each picked five other staff members and two of the oldest campers. Partly on intuition and partly by design, I picked Linda Price to be our tenth player. I knew she was competitive, and I could tell from watching her swim and pitch to her group that she was a good athlete. I also knew that choosing Linda wasn't going to hurt me any—with either her or her two girlfriends.

I was so keyed up that I couldn't even sit on the bench between innings. I coached third base and never once looked up at the kids, staff members, or the parents in the bleachers. I stayed alert to every nuance and detail on the field, all the while imagining that Joanne and Julie were watching every move I made.

On the field and at bat I played fully on instinct. I anticipated every ball hit to me at short, I got three hits, and I hit the game winning home run, a long fly ball that carried over the fence and landed in the swimming pool. Even the last play of the game couldn't have been better scripted. Linda made a running catch of a fly ball with the tying run on third base. That hunch, too, had paid off.

When the kids and staff came streaming out of the bleachers, Julie and Joanne gave Linda a hug. Then all three of them hugged Steve and me. My stomach was flip-flopping. Steve had known all along exactly what he was doing.

Just before the picnic started, Julie asked if Steve and I would pose for a picture. I was glistening with sweat and still in a state of mild euphoria.

"Take off your shirts, you guys," she said. "I've wanted to take this picture all summer."

"I bet you have," Steve whispered to me under his breath. He squeezed my arm as if to say, "She's the one. Go for it."

Julie circled her lips with her tongue and pointed her Brownie box camera at us. Next, she posed us individually—Steve first, then me. As we changed positions he whispered, "She's using me to get to you."

I tried to act composed, even nonchalant. But I was so flushed, I could hardly stand still for the picture. So this is what it feels like to be pursued.

Later on, Ellen showed up at the picnic wearing a pair of skin-tight white shorts and a form fitting red halter top. All afternoon Ronnie and Rob followed her everywhere she went. I was laughing to myself, knowing they'd be all over me with questions on Monday morning. Even Steve, who'd brought Annie with him, hung around the food table flirting with Ellen. She thrived on the attention. And why not? It was her reward for going along with our scheme—the quid pro quo Steve had had in mind all along.

Before the picnic was about to break up, I grabbed Ellen's hand, marched up to the three girls, and proudly introduced her. I watched them coldly eye her up and down. Ellen didn't even flinch. She was playing her role to the hilt. The day had already gone way beyond my expectations, but there was more to come. As we were all packing up, Steve volunteered to drive us to Cairo's. This was going to be a real treat. Cairo's had even more of a mystique than the State Diner. I'd heard so much about it that it had assumed almost mythical stature in my imagination. Cairo's was located in the roughest part of Inwood. The owners, Teddy and Frank, were rumored to have Mafia ties. On weekends, Five Towns studs and Far Rockaway jocks took their girlfriends there "to be seen."

The restaurant itself was an unimposing storefront, the ground floor of an old restored clapboard house. You could smell the aroma of wood fired pizza as soon as you got out of the car. When we walked through the foyer, it was like entering an exclusive inner sanctum. The dining room was just past the bar, to the left. It was brightly lit and alive with the hum and buzz of animated dinner talk. The small, square tables, most of them two and four tops, were draped with standard red and white checked tablecloths. Each one had a wicker Chianti decanter that served as a candleholder. Dozens of framed black-and-white photos hung on the polished, knotty pine walls—pictures of former Lawrence and Far Rockaway High athletic heroes, and autographed photos of celebrities who'd visited the restaurant.

When we arrived, Julie, Joanne, and Linda were comfortably ensconced in their natural habitat—holding court at a center table, smoking, laughing loudly, and drinking beer. They were decked out in white linen pants and gauzy see-through tops. All three were surrounded by a knot of preppy looking cabana boys who had on white ducks and Topsiders with no socks. They each had a V-neck sweater draped around their El Patio T-shirts. All of them—the guys and the girls—looked like they'd just gotten off their parents' yachts.

As we passed their table, Steve and Annie stopped to talk. I made sure to catch all three girls' eyes before giving them a perfunctory wave. Later, when Ellen got up to go to the bathroom, I caught the El Patio guys eyeballing her. She did look sexy. For a second, I felt a twinge of desire. Maybe I was making a big mistake.

All evening the three girls kept turning around and shooting glances in our direction. I even heard one of the El Patio guys imploring Julie to invite us over to the table. For that one evening, everything was working right.

All weekend I was worrying about what to do next. Which one should I ask out? How should I go about it? If I asked one, how would the other two feel? Then, I stopped myself. How presumptuous it was to think that all three were interested in me.

Steve had no such hesitations. "Go out with all of them and then decide."

Of course he'd say that.

"I'd never have the balls to ask *all* of them out," I told him. But I was being partly disingenuous. The seed had already been planted.

On Wednesday, just before free swim, Steve whispered, "Before you do anything, check out the girls' locker room."

I couldn't concentrate for the rest of the afternoon. I waited until all the cars and buses had begun to fill up before I let myself into the locker room. It was dingy and dank, and it reeked of wet towels and stale perfume. I pulled the string above the bare light bulb. Taped just above one of the lockers was the photograph that Julie had taken of me last Saturday. I stood there, transfixed. Was it really me? The guy in that picture had a jet-black flattop, a trim waist, tapered hips, and tightly muscled thighs. It was me, all right. But it wasn't the image I saw every day when I looked in my bedroom mirror.

It was one of those fleeting, serendipitous moments where you see yourself exactly as you've always wanted others to see you. It was such a shock because I'd lived for so long with the opposite image of myself, the one that had been imprinted on my psyche since I was a kid. Looking at that photograph was like seeing a hologram, a mirage that could vanish or shift at any moment.

I remember the precise moment that Julie took the photo. She was kneeling on one knee, looking up. That's why the broad-chested guy in the picture looked so tall and lean. I noticed for the first time that he had a confident, almost cocky look on his face.

I knew right then that I'd better take advantage of the moment. How likely was it that I'd ever see myself in this light again?

◆

_ 14.

The staff swim party on Thursday night was a continuation of the week's unreal events. Within the course of a half hour, all three girls had asked me to dance. It was such a dramatic reversal from the humiliating scenario at the sixth grade dance. Clearly, the girls were waiting for me to make a move.

I was standing at the lip of the pool trying to puzzle out what to do when Julie came up to me and said, "'Time's up."

I flinched, but I knew exactly what she meant.

She extended her right hand and asked me to pick one of three balled-up pieces of paper that were resting in her open palm.

"What kind of game is this?" I said, stalling for time.

"Open it up," she said.

I fumbled with the paper. My hands were shaking, my heart was racing.

"What's it say?"

"Linda."

"Next one," Julie said.

"Joanne."

The last of course had Julie's name on it.

"So, what's this about?" I asked her—half-anticipating her answer.

Julie was just the emissary here. All three of them, it seems, had gotten together and decided that each one would go out with me over the span of three nights. When Julie walked away, I was in a panic. I looked around the patio. Where was Steve? I bet he was in on this.

For a moment, all the old insecurities came rushing back. Maybe the girls hatched this scheme to satisfy their curiosity. Maybe they were just toying with me. Maybe it was all just a silly game to them. But whatever it was, they'd done everything they could to draw me out. I had no choice but to take them up on it.

On Friday, Steve wasn't at camp. Without his counsel, I'd be flying blind all weekend.

My three-day odyssey began on Friday night at seven, when Linda picked me up at the Far Rockaway/Lawrence border. She was driving a white Fairlane convertible and wearing an all-white tennis outfit. Linda always had a spoiled rich girl air about her that reminded me of Jordan Baker, Nick Carraway's sometimes confidante in *The Great Gatsby*. Blonde, athletic, and well tanned, she was about five foot seven, with a swimmer's broad shoulders and well muscled calves and thighs. She even walked like a jock— slightly pigeon-toed and with a little swagger to her step.

Before I had a chance to ask what she'd like to do, she launched into what sounded like a pre-rehearsed monologue. I knew that Linda had a deep competitive streak in her, so I wasn't all that surprised when she let me know in no uncertain terms that she was indeed a competitive swimmer, as well as a tennis player, horseback rider, and accomplished golfer. I half expected her to tell me next that she was a world champion croquet player.

That night, she drove me all over the Five Towns, pointing out all her old haunts. We drove past the golf course, the Hewlett duck pond, the tennis courts, and the yacht club. We cruised with the top down though narrow, winding roads lined with quaint old-fashioned street lamps and evocative names like Ivy Hill Road and Mill Pond Lane. I gawked like a tourist at the huge mansions with spotlights set atop sloping, manicured lawns—each house surrounded by lush vegetation and weeping willow trees. Everything about this scene was almost exactly as I'd imagined it.

Later on, while we were sitting in her car, she suddenly turned toward me and presented her bare right thigh for inspection.

"Squeeze it," she said.

It didn't take a genius to see that this wasn't a sexual overture. Linda literally wanted me to feel how strong her thigh muscles were. It was her perverse way of letting me know that this was as far as I was going to get. But it was a wasted set-up. I had absolutely no designs on her. Attractive as she was, she'd already talked me out of any interest I might have had. Steve had Linda pegged, all right. She was an exhibitionist—big time.

It was the weirdest date I'd ever been on. And it would get odder. Without so much as asking, Linda drove back over to the tennis club to take a half-hour lesson from "Carlos," the tall, swarthy looking club pro. What was Steve thinking when he made the trophy comment? At the moment, I felt more like I ought to be wearing a dunce cap. If all three girls acted like this, I wouldn't have to worry about making *any* choices.

While I was waiting, I looked up and saw the orange glow from the club's ballroom. I half expected to hear the "yellow cocktail music" that Nick Carraway had described so evocatively in *Gatsby*. It was my first close-up view of a world I'd been conjuring in my imagination for years. And except for Linda herself, I was intoxicated by everything I'd seen.

After a half hour had passed, I toyed with the idea of walking to the train station before Linda came back from her lesson. But masochist that I am, I stuck it out. I was curious to see what Linda might come up with next.

On the way home I was thinking that maybe my initial fears were right. Maybe this was all a big game to them. I couldn't help but worry about what was in store for me the next night. Joanne, after all, was the most distant and aloof of all three.

Joanne's demeanor at camp always made her seem so unapproachable. She never socialized or flirted with any of the male counselors, which made me wonder why she'd bothered to participate in this strange little drama in the first place.

Physically she resembled a fashion model—tall and reed slim, with slender legs, small breasts, and narrow shoulders. She had a long elegant neck and wore no makeup. Her dark brown hair was styled in a neat, shoulder-length pageboy. Despite the sophisticated look, Joanne had a coltish, tomboyish quality that attracted me. She wore baggy and rumpled clothes to camp, as if she was deliberately camouflaging her body. I had a hard time picturing her as a cheerleader.

Joanne's family lived in an unpretentious white frame two-story ranch house, surrounded by immaculately pruned trees and flower gardens. It was tasteful but modest—by Woodsburg standards anyway. In my neighborhood, that house would have stood out like a palace.

Joanne's parents—perhaps in their mid-forties—were polite and reserved. They dressed casually—in shorts and sneakers—as if they'd just gotten off the back nine. We talked about school, my plans, colleges—the usual polite conversation you'd expect. It hadn't occurred to me until now that Linda never even invited me in to meet her parents.

When they left to take a walk, Joanne and I awkwardly debated about where we'd go and what we'd do—a movie, bowling, a hamburger and malt at Dave Schor's, the local hangout. Instead, we took a walk into town and then came back and sat in her screened porch and talked—and talked and talked and talked—about books, jazz, even rock and roll.

I was relieved to see that this wasn't going to be a facsimile of last night's fiasco. I was also pleasantly surprised to see that Joanne was so receptive, and that we had some interests in common. I think she was also happy to see that I wasn't just a dumb jock. Maybe Donna's severe tutelage had been useful, after all.

Once she relaxed into it, Joanne began to talk about her passion for opera, ballet, and classical music. It was the first time she'd really let her guard down. I was fascinated by how animated she was, and impressed by how much she knew. But after a while, I began to feel like I was out of my depth.

By the time we wound down, it was close to midnight. The train whistle jolted me back to reality. I had to make the 12:30 to Far Rockaway or else I'd be stranded. We both stood up at the same moment, paused, and awkwardly kissed. It was a deep and passionate kiss, and I wanted it to go on and on. Just before we pulled away, Joanne said, "I hope we can see each other again."

I was dumbfounded. This was the last thing I expected to hear. I didn't know how to respond.

"I wish I'd never agreed to do this," she said. "It was all Julie's idea. When it's about guys, she always gets what she wants."

This complicated everything. Was Joanne really drawn to me? Or was there some kind of competition going on between the two girls? And where did Linda fit into all this? On the bus ride home, I was trying to dope it all out. Joanne and Linda had played two different hands. And just what did Joanne mean when she said that Julie always gets what she wants when it comes to guys? Then I caught myself. Three days ago this was an improbable fantasy. Where did I suddenly find the temerity to even be entertaining such thoughts?

Julie's house was by far the most ostentatious of the three— a sprawling split-level ranch that sat up on a hill adjacent to the country club golf course. It had faux white columns, a terraced lawn, and a circular driveway. Two shark finned '57 Cadillacs, a white El Dorado, and a black Fleetwood Brougham, were parked out front. Above the garage was a backboard and a netted orange

Girl scenes have more punches, visuals than the baseball pictures.

basketball hoop—the kind of set-up I'd always wanted in my own driveway.

I walked up the flagstone steps, still trying to sort out the past two night's events. But as soon as Julie opened the door, my confusions melted away.

Julie was wearing a form-fitting canary yellow shift with a tightly belted sash. The outfit was clearly meant to call attention to her tapered waist and shapely hips. Her chestnut brown hair was pulled back in a tight ponytail tied neatly in place with a yellow bow. I stood there, wide-eyed. Was this the same girl who wore oversized T-shirts and grubby denim shorts to camp every day?

When she turned to walk into the hall, I could see her breasts flexing against the cotton fabric. My pulse was racing and my breath came in short, ragged bursts. Steve and Joanne had alerted me that Julie could play the temptress. Until now, I hadn't understood what they meant.

As she led me into the study, I shuffled along slowly, trying to compose myself but unable to take my eyes off her swaying hips and rounded derriere. If she was deliberately putting on a show, it was working. My face was flushed and hot, and my legs were rubbery. I felt like I was walking on a trampoline. Not exactly the ideal conditions to meet someone's parents for the first time.

The dimly lit study was framed by floor-to-ceiling oak bookcases. I scanned the shelves desperately searching for a familiar title. All I saw were *Reader's Digest* condensations and Book of the Month Club selections. The leather bindings even looked like props from a movie set. And *I* was worried about not being educated enough to impress *them?*

Julie's parents were a real piece of work. Her father, a slender, slightly balding, dark complexioned man—was sitting on a peach-colored divan wearing a red satin bathrobe and scarlet house slippers. He had a glass of scotch on the rocks in one hand and he was holding up the *Wall Street Journal* with the other. When Julie introduced me, he muttered something under his breath and absently shook my hand without lifting his eyes from the paper.

Julie's mother was a severe looking, stocky peroxide blonde. She fired a litany of questions at me; where did I go to school, what did my father do, where did we live? She nervously chain-smoked and avoided eye contact whenever she addressed me. As soon as I'd begin to answer one question, she'd cut me off and move on to the next. In the meantime, Julie's father acted as if I wasn't even in the room. It was as unnerving as getting the silent treatment from Kerchman.

"Don't pay attention to them," Julie said when we were out the door. "They never like any of my boyfriends."

Great. Was that supposed to make me feel better?

All evening I felt like I was off balance. All I recall are a series of impressions—like jump cuts in a movie. I remember that Julie drove us to Jahn's ice cream parlor in Cedarhurst. I know we sat at a white marble table and listened to Buddy Holly's "That'll Be the Day" many times over on the jukebox. I remember thinking how odd it was that every time we heard the refrain, "That'll be the day when you say goodbye, that'll be the day when you make me cry," she would tease me about who would leave who first. I wondered what conclusions I was supposed to draw from that.

Julie's persona confused me. The provocative way she dressed, the elaborate makeup, the beguiling persona, the rumors about her seductive manipulations—none of it meshed with the captivating, childlike manner she displayed at the ice cream parlor. We made the most mundane small talk: school, friends, people we knew, camp gossip. It was the kind of nonconversation that should have bored me to death—especially compared to the highbrow exchange I'd had with Joanne the night before. Yet I was taken by everything Julie said, no matter how trivial or inconsequential it seemed. It was almost as if she was hypnotizing me. Or, was I hypnotizing myself? In less than an hour, we'd established a familiarity and ease that made me feel like we'd been dating for years. At the same time, there was an undeniable sexual undercurrent to everything we said.

Every time I looked at her, Julie's deep brown eyes seemed to be probing right inside me

I was still pretty spacey when we left Jahn's. As we walked to the car, Julie grabbed my hand, and then she drove us down to the yacht club basin, a mile from her house. She cut the lights and turned on the radio. The parking lot was the designated neighborhood make-out spot. Everyone's windows were open, and you could hear the same strains of music coming from the other car radios. We were all tuned into the Murray the K Show.

Murray the K spun an uninterrupted string of rock and roll summer love songs, like "Long Lonely Nights," "In the Still of the Night," and "Tonight, Tonight," while Julie and I made out for what seemed like hours. This DJ knew his audience, all right. He dedicated every love song "to all you submarine race watchers out there."

It reminded me of all those Saturday nights when I listened to some of the same songs alone in my room, aching to be with Cindy Levine or some other unattainable girl. I thought about all those rejections and humiliations; and now, here I was, almost to third base with a pretty, popular cheerleader from the Five Towns.

As I rode home on the bus, I replayed every moment. Somehow Julie had managed to make the evening seem sportive and inviting. Even when we were making out, her playfulness put me at ease. The whole adventure felt like a dream.

But late that night, just as I was approaching my house, a chilling dread crept over me. I looked up and down the street at all the modest homes. Who was I kidding? All of these girls were far more worldly than I was. They had more experience with sex and romance. They had prep school suitors and college boyfriends. They'd been going to lavish, upscale parties since grade school. They had elegant wardrobes, and they drove their own cars. For their entire lives, they'd been bred to attend the top schools and marry the right kind of men. Yet here I was, about to embark on a courtship with one of them, a girl who only a month ago I thought would never even deign to give me a second look.

That night I didn't get any sleep. I weighed all the pluses and minuses. Of the two girls, Joanne was the closest to my imagined ideal: smart, reserved, well-bred, and pensive. Her parents didn't seem to mind that I was from a lower-income family. And let's not forget that unexpected kiss. Intellectually though, Joanne was too far out of my league. In a few years she'd be studying at the Sorbonne or on scholarship at Holyoke, Smith, or one of the other "seven sisters" schools.

No matter how I rationalized it, my feelings for Julie were so intense, so overpowering, that it didn't seem as if I had a choice. Yet, I kept thinking about what I was losing by letting Joanne go.

I talked it over with Steve on Monday morning. He already knew the story. It seems that both Julie and Joanne had called Annie. When I asked his advice, Steve was uncharacteristically hesitant.

"I don't want to get near this one," he said. "It's gotta be your call."

This was a new role for me. I'd never been the heartbreaker; never the leaver, always the leavee. When the moment arrived, I couldn't find the words to express to Joanne the bewilderment and regret I felt. We both stammered and stuttered a lot of platitudes about still being friends. But neither of us really believed that that would happen.

After it was over, I felt guilty and foolish. When I told Julie the next night, I held my breath until I saw the smile on her face. I'd gotten what I wished for, but I still didn't know if this was what I really wanted.

With everything else going on, I hadn't been paying much attention to the Dodgers' situation. In late July, O'Malley had announced that strong business interests in Los Angeles were urging the team to move out there. With each new disclosure, it was getting harder to fool myself.

At home games, of course, it was the only topic we could talk about. Everyone sensed what was coming. But none of us wanted to acknowledge it. We blindly kept on denying reality, hoping that something or someone would deliver us from our misery.

In early August, O'Malley's negotiations with city administrators hit an impasse. Robert Moses, the most powerful of all city officials, staunchly opposed the new ballpark. Moses was like a czar. He was commissioner of parks, and he had jurisdiction over all city highways and urban projects. The new stadium, Moses said, would create a traffic hazard in downtown Brooklyn. His counter offer was a parcel of land in Queens, at Flushing Meadows, the site of the old 1939 World's Fair. O'Malley refused, claiming that he wanted to keep the team in downtown Brooklyn. Today, of course, Flushing Meadows is where the Mets and Shea Stadium reside.

By mid August nothing had been resolved. We didn't know yet that the move to L.A. was already a done deal. We wouldn't find out for two more months that the whole scenario had been an elaborate smokescreen.

At the beginning of August, our American Legion team made it to the regional finals. It was gratifying to get that far—in more ways than one. I was still intermittently brooding about Kerchman. The longer we kept on playing, the less time I'd have to fret about him, or about what was likely to happen next. That was reason enough to want the season to keep on going.

In the championship game we faced Hank Fischer, a hard-throwing high school All-American, who a few years later would be pitching for the Milwaukee Braves. We were overmatched from the start. Zeidner started, and I relieved him in the top of the seventh. We were behind 5-0, but I pitched those last three innings with the same intensity and concentration as if it was a scoreless tie. The only hit I gave up was a monster homer by Fischer. No excuses. He hit a good sinker almost 400 feet.

The minute the game was over, that old hollow feeling overcame me again. What if this was the last time I'd ever pitch? The last time I'd ever wear a baseball uniform? I'd been dreading the moment since I had decided to quit the high school team.

On August 19th Giants owner Horace Stoneham announced that at the end of the season the team was leaving for San Francisco. It confirmed all my worst fears. The Dodgers were certain to leave next. I had so many mixed emotions running through me, I didn't know what to feel.

That night, my brother and I were watching a Dodger game on TV. Suddenly I began shouting so loudly that Alan sat up in his chair.

"That asshole could have used me next season," I screamed. "I could have been his fucking Sal Maglie."

I ranted on, as if no one was there. "But screw him. It's his god-damned loss. He'll never see my goddamn ass again, that's for sure."

Stoneham's announcement and my final Legion game had triggered all the pent-up rage and frustration that had been building inside me since the baseball banquet in June.

Alan crossed his arms and stared at me as if to say, "Are you having a nervous breakdown?"

The last ten days of August were like a jubilant binge. Julie and I saw each other every night. Her reason for letting loose was, she said, to get back at her parents. Since mid July we'd been pushing against their disapproval—which of course drew us even closer together.

The family skirmish began two days after our first date, when Julie's parents abruptly grounded her. To retaliate, she cooked up a scheme with Virginia and Joe, the maid and handyman—both of whom adored Julie and hated her parents. One night, as soon as her mother and father had gone to sleep, Virginia and Joe snuck me in through the basement door. Julie and I spent the night down in her basement rec room, making out. They snuck me out at sunrise.

After Julie's parents gave her back the car, she'd meet me at the train station and we'd park at the yacht basin. Other nights we'd double date with our allies, Steve and Annie—both of whom were already veterans of this war.

Some nights we'd buy a couple of six-packs of beer, crank the top down on Annie's convertible, and at sunset we'd head out for the beach. Annie and Steve would take turns driving fast on the winding back roads, while Julie and I careened from one side of the backseat to the other, laughing and grabbing at one another. The tires squealed and the brakes screeched as we leaned into the sharp curves. The summer wind whipped our hair in our faces, and we all sang along at the top of our voices to songs like "Whispering Bells," "Whole Lot of Shakin' Going On," "Teddy Bear," "Long Tall Sally," and "Jenny, Jenny."

It was all so new and exhilarating. I'd never cut loose like this before, never allowed myself to be so reckless and uninhibited. Part of it was a celebration of my good fortune. The other part was an escape from all the painful setbacks of the past three months.

On the last Saturday night in August the four of us bowled a few frames at Falcaro's on Rockaway Turnpike, and then we drove out to the Sunrise Diner at midnight for hamburgers and shakes. We ended up back at Annie's house, drinking wine and beer, and dancing to the Chuck Berry, Little Richard, Buddy Holly, and Elvis records we were playing on Annie's stereo.

After Steve and Annie snuck off to Annie's bedroom, Julie and I made out for hours on the living room sofa. I couldn't help but wonder what was going on up there. But I wasn't about to bring it up to Julie. A few nights before, in the front seat of Julie's Buick, we were both down to our underwear when she called a timeout. I was frustrated and disappointed, but I didn't put up an argument—or even try and talk her out of her decision. I was too afraid to risk doing anything that might queer what we had going. And I was a bit uncertain about how I'd react if we did agree to go all the way. I still carried the memory of how it all turned out with Karen back in eighth grade. Somehow I felt like I needed to erase that failure before I could move on.

Without baseball to distract me, and with nothing to anchor me until school began, I had sex on the brain again. And being at camp each day didn't help matters any.

Lately, whenever Ronnie and Rob bragged about their sex lives, it made me even more self-conscious about still being cherry. Both of them, and Peter too, had made it this summer with Sandy and Lynn from the kitchen staff. Rob said that there was still time for me to take a shot at both girls. He even offered to wire up the deal in exchange for Ellen's phone number. I thought about it. But everyone at camp knew I was going steady with Julie. It would be too risky.

It's funny how quickly perceptions change when it comes to girls and sex. Ever since the picnic, both of those guys had been buddying up to me—inviting me to parties and offering to drive me to work in the morning. It was all because they believed I was sleeping with Ellen and Julie. I can't deny that I was enjoying their solicitations. But holding on to my secret was beginning to wear on me. It was time for another heart-to-heart with Steve.

It was the last week of camp, and for the past ten days Steve had been after me for details about what was happening between Julie and me. I wanted him to think we were sleeping together, but he was bound to find out the truth from Annie sooner or later.

I'd put it off for too long. Next week we'd all be back in school. Who knows if I'd get a chance to talk about this again? So on the last day of camp, I came clean with him.

Steve being Steve, he simply said, "We gotta get you in the saddle right away."

He didn't waste a minute. Later that day, he told me that we had an eight o' clock appointment in the city.

"You mean hookers"? I said.

"Not hookers, prostitutes. Two classy call girls. Julie and Annie will never know."

It was true. Annie was already up at Kutcher's with her parents. Tonight Julie would be going to the Catskills with her family.

There was no backing out of this one. Neither of us had anything planned for the weekend. Steve was playing Tom Sawyer again to my Huck Finn. But I allowed it for good reason. If I could get past this last hurdle, maybe I'd be ready to pilot my own course.

On the subway ride into the city, Steve was already into his role. He explained, in graphic detail, how it had taken almost a year before Annie finally "came around." He described his tactics with great animation, and proceeded to regale me with strategies for "breaking down Julie's resistance."

His m.o. fascinated me. Sex was like a system to him.

"If you hang in there," he said, "it's bound to happen with Julie sooner or later."

Then, with his usual enthusiasm, he filled me in on the details for tonight. Gus and Sally Cole were sisters, he said. They "specialized" in taking on prep school boys and guys from Ivy League colleges. I loved the way he used the word *specialized.* Then he recounted how he and his best friend, David Bernstein, had arranged a visit to the Cole sisters over a year ago.

"We called up and told them that we were Steve and David Carter, and that our father owned Carter's Little Liver Pills."

"And who are we tonight?" I asked.

"We're seniors at Andover, and we're headed back to school on Monday."

By this time I was starting to worry whether I'd be able to go through with it.

"Suppose they're old or homely?" I said.

But he didn't bite. "You'll see when we get there," he said.

How could he be so damn composed?

When we got off at West Fourth, we had about a half hour to kill, so we walked around the Village, stopping to comb our hair in the store window reflections. At eight, we found the old brick apartment building on Bleeker. Steve rang the bell, and the buzzer sounded. We pushed open the creaking wooden door and headed up the stairs. My stomach began to turn over. The hallway reeked of stale onions and decaying plaster. A door at the top of the stairway swung open and in the backlight I could make out the silhouette of a tall, slender girl with a ponytail. That's when it became real to me. I felt my windpipe tighten. I could hardly breathe. As she ushered us into the apartment, I was thinking, "Please God, let me get through this."

When we stepped onto the faded Persian rug, small plumes of dust spiraled up from under our shoes. The only pieces of furniture were a faded grey love seat against the far wall, a beat-up old coffee table, and two wooden dining room chairs. The room was lit by two old table lamps draped with colored scarves. The tiny room was stuffy and hot.

The girl took our jackets and shook our hands.

"Hi, I'm Sally," she said.

I'd always envisioned prostitutes as dark-haired and stocky, wearing tight black skirts, fishnet stockings, and black sweaters that camouflaged large, sagging bosoms. But Sally looked like she was in her late twenties or early thirties. It was hard to make out her facial features in the dim light. She was wearing a pair of form-fitting black slacks, a white satin blouse buttoned at the top, and tan ballet slippers. I thought the slippers were an exotic touch. I wondered if she was a model or maybe even a dancer.

Her outfit was modest, but it highlighted her smallish breasts, firm rear end, and long legs. Her honey-colored hair was pulled back over her ears, and she wore a yellow ribbon tied in a bow where the ponytail broke off. I felt something stir inside. The ponytail, the ribbon—both reminded me of my first date with Julie. For a second I imagined Sally standing there with all her clothes off except for the yellow ribbon and the ballet slippers.

"We have beer, wine, or soda," she said.

"Two beers," Steve said—a little too eagerly, I thought.

Sally asked us a lot of small-talk questions: Where did we go to school? What were we studying? Where did we want to go to college? What did our fathers do for a living? It struck me as odd that the prelude to having sex with a prostitute was not much different than being interviewed by Julie's and Joanne's parents.

I was relieved that Steve didn't launch into the Carter's Little Liver Pills routine. But I was also thankful that he did do most of the talking. I was too nervous. I don't think I could have gotten a coherent sentence out.

Then Gus came in and introduced herself. The name Gus put me off. She was dressed in tan slacks, a tight black sweater, and those same ballet slippers, only in black. She had dirty-blonde short hair that was shaped like a football helmet. Gus was huskier and sterner looking than her "sister."

They excused themselves and disappeared down the darkened hallway. In a few seconds they returned, followed by two huge black cats, both of which had long, sharp claws. When she saw the look on our faces, Gus said, very softly, "Oh don't be afraid, they're black panthers—quite domesticated though. We keep them around in case guys don't pay up or try and get rough. Happens sometimes."

The message was, "Let's be very clear here. This is business."

"By the way," she said. "Could you leave the thirty on the table over there? You'll each get a buck back for good behavior." I thought that was an interesting touch.

They left us alone to make our decisions. I'd already made up my mind. Gus reminded me too much of my old grade school teachers. Besides, Sally had the yellow ribbon.

"I want the younger one," I said. I was startled by my own assertiveness.

"Nope, she's mine" Steve said, like it had already been decided. "I did the leg work, I get to pick."

My heart sank. I thought this was about getting *me* laid.

Sally padded back into the living room.

"Just follow me boys," she said.

As she led us down a long, dark hall, she looked back at Steve and pointed to a door on the right. How did she know? The bastard shot me the thumbs-up sign and went in. My heart was pounding. Then I saw a crack of light creeping out from under a door.

"Good luck, sweetheart," Sally said.

I cringed. Why couldn't it have been her?

The room was spare and dingy. Another lamp with a scarf draped over it gave off the only light. Against the wall was an old army cot with the bed covers rolled back. The wooden floor creaked with each step I took. Gus shouted from behind the bathroom door, "Take your clothes off honey and get comfortable—I'll be right out."

I took off everything but my jockeys. My stomach was queasy. It was just like the dread I felt on the first day of grade school.

I heard the toilet flush, and Gus stepped into the bedroom wearing only a transparent nightgown that came down to her knees. Underneath, I could see the contour of her body—full breasts, a thatch of dark pubic hair, hefty thighs. She undid the string at the neck of her nightgown, and her breasts floated free. I remembered the night I spied on my neighbor Diana through the open window. I desperately wanted to feel that same wonder and awe. Instead, my hands and feet were freezing and I felt a knot balling up in my stomach.

"Just relax," she said. "I've broken in a lot of boys just like you."

She led me over to the bed and pulled off my jockeys. She fiddled around with my limp penis, then took it into her mouth. I started giggling—a nervous reaction. My stomach was tight as a coiled spring.

"A little ticklish, are we?" she said. She was being generous.

"I know you're cherry, and I know you're scared. It's okay. Just let me do the work."

It would have been stupid to lie to her. I closed my eyes and sunk back on the bed. She continued to stoke my penis and move her tongue slowly up and down the shaft. I thought about Sally, wearing nothing but those ballet slippers. I began to feel a tingling sensation deep in my belly.

"You're doin' real good," she said. "Now, I want you to think about the sexiest girl you know, the one you're dying to go to bed with. Then, make believe I'm her."

It was as if she was reading my mind and giving me permission at the same time. I closed my eyes and slowly called up my old recurrent fantasy of Cindy Levine lying on her back under the board-walk, dress hiked up over her hips, panties rolled down to her ankles. When my erection was at half-mast, Gus rolled a condom over my penis. It broke the reverie, but when she climbed on top and slid it between her thighs, the image that flashed into my mind was of Julie floating toward me, completely naked, except for the yellow ribbon in her hair.

Gus knew exactly when it was time. She started to rhythmi-cally gyrate and pump, slowly and then faster, then up and down like a bucking horse. I held on tight, Julie's image still clear in my mind. When it was over, I was so elated I wanted to kiss her. I didn't care that it was all business. If all prostitutes were like her, they should be charging analysts' rates.

An indolent fatigue set in—a pleasant exhaustion, a feeling of being completely spent—the kind of sensation that ball players describe when they say that they "left it all out on the field."

When we got back in the living room, Steve and Sally were dressed and sitting on the love seat.

"What took you so long, stud?" Steve laughed. Why was he still pulling rank on me?

Sally said, in a mock Southern Belle tone, "Sugar, the best lovers know how to take their time."

She looked right at me and winked. I'll bet it was all part of their schtick. Sally, the actress—Gus, the shrink.

When Steve got up to go to the john, Sally came over to me and whispered, "That one is all talk. He never even got it up."

By the time we were on the subway, I was flushed with my success. I had no idea whether what Sally said about Steve was true or not, but it was reassuring to think that my fears weren't so unnatural after all—that even a stud like him might not succeed at sex every time. It was one more myth I could now put to rest.

◆

_ 15.

When school resumed in the fall, I was still giddy from the afterglow of the summer's escapades. Plus, everything I'd been longing for was now coming my way. I had my own column and full supervision of the new reporters. The high school sports editors at the *Times* and *Herald Tribune* assigned me to write up the football games, this time for a small honorarium. During the first week of classes, I was chosen for Arista, the honor society. Then Mr. Rosenthal, the senior play advisor, invited me to help write the script and play a role in the actual production.

It was almost if I'd had blinders on for the last five years. I'd talked myself into believing that making the varsity would be my only avenue to popularity and recognition The reality was that baseball wasn't responsible for any of the honors and distinctions I'd recently earned. Or for my relationship with Julie. Or even for losing my virginity. None of this would have happened, in fact, had I persisted in seeking out Kerchman's approval.

A week after football practice began, I was in *The Chat* office revising my first column when the phone rang.

"Where the goddamned hell have you been?" Kerchman snapped. "You're my head football manager, get your ass down here."

What chutzpah! And how had he found me? Did Kerchman really believe I'd jump at the chance to be a gloried water boy? Again? Did he have no memory? No conscience? In his twisted scheme of things, there was probably no reason why I shouldn't have been honored by his invitation. But I couldn't risk a face-to-face meeting—couldn't let him get to me again. I had too much to lose.

When Kerchman wanted to be a bastard, he could browbeat you without feeling an ounce of remorse. But he could also be a sweet talker. I'd seen it up-close too many times. Oh how I ached for the opportunity to turn him down. I'd been thinking about this moment since June. All summer, I'd been rehearsing what I'd say. I'd tell him point blank that if he'd given me the varsity letter, I'd have been happy to help him out. And the truth is that I would have—in a blink. Even if I didn't want to do it.

But now that the moment had arrived, all I could do was stammer a polite, weak-ass excuse about having already made other commitments. I braced myself for the fallout. All he said though was, "I see," and he hung up. Just like that, it was over and done with. Okay, I'd reclaimed my dignity and pride. I'd vindicated myself. Why then did I feel so guilty—as if *I'd* somehow undermined *him?*

For the next hour I couldn't concentrate on the column. Every five minutes I fought off the impulse to call him back. Why did he still have such a stranglehold over me?

I'd just about talked myself out of calling him back, when Andrew Makrides dropped the news on me the following morning. Two days ago Henry Koslan had died of leukemia. The whole team would be attending the memorial service the next day. "Kerchman wants you there too," Makrides said. Coach K, it seems, had known about Koslan's condition for almost a year. But he'd promised the family he wouldn't tell anybody.

So that's why he started Koslan in that last game. And that's why Koslan got his letter and I didn't. Despite it all, I still didn't want to give in. I earned that letter. And why couldn't he have explained it to me—even after the fact? Why did I have to hear it from Makrides? Apparently, this little dance wasn't over yet. Certainly not in Kerchman's mind. Maybe not in mine either.

I was never very close to Koslan. In fact, because of our similar roles, I always tried to disassociate myself from him. But his death was a numbing reminder of just how quickly and suddenly your whole life can change. It made everything feel just a little bit more urgent.

On September 27th, a sunny, chilly afternoon, I journeyed alone to Ebbets Field—for what I sensed would be the last time. The 6,702 other Dodger fans in attendance seemed to think so too. We all watched in gloomy silence as Danny McDevitt, a promising left-hander, shut out the Pittsburgh Pirates, 2-0. In a curious twist of fate, the Pirate team president at the time was Branch Rickey, the ex–Dodger owner who, in 1947, had signed Jackie Robinson to a Major League contract.

I can't recall feeling so listless and melancholy at a Dodger game before. Even Tex Rickert's voice on the P.A. didn't have its usual resonance and pizzazz. Between each inning, the organist, Gladys Gooding, played a selection of sad, torchy songs: "Am I Blue," "What Can I Say Dear, After I've Said I'm Sorry?" "Thanks for the Memories," "When I Grow Too Old to Dream." She capped the medley during the seventh inning stretch with a solemn rendition of "Auld Lang Syne." It was only the second time I'd cried over a major league ball game. The first was Bobby Thomson's home run. But back then, I was only eleven.

Most of the crowd left before the game was over—in protest of O'Malley's still-pending announcement of the move. I stayed until the end, wishing that I could stamp all my Dodger memories in my imagination forever.

As the players ran off the field for the last time, I stood up with the few thousand remaining diehards cheering my old heroes, tears

you are here this adult voice put it doesn't

no's for true me me

streaming down my cheeks. One second I'd be overcome by a feeling of pride and admiration for all their achievements, and the next
moment I felt bitter and resentful. Until, finally, a profound sadness
set in. In addition to the Dodgers, I was mourning Henry Koslan's
untimely death. In the larger scheme of things, I was unconsciously
grieving the loss of my childhood.

A few days after Koslan's funeral I went down to Kerchman's
boiler room office. I'd had a week to think it over. Naturally I was
curious to see what he had up his sleeve. But I was also testing my
own resolve. This time it would be my call. No more trade-offs. If I
didn't like the deal, I'd walk.

I made it as tough on him as I could—or so I thought. I told him
I'd take the job, but only if I got time off to write my column and
make the four campus visits I'd already scheduled. I even wrote the
dates out and handed the piece of paper to him; "Trinity/Hartford in
mid October; Syracuse in late October; Boston U in early November;
Columbia, right before Thanksgiving." I deliberately made no mention of baseball. And neither, to my slight disappointment, did he.

Kerchman readily agreed to my demands. A bit too readily, I
thought. He said "Okay" like it was no big deal. For a minute I felt
like he'd trumped me again—that he'd gotten just what he'd wanted.
But to hell with what he thought. I'd already made the deal. I'd wait
and see what happened next.

The following day Mr. K held a special squad meeting in the
boy's showers. He had only a single item on the agenda.

"Anybody gives Steinberg here any flak," he told the troops,
"you'll answer to me." It was the first time he'd ever pronounced my
name correctly.

He'd never said anything like this about Krause or the other
student managers. I was flattered, of course. That was his intent,
wasn't it? Still, I decided to reserve my judgment.

As head football manager I delegated all the menial jobs to the new assistants. I also cut out of practice early on the days when we had editors meetings at the paper, and when we did page proofs and layout. I even missed two games because of my campus visits. But he never said a word to me about any of it. Whatever else he might have thought, Kerchman kept up his end of the bargain.

Over the course of the season I became an unwitting accomplice to this obsessed, inscrutable coach. While the other managers scurried around servicing the players and doing their bidding, I stood next to Kerchman, taking notes on a clipboard while he muttered complicated strategies to me—all of which I somehow comprehended. I felt a secret pride at being taken into his confidence, even as I was annoyed with myself for feeling so beholden to him.

On October 9th—the day before the Yankees and Braves would play the seventh game of the World Series, the Dodgers held a press conference. Arthur Patterson, one of O'Malley's front office minions, read a curt, generic statement to the press: "The stockholders and directors of the Brooklyn baseball club have today met and unanimously agreed that the necessary steps be taken to draft the Los Angeles territory."

I knew it was coming, but I was stunned by the presentation. It was all double-speak. No apologies, no farewells, no concessions of any kind. No acknowledgment of the allegiance of an entire borough. No statement of gratitude to the millions who'd supported this team since the turn of the century. Only a bland, businesslike memo.

The next day, the Braves beat the Yankees in the seventh game. It was an all too abrupt ending to the city's ten-year period of entitlement, a remarkable decade during which a New York team had won the World Series eight times, and two of the city's three teams had played one another for the world championship seven times.

The move to LA would turn out to be the precursor to major league expansion, as well as to the eventual commodification of the game itself. It would also foreshadow a radical shift in the culture's values. But at the moment I was too caught up in my own personal drama to comprehend any of it.

My main preoccupation that fall was my evolving relationship with Julie. At the time of the Dodgers' move we were still in that goofy, euphoric, puppy love stage. From the minute school began, we were sending silly love notes to one another, exchanging cutesy gifts, and talking incessantly on the phone. We even adopted Johnny Mathis's mushy ballad, "Chances Are" as "our song." On Friday nights I'd go to the Hewlett High football games and watch Julie cheer. Saturdays we'd go bowling with friends or see a movie. At the end of the evening we'd either park at the yacht basin or sneak into Julie's den after her parents had gone to bed.

Now that summer was over it was much harder for us to see each other. On top of her parents' objections, there was another obstacle—how to get from Belle Harbor to Woodsburg and back each weekend. I still couldn't drive at night without an adult in the car. And even if I could, my father would never have considered loaning me his '56 Olds, our family's only vehicle. Julie had a license, but she could only drive inside the Nassau County line.

So I started bumming weekend rides with Harris Bookbinder and Danny Alpert, two classmates I'd never socialized with before. Harris was reputed to be one of the richest kids in Neponsit, and Danny was an ambitious social mover who still aspired to be part of the clique. Harris had a steady girlfriend who lived in Cedarhurst, just a few miles from Julie's house. And, on an impulse born of guilt and self-interest, I'd fixed Danny up with Joanne, never dreaming that in less than a month they'd be going steady. Uncharitable as it was, I felt a tinge of envy that they'd taken to one another so quickly.

Both Harris and Danny were driving illegally, but with their parents' permission. Those weekend excursions often qualified as a form of low comedy. Whoever drove, Harris or Danny, he would always wear the same costume: sunglasses, a brown fedora, and a dark trench coat with the collar turned up. They both believed that the disguises made them look older. I thought they were a dead give-away; yet we were never stopped by the police. The rumor was that Harris's father, a big-shot in the importing business, had made an "arrangement" with the local cops.

When we were still within the city limits, neither of those guys ever exceeded the speed limit. But the minute we crossed the bor-der into Nassau County, they'd punch it up to 75 on the back roads. It was partly because they were so giddy from their outlaw triumph, and partly because they knew it scared the hell out of me.

My dependence on them created other hardships. Some nights they'd pick me up at Julie's after midnight. Other times they'd show up at two or three in the morning. Once in a while Julie would have to drive me to the station or to the county line so I could catch the last train and bus home. Once I even had to sleep on her living room sofa—a maneuver that didn't go over very well with her parents, both of whom continued to make me feel as welcome as a gate crasher.

It was not in Julie's nature to be willfully rebellious. Like me, she went out of her way to try and make people like her. I know she tried her best to convince her parents that they had a mistaken impression of me. But the more strenuously they resisted, the more Julie continued to subvert them.

At first I had kind of enjoyed playing the role of the boy from across the tracks. Sneaking around behind her parents' backs was a heady adventure. But now that Julie and I had become so close, it bothered me that her parents saw me as a disruptive influence. I tried being overly polite, I tried to engage them in conversation, I even suggested that they meet my parents. But nothing I did seemed to change their perceptions.

Naturally, my parents were apprehensive about my dating a rich Five Towns girl. Julie's background made them suspicious, even a bit defensive. But, over time, she managed to win them over—just as I knew she would. Julie was like a lightening rod that way.

It amused me how she could always flatter and disarm my father—who under most circumstances was a hard sell. And my mother treated her as if she was the daughter she never had. They shopped, gossiped, and went to lunch together. My parents virtually adopted her as a member of the family. And she took to them just as readily—which of course created even more friction for her at home.

I was surprised to find that in the exclusive Woodsburg circle Julie was something of an outcast. Compared to her friends, she wasn't particularly sophisticated or artistically inclined. She wasn't a high-powered student in high school, and she had no designs on a finishing school education. Joanne, in fact, once told me that Julie had "no intellectual curiosity." The cruel remark, I'm sure, was supposed to make me feel as if I'd made a big mistake.

Still, Joanne wasn't alone in her assessment. The word on Julie was that her interests and goals were limited to being the cheerleading captain and having a series of steady boyfriends. But none of the malicious gossip made me change my mind or second-guess myself. Given my own history with the popular crowd, I admired Julie all the more for being so unaffected, and so willing to risk her friends' disapproval.

There were times, however, that her lack of curiosity bothered me. When Kerouac, Ginsburg, and the Beats were all the rage, I tried to coax her to go to the Village with me. She indulged me a few times, but I could tell that the Beat scene didn't interest her. She also didn't share my curiosity for literature, theater, or jazz. Whenever Harris and Danny boasted about what play or jazz concert they took their girlfriends to, I always felt a little peeved that rather than accompany me to a jazz club or a play, Julie preferred to watch TV, see a movie, or go to a neighborhood party.

On the other hand, we were both interested in ordinary teenage things like rock and roll. After school we'd watch *American Bandstand* from our separate homes. Then at night, like two groupies, we'd gossip by phone about Frankie Avalon, Fabian, Bobby Rydell, and Connie Francis. We talked about them as if they were class-mates we knew intimately.

Like me, Julie was a sports maven. She'd listen to my stories about the "good old days" when the Dodgers, Giants, and Yankees dominated major league baseball, and she made no attempt to hide the fact that she liked having a jock for a boyfriend. I know that she was disappointed I didn't have a letter sweater for her to parade in around school and she hinted more than once that it might be a good idea for me to reconsider my decision not to play baseball. To remind me, she'd sometimes wear my satin baseball warm-up jacket to the movies or out on a bowling date.

I admit I was proud of the fact that she was a cheerleader and a "head turner." But what I remember most is that Julie was uncommonly affectionate and kind. She had a way of making me feel special and important—which made me grateful—thankful even, to have finally found someone who accepted me—even desired me—for who I was, and not for who she wanted me to be.

That fall I noticed a marked change in Mr. K's attitude, not only toward me, but toward the whole football team as well. Whether it was tactical or genuine, I couldn't tell. He still threw temper tantrums when we lost games that we should have won, and he still inflicted cruel punishments on players who screwed up—though the penalties didn't seem as severe somehow. With so many of his veterans gone, Kerchman had resigned himself to rebuilding the team. Several times that season Mr. K even asked me to counsel some of the more troubled players. I wondered what this was leading up to?

At the banquet in November he gave me the customary "See you in a few months" line and handed me my third useless varsity letter. But this time I wasn't going to get my hopes up. I'd wait and see how I felt when baseball tryouts rolled around.

One blustery afternoon in late January, I was working at *The Chat* when I came across a three-day-old press clipping. Someone on my staff had left it for me with an unsigned note that read, "Thought you'd want to see this."

It was a story that had appeared in the *Long Island Daily Press* sports section—a pretty big feature article about this year's Far Rockaway baseball team. It quoted Kerchman as saying that "in this rebuilding season, the mainstays of my pitching staff will be my two seniors, Mark Silverstone and Mike Steinberg."

I had to read the line again just to be certain it wasn't my imagination playing tricks.

"Silverstone is my number one starter, and juniors, Andy Makrides and Steve Coan, will be two and three," the article read. "About Mike Steinberg," Kerchman went on to say, "the senior right-hander will be my late-inning relief specialist, as well as an occasional starter. He has excellent control and an effective sinker, both important weapons for a closer."

I read the interview over again before it sunk in. A closer? Me? I'd pitched some relief in the past, but I'd mainly been a starter since I was thirteen. Had Kerchman all the while been grooming me for this role?

Two more articles spotlighting Silverstone and me soon appeared, one of them in *The Chat*, written—unbeknownst to me—by my own staff reporter. Add Julie's urgings to the mix, and how could I pass this up? I had to at least call Kerchman's bluff on this one, didn't I? Besides, whatever else I might be, I was, goddamn it, a pitcher. If I went back it would be because I needed to play ball and because I wanted to be part of this team. Of course, in the back of my mind there was this tiny voice reminding me that I still needed to prove myself to Kerchman, this hard-bitten coach whose determination and tenacity were more akin to my own obsessions than I wanted to admit.

It struck me, then, that I'd been preparing for this moment since seventh grade. Six long years of auditioning for coaches, waiting my turn, kissing ass, and taking whatever garbage and humiliation I had to put up with. Now it would finally be my turn.

Right from the start, Kerchman made certain to let everyone know just how important I was to this team. During tryouts I stood next to him and the other vets up on the running track. I was also assigned Jack Gartner's old locker. But most satisfying of all was when Mr. K personally escorted me to the equipment cage and ordered Lenny Stromeyer, our pissant student manager, to issue me a vintage Dodger uniform—one with the little red numbers on the front. I was so giddy, so elated, that I wore the jersey to bed for a week.

Taking their cues from the coach, all the new players deferred to me; classmates—and even some of my teachers—treated me with a respect I'd never experienced before. On Friday nights I sat with the varsity at the State Diner jock table while the freshman and sophomore girls fawned all over us.

It was gratifying to have finally gotten here. Still, I wasn't about to throw any parties. Not just yet. Sure, I'd earned all of it. That much I could acknowledge. But I still had to back it up on the ball field. Until I accomplished that, I wouldn't fully believe that I'd arrived.

In the preseason Mr. K made sure I got to throw the last two innings of *every* game, no matter what the score was. I pitched my way out of most every jam, but the exhibition game that mattered most was the one against Long Beach High.

To everyone else it was just another preseason game. But for me it had a special meaning. The Long Beach shortstop was Larry Brown, the all–Nassau County basketball star, and Julie's former boyfriend. Baseball, I'm sure, was just a sideline to him. He was already headed to North Carolina on a full ride—the first leg of what would become a most successful basketball career—a career that would eventually put him in the Hall of Fame.

I started dreaming about the game weeks beforehand. I imagined myself striking Brown out with the ball game on the line, and Julie sitting in the bleachers cheering. In reality, it didn't quite come down to that. It was close, though. Julie was at cheerleading practice that day, but I did get to pitch to Brown in the last inning. When he came up to bat, we had a 5-4 lead and the tying run was on second.

Ever since the first inning I'd been scrutinizing him carefully. Initially, it surprised me that Brown was only a few inches taller than I was, and that he had a pretty average build. But what impressed me most was his tenacity and determination. He dove for ground balls that were just out of his reach; he slid spikes high, into every base; he chastised his teammates when they screwed up; he shouted taunts and epithets at us from the bench, trying to get into our heads. And at bat, no matter what the situation was, he battled on every count.

When I faced him in that last at bat, it was as if he was reading my mind on every pitch. He had ferocious concentration. He didn't bite on anything that was even a hair out of the strike zone. He was looking for either a walk or for a pitch he could drive out of the infield. I threw everything in my repertoire. But I deliberately held back the sinker, waiting for just the right spot to throw it.

I kept changing speeds and rotations, stepping off the rubber to disrupt his rhythm, moving the ball around—up, down, in, out—probing for a weakness. On a 3-2 count he fouled off seven straight pitches—all of them strikes. In the larger scheme of things, the game meant nothing. But I thrived on this kind of challenge. And evidently, so did he.

One of Yogi Berra's classic malapropisms is that "Baseball is fifty percent physical and ninety percent mental." For me, the psychological battle between a smart hitter and a savvy pitcher is the essence of the game. I was determined to outwit Brown. On the thirteenth pitch, I threw a sinker, knee-high, just a hair off the outside corner. It was right where I wanted it: too close to let go, not good enough to hit hard. Most high school hitters would have been too anxious to take that pitch. But he just watched it go by as casually as if he was waiting for a bus. Before the umpire had even yelled "ball four," he'd already flipped his bat toward the dugout and was trotting toward first base. That's how cocky and smart he was. I could have sworn that he winked at me as he headed up the line.

Pitching to Larry Brown that afternoon was just the reminder I needed. Given my limitations, I'd have to cultivate the same mindset and tenacity that great athletes like him possessed.

By the time we opened our league season, I was aching with anticipation. In the first home game, against Woodrow Wilson, Kerchman started Silverstone. Knowing that two big league scouts were in the stands was all the incentive Mark needed. He pitched beautifully for the first four innings. By the fifth though, he started to leave too many fastballs up—a sure sign that a pitcher is beginning to tire. I started to mentally prepare myself. I studied the Wilson hitters more carefully, looking for tendencies and weaknesses I could exploit.

In the top of the sixth Kerchman sent me down to the bullpen to get loose. I was ready after a couple dozen pitches. For the past two innings Mark had barely managed to get out of a few tough jams. In the top of the seventh, it was a scoreless tie. Just before Silverstone came out to pitch the inning, Kerchman motioned to the bullpen. As I was walking toward the mound, my stomach churning with anxiety, Mark threw a tantrum. In front of the team, fans, and school officials, he screamed, "I'm throwing a fucking shutout here. The scouts came to see me, not Steinberg."

Normally, Mr. K would can a player's ass for a lot less than that. But Silverstone was our best pitcher, and Kerchman needed him. Bringing me in was the only way he could keep his hotheaded ace in line.

This was my first important test in a league game. The ball game was on the line, and my father, brother, and Julie were all in the bleachers watching. Add Silverstone's outburst to it, and I can't remember feeling more unhinged on a baseball field. I don't even recall Kerchman handing me the ball.

I threw my warm ups in a daze, bouncing one pitch in the dirt and throwing another so far off line that it hit the backstop on a fly. I could hardly grip the ball my hands were shaking so badly.

The first batter was Fletcher Thompson, Wilson's pitcher and best hitter. I was sure he'd want to look at a few pitches just to get a line on me. To calm myself down, and also get ahead in the count, my first pitch was a gut shot—a letter high fastball that he took a clean rip at. My heart sank the second I heard the crack of the bat. I knew that he'd suckered me. As I watched the ball disappear over the center field fence, I was sure that Silverstone would come charging out to the mound and strangle me. That is, if Kerchman didn't beat him to it.

My cheeks burned and my jersey was soaked with flop sweat. How could I have thrown him a fastball? I don't even have a fastball. Thinking about it tightened me up even more. I walked the next two men on eight pitches. I looked to the bench then to the bullpen for help. Nobody was throwing. Kerchman was going to leave me in there, even if it meant losing the game.

In that split second, all my tension seemed to dissolve. Just knowing that I wasn't going to get pulled somehow calmed me down. I forgot about the crowd and the home run. I even managed to block out the obscenities that Silverstone was still yelling from the bench. I slowed down and started concentrating on what I knew how to do best: pace the count, keep the ball low, and mix my pitches. I remembered the battle with Larry Brown, and I tried to call up that same mind-set. Once I got my concentration back, I struck out the next two batters and got the last guy on a routine ground ball to second.

After the inning, nobody on the bench said a word. They didn't have to. I knew I'd let us all down, especially Coach K. I was too numb to feel anything. It was getting dark, and the plate umpire told both teams that this would be the last at bats. I sat there, empty, waiting for the end. But with two out and nobody on, our first baseman, Dickie Webb, hit a homer off Thompson on a letter-high curve ball that hung. Thompson knew it the minute he let the ball go. You always do. As Dickie rounded the bases, Thompson kicked at the dirt, furious at himself for making such a lame pitch. I knew just how he felt, though at the moment I didn't have an ounce of pity for him—any more than he had for me when he clocked my first pitch. As Dickie crossed home plate, I was the first one out there to hug him. The game had ended in a tie.

I was relieved to have gotten off the hook. But later that night it ate away at me that I'd almost blown the game. I wondered if this was it—if I'd ever pitch again for Mr. K. I began to feel that creeping, familiar sense of dread. If I didn't get another chance to redeem myself, I'd carry my failure and shame for the rest of the season—and for who knows how much longer after that.

The next game was away, thank God, at Jamaica High. On the bus ride, I sulked quietly at the back. When the game started, I sat on the far end of the bench, watching and taking notes—just in case. We got off to a five-run lead. But Makrides lasted only four innings before they tied it up. I looked over at Kerchman. He'd already signaled for Coan to warm up. No surprise there; it was still the middle of the game. Yet the snub stung like a razor nick. We went ahead again, but Coan couldn't hold the lead. It's an awful feeling to have to root against your own teammate, but when Jamaica got within a run of us I started getting antsy. I wanted to run up to Kerchman, tug on his sleeve and say, "Put me in coach, I'm ready." But I just sat and stewed.

In Jamaica's half of the fifth, with the score tied and the bases loaded, Kerchman signaled me to warm up. I was going to get a second chance. He walked out to the mound to stall for time while I got loose. When the umpire came out there for the second time, Kerchman summoned me in from the bullpen. Just before he left the mound, he put his arm around my shoulder and said, "You're my closer. Show me you've got the guts I think you have."

Then, he gently dropped the ball into my open mitt.

This time, I didn't feel the least bit rattled. Part of it had to do with not having to pitch in front of the home crowd. But it was also a different situation from the one I was in a few days ago. When you come into a tight game with men on base, you don't think the same way as you would when you're starting an inning off with nobody on and nobody out. You have less time to prepare, which means, less time to worry. I'd have to rely here on instinct and experience. I couldn't toy with the hitters or play any head games. I had to stay ahead on the count and keep the ball down. I got my three outs without giving up a run—all three on infield grounders. We scored four more times, and won the game 10-6. When it was over, I'd pitched three hitless innings. Nine up, nine down.

The impact didn't register until the bus ride home. For the first time, I joined in as we yelled and whistled and hooted out the window at the girls on the street. We loudly sang along as Dion and the Belmonts harmonized "I Wonder Why" on the radio. Everyone on the team—except for Silverstone—signed the game ball for me. I didn't let Mark's snub bother me. In my own eyes, and I'm sure in Kerchman's too, I'd redeemed myself.

As I walked home in the dark, it began to rain. I slid the grass-stained baseball under my jacket and clutched it to my chest. When I got to my block I was soaking wet, and I was crying, then laughing hysterically, and singing "I Wonder Why" at the top of my voice.

◆

_ 16.

My new-found confidence was starting to influence my writing. Naturally, I liked seeing my headshot and byline above my column. And of course I savored the attention it brought me. But I was discovering that what mattered most was the writing itself.

From the start, Jagust had left me alone to pursue any subject that interested me. In the fall, I started out tentatively, writing standard stuff: impressions of the football team, player profiles, interviews, predictions of how the basketball team would do in the winter. I got my share of compliments, but the columns felt uninspired and routine.

Right before winter break I decided to try something different. I wrote what amounted to an emotional confession, describing how I felt last October when I heard the news that the Dodgers were leaving Brooklyn. While I was writing the piece I was remembering how angry and insulted I felt about the bland, impersonal statement that the Dodger brass had released. I wanted my column to be just the opposite—passionate and personal. The minute I began the piece, I felt freer, less self-conscious. Soon, the writing seemed to take on a life of its own.

I followed the Dodger piece with a column on my struggles to become a pitcher. I was worried that both columns were too personal, too self absorbed. Yet there were moments when the words seemed to flow without effort. It was like pitching "in the zone." A delightful surprise. The same feeling would return whenever I wrote another column.

It didn't occur to me then, but those columns represented the union of two dominant passions—my love of writing and my devotion to baseball.

Ever since the middle of the summer I'd had an unusual run of good fortune. It was like being on an extended hitting streak, and I was beginning to wonder just how long it would continue.

One evening in mid May, halfway through the baseball season, my father and mother gathered Alan and me and sat us down in the living room. My father then announced that right after my graduation the whole family was moving to Los Angeles. I was stunned.

Back in the fall, I remember hearing him complain that he was fed up with taking orders from incompetent bosses half his age. He was also worried that his decreasing commissions weren't nearly enough to pay the household bills. Back then, I wasn't paying very close attention. I'd heard him say those things so many times before. I'd been so preoccupied that I'd been paying almost no attention to what was going on at home. During football and baseball seasons I'd come home from practice sometimes as late as nine o'clock. I'd wolf down a warmed-over dinner that my mother had left out on the kitchen table, and then try to study for a few hours before bed. The next morning, I'd be up at six and at the bus stop by seven thirty.

My first thought now was that the timing couldn't have been worse. Just the day before I'd received two letters—one from Syracuse (Kerchman's alma mater) and the other from Boston University. Both were acceptances, and both offered partial Journalism scholarships. Those were my two "safe" schools." The ones I really wanted—Trinity and Columbia—were such long shots. Still, I couldn't wait to tell everyone, that is, until my father dropped this news on us.

For years, my father had been struggling with his problems at work. His firm had changed hands twice in the last twelve months. And just this past summer, he'd been told that he had to split his sales territory with a younger, more inexperienced salesman. It cut his commissions in half and forced him to go back to work at the liquor store. The final indignity was when his bosses requested that he break in the new guy.

Still, in my wildest dreams I never imagined us leaving New York. Not for good, anyway. Did it mean I wouldn't be going to college? What about my friends? What about Julie? I'd already envisioned the unchaperoned campus visits, the romantic reunions at Thanksgiving and Christmas.

I tried to comprehend my father's dilemma. He'd been failing himself and us, he said. This move was an opportunity to change all that. In the last ten days he'd taken out a bank loan, put the house up for sale, and signed a partnership agreement with a former client who'd started up a linen business in California. His partner would run the business, and my father would be the sales rep. He'd be based in Los Angeles, and his territory would be the Pacific Northwest: northern California, Washington, and Oregon.

I tried again to see it from his point of view. It was an opportune time to stake out this new territory, he explained. A lot of retailers and manufacturers were moving west. If he didn't take this chance, he said, he might miss his last chance to do something like this.

I sat there, too numb to protest. Even if I wanted to oppose him, it was too late. My mother, never very flexible to begin with, had been firmly opposed to the move from the minute she'd found out. That was about a month ago. Of all of us, she stood to lose the most. She'd lived here almost all her life. Gone to school here. And her circle of friends were all in the Rockaways. So were my grandfather and aunt. Despite it all, she'd failed to dissuade my father from making this move.

A part of me admired him for taking such a big risk. It was something my grandfather might have done. But the more I thought about it, the more depressed I became. The move would cost me everything I'd worked so hard to earn. It also bothered me that this was exactly what Julie's parents had hoped for. That was reason enough to want to stay here.

What troubled me most, though, was my father's inflexible stance. He never bothered to consult any of us beforehand. Nor did he ask us, even after the fact, how we felt about it. Almost all of my old coaches operated in the same fashion. I didn't like it then and I didn't like it now. What was worse was that my father's maneuver also reminded me of the arbitrary, impersonal way the Dodgers had treated their fans when they announced their own cross-country move.

Within a few days, I started to dope out strategies and arguments that I hoped would convince my parents to let me stay here— at least until the summer was over. If I could buy some time, maybe I'd find a way to avoid the move altogether.

Up until my father's announcement, it had been a dream season for me. Of the twelve games we'd won, I pitched in ten—winning three, losing one, saving six.

It still felt strange though, to read my name in newspaper articles, sign an autograph for a neighborhood kid, or hear the cheerleaders chanting "Steinberg, Steinberg, he's our man. . . ." But the recognition wasn't important anymore. Now I needed this season to last as long as it could. And the only way that could happen was for us to get to the city finals.

With a week left, our rag-tag team was in a four-way tie for first place. Due to a series of early season rain outs, it all came down to consecutive road games against the three other co-leaders: Wilson, Jackson, and Van Buren. If we won all three, we'd make the play-offs. Then, anything was possible.

The rematch against Wilson was a scoreless tie for ten innings. We'd managed to scratch out a run in the top of the eleventh on a walk, bunt, steal, and sacrifice fly. In the bottom of the inning, Silverstone walked the first two men and gave up a sacrifice bunt. He'd pitched almost eleven innings of one-hit ball, but Wilson now had the tying run on third and the winning run on second. It was crunch time. All we needed were two outs. I'd been up throwing every inning since the fifth.

With everything on the line, Mr. K brought me in to pitch to, of all people, Fletcher Thompson—the same guy who'd jacked the homer off me in my first game. Silverstone was a lefty and so was Thompson. By bringing me in, Kerchman was going against one of the most time-honored strategies in baseball. Conventional wisdom dictates that Mark pitch to Thompson and I come in to face the right-handed hitter who was on deck. But it was too late to question it now.

While I was throwing my warm ups, I was thinking "suppose the son of a bitch does it to me again?" From the bench Silverstone screamed, "Walk him, asshole."

This time, Mark was right. With first base open, it was the obvious thing to do. But Mr. K had a different agenda in mind. He stood on the mound and ordered me to pitch to him.

"Nothing too fat," he said. The obligatory strategy talk. "If you walk him, make him earn it. Try and get him to fish for one."

Sure, coach, no sweat, I wanted to say. Why do they even tell you stuff like that?

I knew Thompson would be salivating to get another crack at me. Tease him, I told myself. Keep the ball low and away, out of his kitchen. On a 2-1 sinker that was low and just off the outside corner, Thompson reached out and poked a soft fly ball that started to tail back toward the left field line. Ordinarily it would have been a routine out. But Thompson was a lefty pull hitter and the outfielders were shading him to the right. Our left fielder, Ira Heid, had a long way to come. The ball hung up there just long enough. An instant before it touched the ground, Ira dove and backhanded it at his shoe tops. When the runner at third tagged and headed home, Ira bounced up and threw him out at the plate with a perfect one hopper to Milner. The Old Redhead would have called it a "bang-bang play."

The game was over and we were still alive. When I got to the bench, Silverstone was livid; and to tell you the truth, I didn't blame him. He'd pitched an almost perfect game for eleven and a third innings; I threw just four pitches and got the game ball and the next day's headline in the *Long Island Daily Press*. Welcome to the club, Mark.

My only real problem that spring was Silverstone. He'd won five of the six games he pitched. But I'd saved three of them, and he resented me for it. Mark hated sharing the limelight, especially with a former flunky. Every time I came in to relieve him, he took it as a personal insult. He'd yell stuff like, "You better not blow my game, peckerhead." Or, "Keep it low, jerk-off. I don't want my E.R.A. getting screwed because you can't keep the fucking ball in the park."

One home run off me in ten games, and I can't keep the ball in the park? I wonder if he thought these lines up beforehand. It's true that Mark could rattle a corpse. But two years of taking shit from Kerchman had taught me how to shake those taunts off and keep pitching. Maybe all that hazing was a deliberate part of his design, after all.

The following day against Jackson, Kerchman put me in again. Seventh inning, and Coan was pitching with a one-run lead. They had the bases loaded and no outs. Otto Agostinelli was up. Otto was a six-foot-four free swinger who led the league in home runs and strikeouts. My favorite kind of hitter. For reasons I'll never understand, Kerchman waited until Coan went all the way down to three nothing on Agostinelli before he yanked him and brought me in. It was an impossible situation.

"You've got a run to give," he said. "But that's all."

It was a strange comment. Maybe Kerchman was trying to take some of the pressure off me. But I wasn't thinking tie. I wanted to win it now.

Kerchman spat a plug of tobacco juice and tossed me the ball.

With a three-nothing count, I thought that even Otto would be under orders to take the first two pitches. So I threw him two strikes, gut shots with nothing on them. I saw him grimace on the second one. He wanted that pitch back, for good reason. Even I could have hit that sucker. With the count full, I knew I had a chance. He'd be looking for another cripple right down the middle. You never want to let a free swinger extend his arms. So on the three-two pitch, I gambled and jammed him with a middle-in slider that should have been ball four. He swung, thank god, and tapped it off the handle. A weak ground ball to me. Easy force at home. One gone.

There's a kind of seesaw head game that goes on between a new pitcher and opposing hitters. At first, you've got to establish yourself as somebody to be reckoned with. Because from the moment you start warming up, their bench will be all over you, yelling stuff like "come-on cream puff, show me what you got," among other less polite remarks about your mother and your origin of birth. But once you get that first out, the momentum shifts. The pressure is now on them. That's when hitters begin to tighten up. Each one knows that he has to come through or it's all over.

Those are the kinds of situations a relief pitcher thrives on. If you can stay ahead of the hitters, you're in command. I was super careful not to groove anything. The next guy hit a hump-back liner to second base. No damage there. Then the last hitter slapped a hard one hopper to Davey Cohen at third. I exhaled, thinking the game was over. We'd gotten through it again. But instead of stepping on the bag for the easy force out, Cohen panicked and threw the ball high and wide to first. My heart was in my throat. The ball looked like it was headed for the bleachers. But Dickie Webb saved our asses again. He jumped, backhanded the errant throw, and came down on the bag two steps ahead of the runner.

On the bus trip home, I wanted to sink back in my seat and savor what we'd accomplished over the last two days, but I didn't have that luxury. We were tied with Van Buren, and the winner of tomorrow's game would advance to the borough finals.

There was so much tension at home that I stayed in my room as often as possible. It also didn't help that Julie brought up the move almost every time we talked.

The ball games had distracted me, and writing the column also took my mind off the situation. But the night before the last game I found the rejection letters from Trinity and Columbia on my bedroom desk. I'd secretly believed all along that I wouldn't fit in at either school. Still, I was devastated by the news. The letters were as impersonal and off-putting as the Dodgers' October press release. And the timing didn't help either. I never should have opened them before the season ended.

I felt worse the next morning when I found out that the four guys in the clique, in addition to Silverstone, had all been accepted at Ivy League schools. Two of them, in fact, were going to Columbia. Their grades weren't any better than mine. Was it legacy? Family money? An inside string that someone pulled? It was just one more reason why I desperately wanted this season to keep going.

Van Buren had waxed us the first time, 8-1. I never even got up to throw. Their pitcher, Joe Sabbaritto, was one of the top prospects in the city. Scouts were comparing his fastball to the Dodgers' Sandy Koufax, back when Koufax was pitching for Layfayette High. And their three and four hitters, McNab and Schumacher, were one-two in the borough. If we could beat this team, we'd have really earned the title.

The next afternoon we traveled by bus to Alley Pond park in Douglaston—the longest road trip we'd ever taken. For the last thirty minutes of the ride Mr. K gave us the old rah-rah speeches, citing former players who always performed at their best under pressure. As a rule, those speeches never got to me. But this game might be it for us. So I took it all in.

For the first two innings, Sabbaritto was throwing over ninety miles an hour. But he couldn't find the plate, and when he did, his catcher couldn't hold onto the ball. Kerchman knew that if this guy ever found his rhythm, we'd never hit the ball in fair territory again. So we took advantage of every opportunity we got. By the end of the second inning, we'd scratched out five runs on walks, passed balls, bunts, misplays, and stolen bases. We had them rattled. But in the third inning Sabbaritto found the groove and he shut us down. Struck out eight of the next nine hitters.

Meanwhile, they kept pecking away at the lead. When it was 5-3 I was aching to get in there. I finally came in to relieve Makrides in the sixth inning. We were ahead 5-4. Two out and two men on. McNab, a lefty, was up. He'd already gotten two hits off Makrides. This was a perfect spot for Silverstone, I thought. Lefty versus lefty, and Schumaker, another lefty, was coming up. Besides, Mark hadn't pitched for the last two days.

My arm was so sore that my warm-up pitches had nothing on them, plus I didn't have my head in the game yet. I should have stepped off the rubber and taken a second to think. Instead I tried to sneak one past him. I rushed the pitch, hoping to get it down and away. But it was middle-in, up in the letters—right in McNab's wheelhouse. He turned on it and hit a hard single to right. Tie ball game. How could I have done it? It was the worst pitch at the worst possible time. Now it was my game to win or lose. I hoped I had the stamina to keep going.

For the next five innings Sabbaritto got even stronger, striking out batter after batter. In my two at bats I struck out looking each time. Sabbaritto was throwing so hard that his fastball looked like an aspirin tablet as it buzzed past your chin.

The pressure from the last two days was taking its toll on me. I was tired, my arm throbbed on every pitch, and my control was off. Van Buren had men on base each inning. But somehow I'd managed to stagger through it without giving up the winning run. I'd gotten by for five innings on adrenaline overload, concentration, and fear.

From the sixth inning on, there was a strange sense of inevitability about this game. We all felt it. There was very little chatter on the bench. Even Mr. K was subdued, almost as if he'd been hypnotized by what Sabbaritto was doing out there. We were in a tie game with the league title on the line, yet it felt like we were ten runs down.

It was an effort to go out there every inning knowing that unless Sabbaritto had another sudden wild streak, we probably wouldn't score again. But I had to block those thoughts out and just take it one pitch, one hitter, one inning at a time. After the first three extra innings, I created my own private game-within-a-game. If we weren't going to score again, I wanted to see just how long I could make the game last. It was a weirdly exhilarating sensation. Each batter I retired felt like a major accomplishment.

By the twelfth, I was so exhausted that the ball felt like a ten-pound shot put. I was almost pushing it up to the plate, grunting on every pitch. There were moments when I felt so arm-weary I was sure I couldn't throw another pitch. But I couldn't let anyone see how depleted I was—especially not my teammates. The moment I gave into the fatigue, the game would be over. I turned and looked at the four infielders. Like me, they were glassy-eyed and frazzled. Yet for the past six innings they'd been making the plays. I had to keep going. I called on every trick, every little piece of psychology I'd learned—including shutting my mind off and going on automatic pilot. At this point, it was a test of wills, an endurance contest.

With two out in the bottom of the thirteenth, we finally cracked. McNab got to third on a misplayed fly ball. On a two-two count, Schumacher punched a good outside sinker past our drawn in infield for the winning hit. For the last six innings, I'd known it had to end this way—we all did. Still, I was in a daze when it happened. Five years of dreams and struggle, and just like that, it was over. Suddenly, all my energy was gone. As I trudged to the bus, my legs felt rubbery, my forehead was throbbing, and my right arm was on fire.

On the ride home, no one said a word. I sat at the back of the bus, trying to sort out my emotions. One minute I felt a wave of admiration for everyone who'd been part of this marathon. The next minute, I was empty and dejected because I'd lost the season's biggest game. Then, intermittently, I'd be overcome by a rush of elation. Despite the outcome, I'd pitched the seven best innings of my life.

A few days later I realized that we'd gone way beyond even Kerchman's expectations. He knew it too. At the banquet he gave *everyone* a varsity letter. While I was chewing on that injustice, Mr. K began to recite the customary platitudes before giving out the awards. The MVP trophy, I knew, was out of the question. It would go to one of the infielders or outfielders—maybe Dickie Webb. But I was a little disappointed that Davey Cohen, one of Kerchman's football guys, won the most improved player award. What the hell, I thought, I'd already gotten my wish; and I'd had a dream season to boot, hadn't I?

Kerchman always saved the John Kelly award for last. Kelly, it seems, was a star football and baseball player in the '40s who'd been killed in a car accident. The award traditionally went to a graduating senior, often the number-one starting pitcher.

I'd heard Mr. K recite the Kelly monologue so many times that I tuned most of it out. Besides, Lenny Stromeyer had leaked it to several of us that the gold medal already had Silverstone's name engraved on it. We all agreed that Mark was a jerk, but he'd had a great season, and he deserved the award.

I looked over at Mark, and I could read his mind: with one hand he was slipping the medal around some pretty cheerleader's neck, with his free hand he was reaching down her blouse to cop a feel. So when Kerchman announced my name and said to that roomful of people, "Mike Steinberg is a kid who'd made the most out of a little bit of talent, a big heart, and a whole lot of guts," I was too stunned to move.

Before I could stand up, Mark yelled, "I don't fucking believe this." He stuck his middle finger up and stormed out of the restaurant, kicking over empty chairs as he went. Sure he was a bastard and a sore loser, but I half-admired him for giving Kerchman the bird. Last year, in this same banquet room, I'd wanted to stand up and tell Kerchman to take his minor letter and stick it. Instead I let him sweet-talk me into playing. And now, this.

I don't recall how I got to the dais, but I remember standing next to Mr. K, my thoughts scrambled, throat so dry I couldn't swallow. Kerchman had his arm draped around my shoulder, flashbulbs were popping all around me, and everyone was standing and applauding. I squinted through my tears, frantically searching the blurred room for a glimpse of the expressions on the faces of my father and brother.

The shock of winning the Kelly kept me high for several days. But there was a lot more to come. That weekend, I found out I was chosen third team all-city by the *Long Island Daily Press*. The next week I received an honorable mention from the *Journal American*. The biggest surprise of all was when a scout from the Phillies, and another one from the White Sox, offered me a minor league tryout.

It was all so flattering and tempting. But I knew I wouldn't accept. The chances of my playing professional ball—even at the lowest level—were just too remote. Even Zeidner, who was far more talented than I was, had lasted less than two days at a Yankee tryout camp.

To cap it off, on the last day Jagust invited the editorial staff to read his Journalism class's grades aloud; that weekend, I had a bit part in the senior play that got me a lot of applause and some laughs;

and, as the Kelly award winner, I carried the flag at graduation. Except for the dreaded cross-country move, I couldn't have scripted a more fitting ending. For years I'd tried and failed, worked my ass off, and suffered so much humiliation in the service of my dreams. And now, I'd gotten everything I'd longed for.

For the moment, it felt like a just vindication. I forgot about the effort and the waiting, the disappointment and pain—even the bitterness and resentment I'd carried. Even if I didn't fully believe it, I told myself that it was all worth it. That I'd earned it. And that I could not have done it any other way.

A curious thing about the move west was that all my friends and teammates envied me. Some would be going to schools that were close to home. Some would commute. Some wouldn't even be attending college. To them, the idea of attending college in L.A. seemed like a big, glamorous adventure.

I wish I'd had the perspective to see it that way. To me, leaving New York meant that that I'd be starting all over again. I'd be giving up everything I worked so hard to get. Going to Syracuse or Boston U would have been a hard enough adjustment for me, but at least my friends and girlfriend would still be here. And I'd have a roster of accomplishments to build on. It terrified me to think about moving three thousand miles away, especially to a nutty place like L.A., where I knew no one. I'd recently read *Day of the Locust* and *The Last Tycoon*—both of which made L.A. seem even more off-putting.

For the past two months, I'd been trying to think of some kind of scheme that would at least keep me in the east. The partial scholarships at Syracuse and Boston University weren't nearly enough to cover my tuition and room and board. The only way I'd have even the slightest a chance to influence my father was to come up with more money. My first move was to ask Kerchman to write a letter to the Syracuse athletic department, recommending me for a baseball scholarship. It left me with only one more card to play.

It was clear that my mother was still bitter over the move. Lately, whenever I argued with my father about it, she took my side. I knew he'd be leaving for L.A. ten days ahead of the rest of the family, so as soon as he left, I told her my plan.

About a month ago, I'd approached my widowed cousin, Sarah Neiman, with a proposition. Sarah's husband Abe was one of the co-owners of Hymie's old pharmacy. When he died ten years ago, his share of the pharmacy went to her. Sarah agreed to let me stay in her attic apartment if I worked at the pharmacy and contributed a small sum of rent money. But to do this, I needed my mother's approval.

For three weeks she and my father had been turning all my requests down. But now she had to deal with me on her own. I tried to make it seem as if I'd be her proxy here. It was a pretty transparent ploy, but after a week of listening to me whine, beg, and plead, I finally wore her down. It was, at best, a Phyrric victory.

There were moments that summer when I felt like I was living an independent existence. I slept in Sarah's attic, I saw Julie at night, and I played for a traveling semi-pro team on weekends. Other times, I felt like I was thirteen again. While most my friends were driving their own cars, I'd was delivering prescriptions on a borrowed old Schwin three-speed—something I vowed I'd never do again.

I tried to make my father feel guilty for letting me down. I complained and protested long distance. I even asked Julie to intervene. In the back of my mind, though, I knew I was only postponing the inevitable.

On the evenings when I didn't see Julie I was stuck in Sarah's hot, stuffy attic room with nothing to do but listen to rock and roll on the radio. It was like I'd regressed back to junior high. One night, almost by instinct, I turned the dial to WOR, where I used to hear Red Barber's voice broadcasting the Dodger games. I got some DJ instead. That's when it began to register—no more ball games to listen to late at night; no more Saturday pilgrimages to Ebbets Field; no more bickering at dinner or in the school yards about who's the best team in New York. The Yankees were the only team left, and I simply couldn't bring myself to listen to their games. I was getting so wistful that I was even starting to miss Kerchman and all the tsuris he'd caused me.

Separating from Julie was the scene I'd dreaded most. All summer, our relationship had become more intense and desperate. We talked about how much we'd miss each other, and how we'd look forward to Thanksgiving and Christmas holidays. We even discussed the possibility of her coming to visit me in California.

In the last two months, her parents were much more cordial to me. It was spooky. They'd invite me for dinner and put me up in the guest room on nights that I couldn't get a ride home. It would have been nice to think that they were beginning to warm up to me. But the truth of course is that it was only a matter of time before they'd be rid of me. Why not take the high ground?

About a week before I was scheduled to leave, Steve informed me that Julie had a crush on one of the older counselors at camp. He'd heard it of course from Annie. Steve had warned me before that Julie was fickle, that she'd had a different boyfriend for the past three summers. I think he was trying to prepare me for the inevitable break.

As forlorn as I felt, I couldn't really blame her. I was the one, after all, who was leaving. For the final few weeks of the summer, I didn't let on that I knew, and Julie didn't say anything that would make me suspect her. Whatever might happen when I was gone, she was determined that we'd enjoy the time we had left together.

On the day she drove me to La Guardia, Julie orchestrated a dramatic and touching farewell scene. She wore all black—black raincoat, tight black Bermuda shorts, and a black form-fitting sweater. And her bobbing ponytail was tied in a bow with a black ribbon. It's an image that would linger in my imagination for a long time afterward.

On the long plane ride to L.A., I had a lot of time to think. A whole phase of my life was over, and a new one was about to begin. The reality of it had begun to sink in when I was packing to leave. I was rummaging through my stash, looking for my old baseball memorabilia—the Topps and Bowman baseball cards, the Dodger yearbooks and Ebbets Field programs, my collection of *Sports Illustrated* magazines. I couldn't find any of it. When I called my mother to ask where it was, she confessed that she'd thrown everything out before the move.

I felt bereaved, of course, and for a while, inconsolable. During the entire plane ride, I brooded about my losses. Yet just as we were descending, my stomach hollow with fear, I felt a tiny flicker of hope.

It hit me for the first time that I was following the Dodgers again. In the past, their ability to come back from failure and loss had helped me to persevere. I knew, of course, that the Dodgers were only a baseball team. But as the plane touched down, it was momentarily reassuring to think that perhaps I wouldn't be the only New Yorker out here who was starting over again.

◆

Epilogue

In April of 1959, *Mike Mandell, a UCLA fraternity brother, invited me to the Dodgers' opening-day game. Mike's father, Harry, a minor studio exec, had managed to score three field boxes behind the Dodger dugout. Initially, I'd turned the offer down. That piece of my life was over, I told myself. But three days later, my curiosity got the best of me.*

The Coliseum is a one-hundred-thousand seat football palace that in the '50s and '60s housed three teams; UCLA, USC, and the LA Rams. The Dodgers had temporarily moved there because their new park at Chavez Ravine was still under construction. At the local taxpayers' expense.

As a baseball stadium, the place is a spectator's nightmare. The inner structure is a round, dirty white concrete slab with no tiers, no upper deck, and no backs on the bleacher style seats. Like most football stadiums, the interior is a widening band of concentric circles. The higher you sit on the circle, the farther away you are from the game.

And what about these oddities?: there's more room in foul territory behind the plate than on the entire left side of the field; and the left field wall is only two hundred and fifty feet away from home plate. A windblown fly ball to left stood a chance of drifting over the outfield screen. And because the right side of the field angles out away from the plate, a four-hundred-foot fly ball to left or right center is a routine out.

The ceremonial speeches by city officials, turncoat Dodger brass, and a few Hollywood celebs were pompous and self-serving. Except for Duke Snider, Johnny Padres, and Gil Hodges, whose best years were behind them, most of the players I remember either had been traded or had retired.

None of this seemed to bother the fans, though. Once the game began, they acted as if they were mildly charmed by what was happening on the field. Every time a player hit a high pop fly, they cheered like it was a home run. But by the third inning, most of the conversation I overheard was about movie agents, lunch meetings, and script deals. Nobody spoke the old Ebbets Field lingo. Only a handful of people even took the trouble to score the game. Some of the Hollywood types, in fact, couldn't seem to figure out what the numbers in the scorebook mean.

"How come the first baseman is wearing number 14, and the program says he's number 3?" asked a peroxide blonde in pedal pushers and spike heels.

I wasn't even tempted to explain it to her.

I also noticed that there were only a handful of fathers and sons in the stadium. At eighteen, I was one of the youngest males in attendance.

Most of the crowd looked like they'd been shipped over from Central Casting. Many of the older men wore garish, flowered shirts and monogrammed sun visors. Some of the younger ones even brought their surfboards. Several women dressed in gauzy see-through blouses, form-fitting short shorts, and flip flops. And I saw a few in halter tops and bikinis as well. Every two innings, the celebrity wanna-bes would preen for the TV cameras; and all throughout the game there was an unbroken flow of traffic to and from the concession stands. By the seventh inning of a one-run game, the Coliseum was less than half full. When I left that afternoon, I knew I would not return.

In the fall of '59 *I went back to New York and enrolled at Hofstra College. At nineteen, I was a typical college kid; I went to fraternity parties, slept in, and chased girls. I pitched middle-inning relief on the baseball team, majored in English and wrote sports for* The Chronicle, *the school weekly. My vague hope was to someday become a writer and teacher.*

That year I didn't pay a lot of attention to Major League baseball. When I went to Yankee Stadium, I joked to friends that I was only there as a tourist. But in the winter of 1960 I stumbled across a Newsday *article announcing the upcoming demolition of Ebbets Field.*

How could I not attend? Perhaps, I'd find some closure here.

A bone-chilling, *late February morning. For the first time in years, I took the Green Bus Line and Flatbush Avenue IRT to the Eastern Parkway stop. Alone. I walked down Franklin Avenue and saw the light towers of Ebbets in the grey distance. When I reached Empire Boulevard, I instinctively turned left and walked through the marble rotunda, past the boarded up ticket windows, before heading up the third base grandstand ramp.*

The first thing I saw when I reached the portal was the huge, black scoreboard in right field. I gazed around the outfield for a last look at the old Abe Stark, "Hit This Sign and Win a Suit" billboard, and the fire engine red Tydol Flying A sign.

I closed my eyes, and for a moment I was twelve years old again. But the reverie faded when I looked out at the brown outfield grass and saw jagged ruts and bare patches, the residue from two years of stock car races and neglect. Then, below me, I noticed the shabby looking blue box seats, surrounded by faded, chipped red railings.

A sparse crowd, maybe a few hundred men and three or four women, huddled behind the third base dugout. But they weren't waiting for autographs. We'd all gathered here to witness the demolition of Ebbets Field. In the crowd, I recognized two of the old players; Carl Erskine, always a winner, always a classy guy. Standing next to him was the unfortunate Ralph Branca. Who'd have expected that kind of loyalty from Branca, a man who was so unfairly maligned by the fans and press? Was it penance he was seeking here?

Lucy Monroe sang the National Anthem just as she'd done at countless Dodger games. But the speeches were canned eulogies. Some phony Brooklyn politico with bad teeth droned on, inform-ing us—without any sense of irony—that Ebbets Field was now forty-six years old. But I was thinking about Walter O'Malley, the owner who sold out millions of naive, loyal, baseball fans like me. I recalled the scene in The Great Gatsby *where Jay Gatsby intro-duces Nick Carraway to Meyer Wolfsheim, the character who was based on Arnold Rothstein, the gambler who allegedly conspired to fix the 1919 World Series. As Nick shakes Wolfsheim's hand he thinks: "It never occurred to me that one man could start to play with the faith of fifty million people—with the single-mindedness of a burglar blowing a safe."*

The demolition crew were fittingly outfitted in Dodger-blue windbreakers; and as the giant white-washed, red-lined "headache ball" crunched into the third base dugout, chunks of concrete and splintered wood flew in all directions. I felt a terrible ache in the pit of my stomach. Then I caught my breath and closed my eyes again. I could see myself sitting in the centerfield bleachers watch-ing Duke Snider camp under a lazy fly ball. The Duke is casually patting the pocket of his mitt, waiting to gather in what Red Barber used to call "an easy can of corn." In another flashback, I imagined Jackie Robinson crouched between second and first base, hands on knees, waiting for Newk, Ersk, Padres, or "the Preach" to deliver the next pitch.

I was jolted back to the present when the "headache ball" smashed into the right field scoreboard. The concrete beneath me started to quiver. It felt like a minor earthquake.

As I walked slowly back to the subway that morning, I made a promise not to attend another Major League ball game.

After the Coliseum charade *and the demolition of Ebetts, it was easy to stick to my promise. That is, until 1962 when the newly formed Mets moved into the Polo Grounds. I had a brief flirtation with the Mets, but it was mainly because going to the Polo Grounds reminded me of the days when I was still on fire for the game, back when my father used to take us to watch the Giants play here. Once Shea Stadium was built, though, I lost interest again.*

Though I no longer followed Major League baseball, I continued to pitch and play fast pitch softball throughout graduate school and for a good piece of my early teaching career. I finally quit playing at age forty-five.

Kerchman, too, would figure in my life for a long time after high school. When I was in college I'd sometimes stop by to watch the team scrimmage. Occasionally I'd pitch batting practice. Each time I went back, Kerchman made certain to praise me to his players. Sometimes I wondered if that's why I did go back.

After college, I moved to Michigan to attend graduate school. I didn't see Coach K again until the 25th-year class reunion. He seemed mellower, more fragile looking—even somewhat wistful. Kerchman was a year or two away from retirement, and yet it still amazed me how he could recall so many specific games and situations from the years when I'd played for him.

He was as complimentary toward me as he'd been ever since my senior year. He was proud, he said, that I'd become a teacher. Because that's the way he thought of himself, as a coach who tried to set an example for his players. We all have our own myths, I guess.

Ten years ago, *I was rummaging through an old trunk when I found the Kelly award. I cradled the medal in the palm of my hand and read the inscription: "Courage, Character, Loyalty." Next to the small white box was a copy of a short memoir my brother had written about his own high school baseball days. Mr. K, it seems, had treated Alan the same way as he'd handled me. He made him sit on the bench for three seasons before playing him only sporadically in his senior year. When he finally got his chance, Alan made the most of it. That season, 1963, Far Rockaway won its only city championship—thanks in good part to my brother's contributions. So at the season ending banquet, Alan was naturally disappointed that he didn't win the Kelly award. It would have been a most fitting ending.*

As I thumbed through the memoir, I stopped when I came across the following passage:

> *In his locker room speeches, Mr. K talked about this little Jewish relief pitcher whose uniform didn't fit and who didn't have a whole lot of talent. But the boy, he said, always seemed to be at his best under extreme pressure. In fact he'd bring this kid into impossible situations—tie game, bases loaded no outs, that kind of thing—and he'd say to him, "Son, I want you to get me two ground balls and a pop fly." And that pitcher, my brother Mike, would somehow figure out a way to get the other team to hit two ground balls and a pop fly.*

As I scanned the passage, my first response was: a typical Kerchman ploy—the old rah-rah psych job for the benefit of the rookies. But I was moved by what I'd read. Some part of me under-stood—maybe for the first time—that in his own perverse way Mr. K had given me what I had been asking for all along: a nod of acceptance from one kind of Jew to another.

◆